5⁹⁵

Don Green
2280 Ardmore Cove
Memphis, TN. 38127

REMODELING GUIDE FOR
HOME INTERIORS

REMODELING GUIDE FOR HOME INTERIORS

Planning, Materials, Methods

J. RALPH DALZELL

McGRAW-HILL BOOK COMPANY, INC.

1956   NEW YORK   TORONTO   LONDON

Preface

This book was written in response to the tremendous interest in house remodeling encountered among homeowners, mechanics, and real estate people. Such interest is continuing to grow. Some of the more important reasons for its growth are set forth in the following paragraphs.

First, there are the eternal dreams of comfortable and beautiful houses planned to suit the particular needs of families. More often than not, even extensive remodeling is a great deal cheaper than new houses.

Second, there are the desires to use and to enjoy the modern and labor-saving equipment now available for kitchen and laundry activities. There are also desires to enjoy modern bathroom fixtures and a host of other devices, all of which make comfortable and modern living possible. In most cases, some remodeling is necessary before new equipment, fixtures, and devices can be used to the best advantage. For example, many old houses have ceilings which are too high in terms of modern kitchen cabinets.

Third, there are the desires to create and to enjoy new recreation rooms, additional bedrooms for growing families, kitchens with planned work centers, bathrooms which can be used by two people with privacy and at the same time, additional closets and storage spaces, and several other such innovations, which make homes much more serviceable and comfortable.

Fourth, there are the desires to modernize all interior walls, ceilings, and floors. Many new and beautiful materials are available for such purposes. There are also materials available for specific purposes such as nursery and play rooms, where fingerprints and other soil must be taken into consideration.

Finally, because of attachments and associations, many families do not want to leave old neighborhoods in order to enjoy all of the previously mentioned desires in new houses located in "garden" or "development" areas. The answer to this is remodeling.

Most of the older houses, especially those which are from 30 to 40 or more years old, are of sound construction that can be depended upon for many more years. Such houses need only interior remodeling to make them compare favorably with new houses. With such a fact in mind, this book is devoted to the simple but effective interior remodeling operations which most people are capable of doing.

Remodeling is a fascinating project for homeowners. Perhaps no other aspect of homemaking produces the pleasure and comfort made possible by the simple suggestions and procedures set forth in this book. Drab, uninteresting, inefficient and tiring old houses can be transformed into beautiful and pleasant areas where housework is greatly reduced, where there is ample space for all activities, and where modern living can be enjoyed to the fullest extent.

The remodeling suggestions and the how-to-do-it instructions set forth in this book were planned and are explained in such a manner that homeowners can do all of their remodeling work as financial budgets allow. In other words, remodeling work need not be done all at one time. The various improvements can be planned as a whole but carried out as financial ease permits.

Each of the chapters in this book is a story in itself. For example, the basement chapter is devoted to only such suggestions and instructions as pertain to the remodeling of such areas. However, it is advisable for readers to become acquainted with all of the chapters prior to the time they start to plan any particular project. In this manner, all of the important and related considerations will be understood.

This book makes a special effort to point out and explain considerations which must be applied to any remodeling project. For example, the basement chapter contains thorough explanations in connection with frequently overlooked problems and unexpected expense. Readers are urged to evaluate their remodeling plans accordingly.

In any remodeling project, large or small, careful planning must be done before the actual or manipulative work is started. Without such planning many disappointments, delays, and added expenses are likely. This book gives special emphasis to planning, and readers are urged to pay particular attention to it. Never start a remodeling project until such planning as described in this book has been carefully done.

In addition to carefully planning all remodeling projects, readers are urged to obtain preliminary cost estimates, as described in the kitchen chapter, and then to determine if such expense is worthwhile, as described in the basement chapter.

This book contains a great many remodeling suggestions which pertain to all parts of house interiors. However, readers are urged to peruse shelter magazines and manufacturers' literature all as a means of better and more effective planning. The magazines are available at news stands and the literature at lumber yards or manufacturers' show rooms. Literature can also be obtained by writing directly to manufacturers. Their names and addresses appear in magazine ads.

Each of the major remodeling, maintenance, and repair projects explained in this book are set forth in terms of typical problems and their answers. All instructions are in the how-to-do-it form which readers can use as a guide. The various procedures are explained in regular order and by means of procedures recommended by manufacturers and approved of by most city and town building codes.

The author wishes to thank a host of manufacturers for their help and advice during the time this book was being written. He also wishes to thank the many contractors and builders who contributed many and helpful manipulative procedures.

Contents

PREFACE   v

ONE. WOODS   1

Kinds of Lumber   2
    Softwoods · Hardwoods · Availability of Lumber
Hardness of Lumber   3
Grain of Lumber   3
Shrinkage and Swelling   4
    How to Recognize Dry Lumber
Freedom from Warping   6
Ease of Working   7
Paint Holding   8
Stiffness of Lumber   8
Figure in Wood   9
How to Avoid Shrinkage Defects   10
Dressed Lumber   11
Grades of Lumber   11
    Softwoods · Hardwoods · Finish Lumber · Floor Lumber ·
    Grading Rules for Maple, Beech, and Birch
Wood Defects   14
    Checks · Knots · Decay · Warping · Wane · Pitch Discoloration
Board-feet Content   16
Lumber for Various Purposes   18
    Exterior House Trim · Living and Dining-room Floors ·
    Uncovered Kitchen Floors · Covered Kitchen Floors · Porch
    Flooring · Rough Framing · Interior Trim · Roof Boards ·
    Window Sash · Shelving: High-class Natural or Paint Finish ·
    Shelving: Unfinished or Plain Paint Coating · Shingles · Siding
    · Outdoor Steps · Subfloors · Sheathing · Concrete Forms ·
    Gates and Fences · Cabinets · Furring Strips · Sills · Screen
    Frames
Softwood Plywood   21
Hardwood Plywood   21
    Grading · Hardwood Plywood Species
Economical Use of Plywood   26

ix

TWO. FASTENERS   27

Nail-holding Power   28
    Nail Shanks
Nail Sizes   31
Rule for Length of Nails   31
Typical Nail Data   31
Nail Points   34
    Diamond Point · Blunt-tapered Point · Long-diamond and
    Needle Points · Chisel Point · Duck-bill Point
Nail Clinching   34
Nailheads   35
General Nailing Specifications   35
    Figure 2. Two-piece Beam · Figure 3. Double Sill · Figure 4.
    Joists · Figure 5. Joints Bearing on Beam · Figure 6. Subfloor
    and Sill · Figure 7. Plywood Subfloor · Figure 8. Studs · Figure
    9. Joists Bearing on Ribbon · Figure 10. Rafter Ends · Figure
    11. Porch Connections · Figure 12. Diagonal Wall Sheathing ·
    Figure 13. Plywood Wall Sheathing · Figure 14. Singles · Figure
    15. Rafter and Ceiling Joists Supported by Wall Plate
Fastening Decorative Plywood   40
Fastening Furring Strips to Masonry   41
    Concrete Block · Concrete
Fastening Sills to Foundations   43
Miter Stiffeners   44
Joist Hangers   44

THREE. INSULATION   46

What Is Insulation?   48
Kinds of Insulation   49
    Loose Fill · Blanket · Batt · Structural Insulating Board · Slab
    · Reflective
Benefits of Insulation   50
    Less Costly Heating System · Less Costly Cooling Systems · Fuel
    Savings · Power Savings · Decorating Savings · Protection
    against Vermin · Comfort
Insulation Principles   51
    Heat Flow · How Heat Flow Takes Place · How Heat Flows
    through a Wall
How Insulation Functions   53
How Much Insulation to Use   54
Condensation   54
    Attic Ventilation · Crawl-space Ventilation
Suggested Remodeling Projects   56
    Top-floor Ceilings · Attic Knee Walls and Roof · Dormers ·

Roofs · Foundations · Cold Surfaces · Cool and Damp Surfaces · Basement Floors · Floor Slabs · Crawl Spaces · Added Rooms · Ceilings · Floors · Walls · Infiltration · Existing Walls · Frame Walls · Pneumatic Application · Application of Rigid Insulation · Masonry Walls · Flat Roofs · Sound Transmission · New Construction · Existing Floors · Existing Walls and Ceilings

How to Plan and Do Typical Remodeling Projects 70
Top-floor Ceiling 70
Knee Walls 72
Collar-beam Ceiling 74
Crawl Spaces 75
Common Condensation Troubles 76

FOUR. CEILINGS 78

Plaster Defects 79
    Cracks · Natural Conditions · Lumber Shrinkage · Settlement · Expansion and Contraction · Weight Shifts · Wind Force · Unfortunate Conditions · Judging Defects
Plasterboard Defects 84
    Poor Joists · Cracks · Damage Due to Water · Nail Holes
Suggested Remodeling Projects 85
    Repairing Cracked Plaster · New Surfaces over Sound Plaster · Surface Materials · Prefinished Ceiling Tile · New Surfaces over Unsound Plaster · Fastening Tile · Prefinished Ceiling Tile · New Surfaces over Plasterboard · New Surfaces without Plaster · Fastening Furring Strips and Tile
How to Plan and Do Typical Remodeling Projects 95
Repairing Plaster Cracks 95
    Large Cracks · Corner Cracks · Small Cracks · Conclusion
New Surfaces over Sound Plaster 98
New Surfaces over Unsound Plaster 102
New Surfaces without Plaster 105
    Application of Insulation · Application of Furring Strips · Application of Starter Strip · Application of Tile · Painting
Sloping Attic Ceilings 108
Lowered Ceiling 109
    Installation of E Pieces · Installation of 2 by 4 Joists · Application of Furring Strips · Application of Tile
Ladders and Scaffold Planks 112
    Types of Ladders Recommended · Safety Hints

FIVE. WALLS 113

Plaster and Plasterboard Defects 113
Judging Wall Defects 114

Suggested Remodeling Projects   114
    Repairing Cracked Plaster · Repairing Holes in Plaster · Plastic
    Wall Coverings · Fabric Wall Coverings · New Surfaces over
    Sound Plaster · Planks · Blocks · Corrugated and Grooved
    Boards · Panels · Perforated Panels · New Surfaces without
    Plaster · Plywood · Panel Sheet Rock over Plasterboard
How to Plan and Do Typical Remodeling Projects   125
Repairing Plaster Cracks   125
    Large Cracks · Small Cracks
Cracks in Thin Plaster   127
Repairing Holes in Plaster   127
    Small Holes · Large Holes
New Surfaces over Sound Plaster   128
New Surfaces over Foundations   136
Wall-surface Materials on Framing   139
    Block on Framing · Planks on Framing · Soft-surface Planks or
    Panels on Framing

SIX.   FLOORS   142
Floor Defects   143
    Cracks in Wood Floors · Cracks in Concrete Floors · Judging
    Defects
Suggested Remodeling Projects   148
    Repairing Cracks in Wood Floors · Repairing Large Cracks ·
    Correcting Floor Squeaks · Replacing Damaged Boards · New
    Flooring in Place of Old · Repairing Cracks in Concrete Floors ·
    Soft Recreation-room Floor over Concrete · Parquet Squares or
    Blocks over Concrete · Plank Floors for Remodeled Attic Areas
    · Floor-sag Correction · Tile over Plywood in New Attic Rooms
    · Tile over Wood Floors in Bad Condition · New Board-type
    Hardwood Floors over Concrete · New Masonry Surfaces for
    Concrete Floors · Refinishing Existing Hardwood Floors · New
    Hardwood Floor over Softwood
How to Plan and Do Typical Remodeling Projects   153
Repairing Small Cracks in Wood Floors   153
    Preparation · Patching Materials
Repairing Large Cracks in Wood Floors   155
    Preparation · Patching Materials
Correcting Floor Squeaks   156
    Preparation · Materials
Replacing Damaged Floor Boards   158
    Preparation · Removing Boards · Placing New Boards
Soft Tile over Old Wood Floor   160
Soft Recreation-room Floor   163
Parquet or Blocks over Concrete   166

Plank Floor over Wood Subfloor   168
Tile or Planks over Plywood   170
Tile on Plywood over Worn-out Wood Floors   172
Hardwood Flooring on Concrete   173
How to Keep Hardwood Floors Beautiful   176
Safety Features in Connection with the Laying of New Hardwood
    Floors   177
Asphalt Tile over Concrete   177

SEVEN.   BASEMENTS   180

Purpose of Remodeling   182
Remodeling Precaution   183
    Fireplace · New Heating Plant · New Windows · Piping ·
    Water Heater · Water Closet · Washer · Lavatory
Preliminary Considerations   186
    Ceiling Height · Columns · Bearing Partitions · Floors ·
    Windows · Basement Water · Stairs · Wall Surfaces · Pipes ·
    Sweating Pipes · Furnace Location · Basement Temperatures ·
    Sagging Floors · Games · Ceilings · Hot-water Tank · Electrical
    Outlets
Related Projects   190
    Ceiling Height · Bearing Partitions · Floors · Windows · Base-
    ment Water · New Foundation Surface · Stairs · Wall Surfaces
    · Cutting Structural Details for Pipes and Ducts · Existing Floor
    Drains · Basement Temperature · Sagging Floors
Typical Remodeling Projects   207

EIGHT.   KITCHENS   214

Basic Kitchen Types   218
    U Type · L Type · Parallel-wall Type · One-wall Type ·
    Variations
Dining Nooks   223
    L Type · U Type · Parallel Type
Advantages of Remodeling   224
Work Centers   226
Choice of Equipment   227
    Sinks · Ranges · Refrigerators · Base Cabinets · Merry-go-
    rounds · Cutting-board Cabinets · Mixer Cabinets · Wall
    Cabinets · Islands · Suggested Cabinets and Accessories
Cabinet Dimensions   230
Other Kitchen Factors   231
    Lighting · Electrical Convenience Outlets · Future Plans
Cabinet-top Materials   232

Walls and Floors   233
   Walls · Floors
Soffits   233
Hanging Cabinets   236
Filler Strips   237
Kitchen-area Remodeling   237
   Structural Considerations
Preliminary Planning   241
   Plan to Save Steps · Plan for Convenience · Plan for Efficiency
   · Check Points
How to Plan a New Kitchen   243
   Known Shape and Size · Unknown Shape and Size
How to Install Cabinets   247
   Fastening Cabinets to Walls · Checking Walls · Layout · Install-
   ing Wall Cabinets · Installing Base Cabinets · Installing Sink
   Cabinet
Financial Considerations   253
   Outright Payment · Unit-by-unit Purchase · Extended Payment
Typical Projects   255
   Serving Bar · Seat

NINE. ATTICS   257
Reasons for Remodeling   261
Remodeling Considerations   261
   Dormers · Area of Attic Space · Ceiling Height · Condition of
   Roofing · Reroofing · Climbing Suggestions · Disappearing
   Stairs · Heating · Insulation · Chimneys · Joist Direction · Sub-
   flooring · Dormer Flashing · Plumbing
How to Plan and Do Attic Remodeling   275
   Typical Dormer Construction

TEN. BATHROOMS   285
How to Visualize Plan Views of Bathrooms   288
Bathroom Safety   290
   Nonslip Flooring · Bathtub Bottoms · Grab Bars · Thermostatic
   Valves · Towel Bars, etc. · Light Switches · Medicine Cabinets
   · Radiators
Remodeling Considerations   291
   Piping Economy · Bathtub Locations · Bathtub Hangers · Codes
   · Windows · Condensation · Roughing-in Drawings · Cabinets
   · Heating · Sliding Doors · Size of Bathrooms · Shutoff Valves
Advantage of Remodeling   296
Modern Fixtures and Accessories   299
   Lavatories · Water Closets · Bathtubs · Shower Stalls · Medi-
   cine Cabinets · Water Heaters · Ventilation

Location of Bathroom Accessories   301
Minimum-sized Bathrooms   302
Duplex Bathrooms   303
Typical Remodeling Projects   305

ELEVEN. STORAGE SPACES   309

Storage-space Safety   310
    Lighting · Ventilation · Dust Prevention · Access · Reaching
    and Climbing · Seldom Used Articles · Outdoor Articles ·
    Poisons · Locations
Basic Types of Storage Spaces   312
    Clothes Closets · Wardrobe Closets · Prefabricated Closets ·
    Storage Spaces
Closet Fittings   317
Cedar Closets   319
    Application
Closet Doors   321
    Folding Doors · Sliding Doors
Typical Projects   322

INDEX   327

BLUEPRINTS—PLATES I TO VI   341

REMODELING GUIDE FOR
HOME INTERIORS

CHAPTER ONE

Woods

A good basic knowledge of the characteristics and types of woods is invaluable in connection with any form of carpentry work, especially remodeling. The selection of suitable woods has a great bearing on costs, working procedures, and ultimate results.

An expensive grade of lumber is not always necessary or best for a given project; in many instances a cheaper grade may do as well or better. In fact, some of the cheaper grades, especially if they are to be painted or otherwise hidden from view, have the stiffness and other qualities necessary to assure the most durable construction.

Wise selection of woods involves giving careful thought to the requirements of a project. Good judgment in this connection yields high returns in satisfaction. After the requirements have been determined, it is relatively easy to select proper grades of woods. For example, we may be led to believe that a wood of high strength is necessary for a given project, whereas what we actually need are good painting qualities and weather-resisting properties. Or we may think that high strength is necessary, whereas stiffness, dryness, and minimum shrinkage are actually the important points to consider.

There are many other considerations, such as workability, which we should take into consideration before making a selection of woods for a specific purpose. Therefore, the purpose of this chapter is to assist in a careful estimation of the essential requirements for different remodeling purposes, to show how the different kinds of woods meet such requirements, and to emphasize some of the principles frequently overlooked.

KINDS OF LUMBER

The trees commonly cut into ordinary lumber are divided into two broad groups: *hardwood* and *softwood*. Strangely enough, the term hardwood does not always refer to a tree whose wood is hard. Actually, there is no definite or exact means of determining the difference between many trees so far as softness and hardness are concerned. However, many of the so-called softwood trees have wood which is softer than several of the so-called hardwood trees. The custom has developed of calling the coniferous trees softwood, and the broad-leaved trees hardwood. Coniferous trees, generally called *evergreens,* are those with needles or scale-like leaves. Broad-leaved trees are generally called *deciduous* because they shed their leaves each autumn.

Softwoods. The lumber industry includes the following trees in the softwood group:

Cedar	Hemlock	Redwood
Cypress	Larch	Spruce
Douglas fir	Pine	

Hardwoods. The lumber industry includes the following trees in the hardwood group:

Ash	Cherry	Maple
Basswood	Chestnut	Oak
Beech	Elm	Poplar
Birch	Gum	Walnut

Availability of Lumber. The lumberyards in various sections of the country are apt to stock the kinds of lumber that are grown and cut closest to them. This practice saves on transportation expense and makes for more economical lumber prices. Therefore, it is always a good practice to visit local lumberyards to see what kinds of lumber are in stock.

HARDNESS OF LUMBER

Hardness is the property that makes a surface difficult to dent, scratch, or otherwise mar. The harder the wood, the better it resists wear and the better it can be finished or polished. However, the hardwoods are generally difficult to work with and should therefore be used only for flooring or other uses where *wearing* qualities are important.

For ordinary building purposes, carpenters like some woods because of their softness and uniformity rather than because of their hardness. Northern white pine, Douglas fir, basswood, sugar pine, redwood, and ponderosa pine are typical examples. The ease with which these woods can be sawed, planed, and nailed has made them most popular for general use, particularly where remodeling work is involved.

GRAIN OF LUMBER

The *A* part of Figure 1 indicates annual growth rings in a typical log. When such rings are narrow or close together, as in slow-growing trees, the wood is known as *close-grained*. When they are wide and farther apart, as in rapidly growing trees, the wood is known as *coarse grained*. For example, *close grain* is used to describe such woods as birch, pine, and maple, all of which have smooth surfaces. *Coarse grain* is used to describe such woods as oak, walnut, and chestnut, all of which have slightly rough surfaces.

A log is first sawed along the lines *ab*, *bd*, *dc*, and *ca* to produce a square section such as shown in the *B* part of the illustration. The square section is finally sawed into such typical boards as shown at *C* and *D*. Small patterns of the growth rings can be seen in the boards. Depending upon the size of a log and upon the width of boards, various other growth ring patterns, known as *grain* and illustrated at *E*, *F*, and *G*, are created.

When the grain in a board forms an angle of 45 degrees or more with its side faces, as shown in board *E*, the lumber is described as *vertical grain* in softwoods and as *quartersawed* in hardwoods. When the grain in a board forms an angle of 45 degrees or less with its side faces, as shown in board *F*, the lumber is described as *flat grain* in softwoods and *plain-sawed* in hardwoods. *Mixed grain* is indicated in board *G*. Vertical-grain lumber is the strongest.

Side views of grain patterns, such as shown in the *H* part of the illustration, also indicate important characteristics. The straight-grained board is the stronger of the two and should be used for structural details which

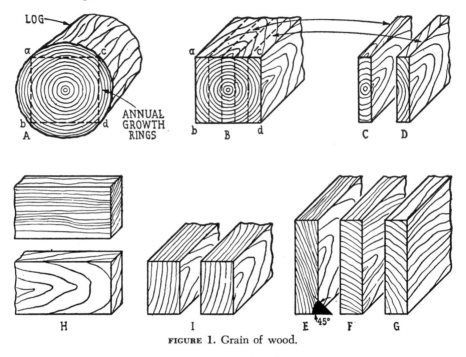

FIGURE 1. Grain of wood.

must support portions of a house. The other board could be used for panels or other facings where its irregular grain is decorative.

We should also examine lumber grain pattern at the top of lumber, as indicated at *I*. Of the two pieces shown, the straight-grained one is likely to be the stronger and more durable. The other, with its grain running off to one side, may split if used as a support.

SHRINKAGE AND SWELLING

In remodeling work, where we often place new wood alongside of or in connection with older wood, it is most important that the new wood be free of shrinkage or swelling tendencies. This is highly important from the standpoint of avoiding ceiling and wall defects, as described in Chapters 4 and 5.

Wood, like many other fibrous materials, shrinks as it dries and swells as it absorbs moisture. As a rule, however, much of the shrinkage and swelling of wood in service is unnecessary and can be avoided by using wood that has been dried to the right moisture content.

In all kinds of wood the shrinkage or swelling in the width of a flat-grained board is nearly twice that of an edge-grained board of the same width. Edge-grained wood of a kind having a high shrinkage will therefore prove as satisfactory as flat-grained stock of the kind with inherently lower shrinkage. Wood has practically no shrinkage or swelling length-wise of the grain.

In the following, several common woods are classified according to their probable amount of shrinkage as they change from wet to dry conditions.

CONSIDERABLE SHRINKAGE

Ash	Birch	Larch
Basswood	Elm	Maple
Beech	Gum	Oak

MEDIUM SHRINKAGE

Cherry	Douglas fir	Poplar
Chestnut	Hemlock	Spruce
Cypress	Pine	Walnut

LITTLE SHRINKAGE

| Cedar | Redwood |

The foregoing classifications according to the amount of shrinkage do not tell the whole story of the shrinkage of different woods. About half the shrinkage is "taken out" of wood through air seasoning and about two-thirds by thorough kiln drying. The taking out of shrinkage in the amounts mentioned is sufficient for the ordinary uses to which wood is put in any remodeling project. Shrinkage does not always stay out when mositure is reabsorbed, but the important thing is to have it taken out prior to the time the wood is built into a house. The rate at which drying and shrinkage occur in different kinds of wood is very important in practical usage. A wood that has a relatively low total shrinkage may dry so slowly that, in actual practice, it commonly gets into use before the proper amount of shrinkage has been taken out. Pieces of some woods, such as larch, cypress, and redwood, frequently are slow to dry and therefore slow to shrink to their ultimate condition. Such pieces are apt to give a greater amount of trouble from shrinkage than the classification previously given indicates. The only remedy consists of making sure that such lumber is dry before being put to use.

How to Recognize Dry Lumber. There are several rule-of-thumb tests which we can employ as a means of recognizing dry lumber.

1. Dry lumber is apt to have small and brittle slivers on it.

2. Dry lumber produces a hollow sound when rapped with the knuckles of the hand.

3. Dry lumber weighs less than moist or wet lumber.

4. Moist or wet lumber has a sharper odor.

5. Dry lumber has more springiness.

6. Moist or wet lumber feels damp to the touch.

FREEDOM FROM WARPING

The warping of wood is closely allied with shrinkage and causes many of the same defects in ceilings and walls. Lumber that is cross-grained, such as shown at *C* in Figure 1, tends to warp, or twist out of shape, when it shrinks. Warping can be reduced to a minimum by the use of quartersawed wood.

In the following, several common woods are classified according to their tendency to warp as they change from wet to dry conditions:

CONSIDERABLE WARPING

| Beech | Elm | Gum |

SLIGHT WARPING

Ash	Cypress	Pine
Basswood	Douglas fir	Poplar
Birch	Hemlock	Redwood
Cedar	Larch	Spruce
Cherry	Maple	Walnut
Chestnut	Oak	

EASE OF WORKING

For some purposes the ease with which woods can be worked, so far as hand tools are concerned, is negligible. For others, and in most cases, the smoothness and facility with which they can be worked have a decided influence in the quality of finished projects. This is especially true where inexperienced mechanics are concerned.

In the following, several common woods are classified according to ease of working:

EASY TO WORK WITH

Basswood	Pine
Cedar	Poplar

DIFFICULT TO WORK WITH

Ash	Cherry	Larch
Beech	Douglas fir	Maple
Birch	Elm	Oak

MEDIUM DIFFICULT TO WORK WITH

Chestnut	Gum	Spruce
Cypress	Hemlock	Walnut
	Redwood	

PAINT HOLDING

Paint holds better on edge-grained or quartersawed wood than it does on flat-grained wood. Knots in pine do not retain paint as well as the sound knots of cedar, hemlock, or larch. Among the flat-grained boards, the bark side is more satisfactory for painting than the side which was nearer to the center of a tree. Under exposure to the weather, cedar, cypress, and the pines hold paint to excellent advantage in any climate. Hemlock can be depended upon in mild climates. Douglas fir and larch cannot hold paint as well as the woods previously mentioned.

STIFFNESS OF LUMBER

As previously mentioned, stiffness of lumber is often of more importance than what is called *breaking strength*. For example, joists made from practically any kind of lumber will safely support a floor if they are 2 by 8 or 2 by 10 inches in size, if they are spaced no more than 16 inches apart, and if bridging is installed between them. But unless the wood has ample stiffness, plaster cracking, as mentioned in Chapters 4 and 5, would surely occur.

If lumber lacks stiffness, it tends to bend or deflect when subjected to a load. For example, if floor joists do not have ample stiffness, they will bend a little each time a piece of furniture is moved across a floor they support. Such bending subjects plaster to stresses it cannot resist and it cracks as a result. Lack of stiffness in floor joists is also likely to cause vibration in a floor as it is walked on. This is another cause of plaster cracks.

The wood used for wall studs must also be stiff in order to resist tendencies of walls to bend under the weights of floors above them.

Differences in stiffness between kinds of wood may be compensated for by changing the size of such structural details as floor joists. Height and length of such details have a greater effect on their stiffness than on strength properties. A change of $\frac{1}{32}$ inch in the thickness of a standard $2\frac{5}{32}$-inch board produces a change of 12 per cent in the stiffness of the board laid flat in a floor. A 2- by 10-inch joist has about one-fourth more wood in it than a 2- by 8-inch joist, but it is more than twice as stiff.

Stiffness is little affected by such defects as knots. Thus, where house remodeling work is concerned, lumber of sound but knotty grades may safely be used.

In the following, several common woods are classified according to stiffness:

HIGH STIFFNESS

Ash	Cherry	Maple
Beech	Elm	Oak
Birch	Hemlock	Pine
Douglas fir	Larch	Walnut

MEDIUM STIFFNESS

Basswood	Gum	Redwood
Cypress	Poplar	Spruce

LOW STIFFNESS

Cedar	Chestnut

FIGURE IN WOOD

The choice of woods for woodwork (trim) that are to have a natural finish (varnish or wax) is usually based upon the character of the figure or pattern of grain in the woods. Figure is due to different causes in the various woods. In woods like yellow pine and Douglas fir it results from the contrast within the growth rings; in others, such as oak and beech, it results from flakes in addition to the growth rings; in maple, walnut, and birch it results from wavy or curly grain, etc. Except where the figure in wood results from flakes, the figure is more pronounced in plain-sawed lumber than in quartersawed.

In the following, several common woods are classified according to the amount of figure they contain:

HIGHLY FIGURED

Ash	Douglas fir	Larch
Chestnut	Elm	Oak
Cypress		Pine

MODULATED FIGURE

Beech	Gum	Redwood
Birch	Hemlock	Spruce
Cherry	Maple	Walnut
	Poplar	

LITTLE FIGURE

Basswood	Cedar

HOW TO AVOID SHRINKAGE DEFECTS

When new walls, floors, and other structural details are being added to existing houses, the woods used must be exceptionally dry. Otherwise, several undesirable shrinkage defects are probable. For example, new walls and floors may shrink enough to be out of plumb or out of level so far as the old walls and floors are concerned. Also, severe plaster cracks may appear at points where old and new walls meet. Thus, the use of exceptionally dry wood is a matter of first consideration in any major remodeling project.

In general, careful observance of the following rules will help materially to prevent shrinkage defects:

1. Secure exceptionally dry lumber and keep it in that condition prior to and during remodeling operations.

2. Use paint or other protective coatings as soon as possible. Such coatings seal woods and eliminate moisture absorption.

3. Select woods having low inherent shrinkage.

4. Wherever possible, use vertical-grain or quartersawed lumber in preference to the flat-grain type.

DRESSED LUMBER

Most of the lumber used in ordinary remodeling projects is *surfaced* on both sides and both edges. Such lumber is known as *dressed* lumber because it is ready for use without reworking so far as its sides and edges are concerned.

When lumber is dressed, it is reduced from the size it was when it left the sawmill. For example, a piece 2 inches thick and 8 inches wide is known as a 2 by 8. When it is dressed, the planing (surfacing) reduces it to 1⅝ by 7⅝ inches. However, it is still called a 2 by 8. All ordinary lumber is thus reduced somewhat in size. Such reductions should be taken into consideration when planning remodeling work.

GRADES OF LUMBER

Because any kind of lumber is apt to contain various defects and blemishes, the National Bureau of Standards formulated what is known as the *American Lumber Standards*. The purpose of setting up such standards was to ensure uniform grading throughout the country. There is now a growing practice to put indelible marks on all building lumber at the sawmill, stating the grade, kind, size, degree of seasoning (dryness), and identity of the supplier. This grade- and trade-marking program is distinctly in the interest of users.

Softwoods. There are several ways in which softwood lumber is graded. We shall discuss the most important of such ways.

AMERICAN STANDARD GRADES. Table 1 shows the various grades of lumber from the standpoints of quality and recommended uses.

STANDARD LENGTHS. Most ordinary lumber is sold in what is called standard lengths. All such lengths are multiples of 2. As far as possible, remodeling projects should be planned to make use of standard lengths so as to avoid waste. Local lumberyards will supply information in connection with the standard lengths available.

STANDARD WIDTHS AND THICKNESSES. Various standard widths and thicknesses are available, but they vary somewhat, depending upon kinds

TABLE 1. American standard softwood yard lumber grades[*]

	Yard lumber		Grades
Total products of a typical log arranged in series according to quality as determined by appearance	Select lumber	Suitable for natural finishes	Grade A (practically free from defects) Grade B (allows a few small defects or blemishes)
	Finish items (lumber of good appearance and finishing)	Suitable for paint finishes	Grade C (allows a limited number of small defects or blemishes that can be covered with paint) Grade D (allows any number of defects or blemishes which do not detract from the appearance of the finish, especially when painted)
	Common lumber (lumber containing defects or blemishes which detract from the appearance of the finish but suitable for general-utility and construction purposes)	Lumber suitable for use without waste	No. 1 (sound and tight-knotted stock; size of defects and blemishes limited; may be considered watertight lumber) No. 2 (allows large and coarse defects; may be considered graintight lumber)
		Lumber permitting waste	No. 3 (allows larger and coarser defects than No. 2 and occasional knotholes) No. 4 (low-quality lumber admitting the coarsest defects, such as decay and holes) No. 5 (must hold together under ordinary handling)

* Recommended by the U.S. Department of Agriculture "Wood Handbook."

of lumber. Local lumberyards will supply information in connection with the widths and thicknesses available.

Hardwoods. The most desirable grades of hardwood are known as *firsts*. The next grades are known as *seconds*. Both firsts and seconds, which are generally combined, are known as *FAS*. The third-best grade is called *selects*, followed by *No. 1 common, No. 2 common, sound wormy, No. 3A common*, and *No. 3B common*.

STANDARD LENGTHS. Little standardization exists because of the scarcity and size of hardwood logs.

STANDARD WIDTHS AND THICKNESSES. No standards have been established.

Finish Lumber. Such lumber, to be used for fine cabinets and other finish items, can be purchased at most lumberyards. However, we must remember that so-called 1-inch stock will actually be less than 1 inch after dressing.

KNOTTY PINE. This specialty lumber, as used for wall surfaces, is generally available ¾ inch thick and 5½, 7½, 9½, or 11½ inches wide. The boards are known as *1 by 6, 1 by 8, 1 by 10,* and *1 by 12.*

RED CEDAR. Ordinarily, red cedar can be purchased ⅜ inch thick, 3¼ inches wide, and in random lengths. It is supplied in bundles of about 40 feet board measure. Each such bundle will cover about 30 square feet of wall area.

Floor Lumber. The wood of hardwood trees, such as oaks, birches, maples, and beeches, is graded so as to take into account the yield and size of cuttings, with one clear face, that can be sawed from the lumber. The chief grades in maple are *first, second,* and *third.* The grades in quartersawed oak are *clear, sap clear, and select.* The grades in plain-sawed oak are *clear, select,* and *No. 1.* The flaked grain of quartersawed oak is generally preferred to the figure of plain-sawed oak. The following grading rules are typical of all hardwood flooring:

Grading Rules for Maple, Beech, and Birch. The beech and birch flooring show slightly more grain pattern than maple but all three are nearly alike.

FIRST GRADE. This grade is the highest standard grade and assures the most beautiful floors. The surface is practically free from defects.

SECOND GRADE. This grade has some tight, sound knots and slight imperfections. It is especially suitable for recreation rooms where absolutely perfect floor surfaces are not required.

THIRD GRADE. This is an economical grade which contains more imperfections. It is especially suitable for cottages or dens where unusual coloring and irregularities are not serious.

BOARD LENGTHS. The better the grade of such flooring, the longer the average board length. It is cheaper to use standard lengths, as they ordinarily come in bundles, than to request all long lengths.

BOARD THICKNESSES AND WIDTHS. Several such dimensions are available. Typical thicknesses are $^{25}\!/_{32}$, $^{53}\!/_{32}$, $\frac{3}{8}$, $\frac{1}{2}$, and $\frac{5}{8}$ inch. Typical widths are $1\frac{1}{2}$, 2 and $2\frac{1}{4}$ inches.

The $^{25}\!/_{32}$-inch thickness is most commonly used for all general purposes.

The $^{53}\!/_{32}$-inch thickness is used when floors are to be subjected to extraordinary strain and wear.

The $\frac{3}{8}$-, $\frac{1}{2}$-, and $\frac{5}{8}$-inch thicknesses are satisfactory for light service and especially in remodeling projects where existing floors are to be resurfaced.

NOTE 1: See explanations relative to the use of second grade flooring in Chapter 6.

NOTE 2: There are national associations, in connection with various kinds of flooring wood, which supply all sorts of helpful information upon request.

WOOD DEFECTS

Since wood, unlike steel, is a natural product developed through many years of growth in the open air where it is exposed to varying conditions, it is likely to contain some defects. Such defects cannot be corrected. Therefore, wood should be inspected before use. Some of the commonly encountered defects are set forth in the following and illustrated in Figure 2.

Checks. See *A* part of illustration. A lengthwise separation of wood tissue between growth rings is known as *check*. Such defects should be avoided where strength, stiffness, and good appearance are required.

Knots. See *B* part of illustration. As previously explained, knots are not serious if they are sound and confined to lumber used where it does not have to be painted or otherwise finished.

Decay. See *C* part of illustration. Decay can be recognized by the punky, soft, spongy, stringy, or crumbly condition of woods. Boards showing such symptoms should be avoided.

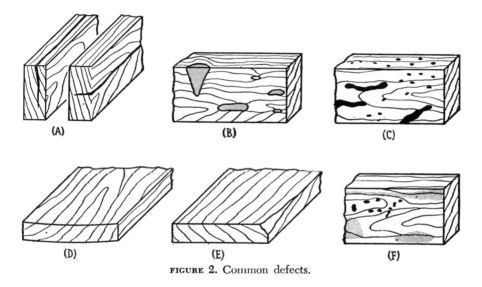

FIGURE 2. Common defects.

Warping. See *D* part of illustration. In some instances, boards develop a curve across the grain as they dry out. Slight warping can be corrected in rough structural details, but warped boards should never be used for visible details such as cabinets.

Wane. See *E* part of illustration. This is a defect on the corner or edge of a board due to lack of wood or bark. Such boards should not be used except for subfloors or in other locations where the defect will not be visible.

Pitch Discoloration. See *F* part of illustration. Owing to a moldlike fungus, discoloration sometimes appears in boards. Such a defect does not impair strength or stiffness but is objectionable for painted or natural finishes.

BOARD-FOOT CONTENT

Lumber is always sold by the board foot. A board foot consists of a unit that measures 1 by 12 inches, as shown in the *A* part of Figure 3. Both of the units shown in the *B* part also contain 1 board foot.

FIGURE 3. Board-foot content.

The number of board feet in lumber of any dimension can be found by means of the simple formula

$$\frac{T \times W \times L}{12} = \text{board feet}$$

where T = thickness of lumber in inches

W = width of lumber in inches

L = length of lumber in feet

EXAMPLE. Find the number of board feet in a 2 by 6 that is 12 feet long.

SOLUTION. Substitute numerical values for the letters in the formula.

The value of T is 2. The value of W is 6. The value of L is 12. Thus we have

$$\frac{2 \times 6 \times 12}{12} = \frac{144}{12} = 12 \text{ board feet}$$

This checks with the answer shown in Table 2.

TABLE 2. Board-foot content

Size, inches	Length, feet							
	8	10	12	14	16	18	20	22
1 × 2	1½	1⅔	2	2⅓	2⅔	3	3⅓	3⅔
1 × 3	2	2½	3	3½	4	4½	5	5½
1 × 4	2⅔	3⅓	4	4⅔	5⅓	6	6⅔	7⅓
1 × 5	3⅓	4⅙	5	5⅚	6⅔	7½	8⅓	9⅙
1 × 6	4	5	6	7	8	9	10	11
1 × 8	5⅓	6⅔	8	9⅓	10⅔	12	13⅓	14⅔
1 × 10	6⅔	8⅓	10	11⅔	13⅓	15	16⅔	18⅓
1 × 12	8	10	12	14	16	18	20	22
1 × 14	9⅓	11⅔	14	16⅓	18⅔	21	23⅓	25⅔
1 × 16	20⅔	13⅓	16	18⅔	21⅓	24	26⅔	29⅓
2 × 4	5⅓	6⅔	8	9⅓	10⅔	12	13⅓	14⅔
2 × 6	8	10	12	14	16	18	20	22
2 × 8	10⅔	13⅓	16	18⅔	21⅓	24	26⅔	29⅓
2 × 10	13⅓	16⅔	20	23⅓	26⅔	30	33⅓	36⅔
2 × 12	16	20	24	28	32	36	40	44
4 × 4	10⅔	13⅓	16	18⅔	21⅓	24	26⅔	29⅓
4 × 6	16	20	24	28	32	36	40	44
4 × 8	21⅓	26⅔	32	37⅓	42⅔	48	53⅓	58⅔
4 × 10	26⅔	33⅓	40	46⅔	53⅓	60	66⅔	73⅓
4 × 12	32	40	48	56	64	72	80	88
4 × 14	37⅓	46⅔	56	65⅓	74⅔	84	93⅓	102⅔
4 × 16	42⅔	53⅓	64	74⅔	85⅓	96	106⅔	117⅓
6 × 6	24	30	36	42	48	54	60	66
6 × 8	32	40	48	56	64	72	80	88

LUMBER FOR VARIOUS PURPOSES

In the following, several typical uses for various kinds of woods are suggested:

Exterior House Trim. The usual requirements are decay resistance, good painting and weathering characteristics, easy-working qualities, and freedom from warp.

SUGGESTED WOODS. Cedar, cypress, and redwood where decay hazard is high. Pine where decay hazard does not exist. Heartwood is preferable.

Living- and Dining-room Floors. The usual requirements are resistance to wear, attractive figure or color, minimum warp and shrinkage.

SUGGESTED WOODS. Beech, birch, maple, and oak.

Uncovered Kitchen Floors. The usual requirements are resistance to wear, fine texture, ability to withstand washing, and minimum warp and shrinkage.

SUGGESTED WOODS. Beech, birch, and maple.

Covered Kitchen Floors. Where linoleum or soft tile are to be used as surfaces, softwood plywood serves the purpose to excellent advantage.

Porch Flooring. The usual requirements are minimum decay resistance, medium wear resistance, and freedom from warping.

SUGGESTED WOODS. Cypress, Douglas fir, larch, pine, and redwood.

Rough Framing. The usual requirements are stiffness, nail-holding power, hardness, and freedom from shrinkage and warp. Dryness is the most important requirement.

SUGGESTED WOODS. Douglas fir, larch, and pine. Cypress, redwood, ash, and beech can be used when the previously mentioned kinds are not available.

Other woods, such as chestnut, elm, gum, and poplar, may be used, but they are not recommended.

Interior Trim. The usual requirements are pleasing figure, hardness, and freedom from warp.

SUGGESTED WOODS. Ash, birch, cherry, chestnut, and oak constitute the most desirable materials where natural finishes are desired.

When trim is to be painted, the following woods are suggested and listed in the order of desirability:

Hemlock	Basswood	Douglas fir
Redwood	Cypress	Gum

Roof Boards. The usual requirements are stiffness, nail-holding power, small tendency to warp, and ease of working.

SUGGESTED WOODS. Douglas fir, larch, and pine are commonly used. Cypress, ash, beech, chestnut, and hemlock may be used with somewhat less assurance of stiffness.

Window Sash. The usual requirements are moderate shrinkage, good paint-holding qualities, freedom from warping, ease of working, and screw-holding power.

SUGGESTED WOODS IN DRY LOCATIONS. Northern white pine, cypress, and redwood. Douglas fir, larch, and yellow pine can be used but with less assurance of requirements being met.

SUGGESTED WOODS IN MOIST LOCATIONS. Northern white pine. Douglas fir and larch can be used with less assurance of requirements being met.

Shelving: High-class Natural or Paint Finish. The usual requirements are stiffness, good finishing qualities, and freedom from pitch and warp.

SUGGESTED WOODS. Ash, birch, maple, oak, and walnut are suitable for natural finishes to match other interior trim. Cypress and northern white pine are suitable for paint finishes.

Shelving: Unfinished or Plain Paint Coating. The usual requirements are stiffness, ease of working, and freedom from pitch and warp.

SUGGESTED WOODS. Northern white pine, cypress, hemlock, redwood, basswood, and poplar.

Shingles. The usual requirements are high decay resistance, small tendency to curl, and freedom from splitting when nailed.

SUGGESTED WOODS. Cedar, cypress, and redwood; No. 1 shingles (all heart, edge-grain clear stock) should be used for long life and greatest ultimate economy.

Siding. The usual requirements are good painting characteristics, easy-working qualities, and freedom from warp.

SUGGESTED WOODS. Cedar, cypress, northern white pine, and redwood.

Outdoor Steps. The usual requirements are decay resistance, non-splintering, bending strength, wear resistance, and freedom from warping.

SUGGESTED WOODS. Cypress and Douglas fir. Larch and redwood are good second choices.

Subfloors. The usual requirements are high stiffness, medium shrinkage, small warp, and ease of working.

SUGGESTED WOODS. Douglas fir, larch, and pine.

Sheathing. Same as subfloors.

Concrete Forms. Same as subfloors.

Gates and Fences. The usual requirements are moderate bending, medium decay and weather resistance, high nail-holding power, and freedom from warp.

SUGGESTED WOODS. Cypress, Douglas fir, pine, redwood, and oak. Cedar, northern white pine, chestnut, and poplar can be used with al· most as much assurance that all requirements will be met.

Cabinets. Same as shelving.

Furring Strips. Same as sheathing.

Sills. Same as sash.

Screen Frames. Same as sash.

SOFTWOOD PLYWOOD

In most remodeling work where panel plywood is used, Douglas fir is considered one of the best. Douglas-fir plywood is a built-up board of laminated veneers in which the grain of each piece is at right angles to the one adjacent to it. Kiln-dried veneer is united under high pressure with a bonding agent, which makes the joints as strong as the wood itself or stronger. The alternating direction of the grain with each contiguous layer of wood equalizes the strains and in this way minimizes shrinkage and warpage. It also prevents splitting.

Plywood panels, 48 inches wide and 96 inches long, are very popular in the building of houses. However, they are made in many other sizes, such as 30 inches wide and 144 inches long, and in various thicknesses. Thicknesses are from $\frac{1}{4}$ to $\frac{3}{4}$ inch. Still other sizes are specially made. The stock-panel width of 48 inches as well as the popular 8-foot lengths are multiples of 16 inches, which is the accepted spacing for studs and joists.

In building construction, plywoods have many uses. They are extensively used in the following types of construction:

1. Kitchen cabinets, bookcases, shelves, linen closets, utility-room cabinets, supply cases, and many other types of cabinet work
2. Interior wall paneling, partition walls, and for decorative purposes
3. Exterior wall sheathing
4. Exterior roof sheathing
5. Subflooring and underlays
6. Outside wall siding
7. Concrete formwork
8. Outside decorations, soffits, etc.

HARDWOOD PLYWOOD

Hardwood plywood is made with two types of cores—veneer core and lumber core. *Veneer-core plywood* is made of thin veneers, the face veneers running parallel to the length of the panel and the alternating plies at right angles. An odd number of plies (3, 5, 7, etc.) is used. In *lumber-core* construction, the plywood is made of narrow strips of sawn lumber with crossbands and face veneers on either side.

Veneer-core plywood has somewhat more resiliency and strength per pound than lumber-core plywood, but the latter possesses practically the same dimensional stability and is generally used for woodworking projects which call for doweled, splined, or dovetail joints, exposed edges or butt hinges.

Grading. The Hardwood Plywood Institute has adopted four grades governing the backs and faces of hardwood plywood:

GOOD GRADE (Grade 1). Used for a great variety of projects where appearance is a factor, this grade is free of obvious defects and will take a beautiful natural finish. If formed of more than one piece, it can be matched at the joints to avoid sharp contrasts in color and grain.

SOUND GRADE (Grade 2). Intended for smooth paint surfaces, this grade is free from open defects in order to provide a smooth, sound surface for the paint. It may contain defects of the kind that will be completely covered by the paint, such as mineral streaks, stain, discoloration, and patches.

UTILITY GRADE (Grade 3). A strong, serviceable material for backs, concealed constructions, and other uses where appearance is not a prime factor, this grade may contain any number of defects which do not actually weaken the material structurally. This includes knotholes up to ¾ inch in diameter, and wormholes, splits, or open joints not exceeding ³⁄₁₆ inch.

REJECT GRADE (Grade 4). This lowest grade may be used for the same purposes as utility grade inasmuch as the same defects are allowed, but the defects are permitted to be larger. For example, knotholes may be as large as 2 inches in diameter, instead of ¾ inch as in utility grade, and splits and wormholes may be ¼ inch wide if they do not exceed one-fourth of the length of the veneer. The limitations ensure that the strength and serviceability of the panel are not seriously impaired.

In addition to specifying one of these five grades, a buyer of plywood may also specify plywood by adhesion type, although it is generally enough to state whether the material is to be used for exterior or interior purposes. The three types are based on the adhesives used in joining the layers of the plywood together. Type 1 is fully waterproof, intended for outdoor and marine uses. The bond will withstand full weather exposure and will be unaffected by microorganisms. Type 2 is highly water-resistant, retaining practically all its strength when subjected to an occasional thorough wetting and drying. Type 3 is dry bond, suitable for uses not subject to water, dampness, or high humidity.

Hardwood Plywood Species. This type of plywood is produced in a full range of American hardwoods in addition to such imported hardwoods as mahogany. Six hardwood species rank above all others in plywood popularity. They are:

Gum	Mahogany	Walnut
Birch	Oak	Maple

SIZES AND THICKNESSES. Hardwood plywood is available in a great many sizes and thicknesses, but only panels in the most commonly used dimensions are customarily carried by neighborhood lumberyards. Hardwood plywood distributors, found in every good-sized city in the United States, carry a complete line of all sizes, and they will fulfill special orders as requested by the retail lumber dealer.

Panels come in widths of 2, 2½, 3, 3½, and 4 feet, and lengths of 3, 4, 5, 6, 7, and 8 feet. Standard veneer-core-plywood thicknesses range from ⅛ to $1\frac{3}{16}$ inch in 3, 5, or 7 plies. The most popular veneer-core-plywood thicknesses are ⅛, ¼, and ⅜ inch.

Lumber-core plywood is generally thicker, ½ inch and upward. Approximately six times more veneer-core plywood is sold than lumber-core.

CHOOSING PLYWOOD PANELS. One of the big advantages in working with hardwood plywood lies in the great diversity of sizes, species, grades, and prices in which the material may be obtained.

The species and grade, and consequently the price, will be governed by the nature of the project and the type of finish desired. If the user wants a paint finish, he can buy Sound Grade plywood, but if a natural wood effect is desired, he should move up to Good Grade for better results. A saving can be effected by obtaining Utility Grade for backs and concealed construction.

Economy comes into the picture again in laying out the work. By careful planning, the craftsman often can fit all the pieces of his project into one good-sized rectangle, say, 3 by 6 feet. This means that he need purchase only a single panel of that size, and that he will have a minimum of waste.

SAWING HARDWOOD PLYWOOD. Correct sawing procedure is an important factor in producing a close-fitting, well-built job. With plywood, best results are obtained by using high-speed power saws with little or no set and as much lead to the teeth as possible. If both edges of panel are to be exposed, place the panel on a plywood scrap and saw through both layers to eliminate the possibility of fuzzing. A circular saw should be 10 or more inches in diameter. A combination-blade type is the best to use. It is advisable to saw with the best side of the panel up, except when using a portable circular saw. Ordinary hand saws can also be used. Their teeth should be fine and sharp with little set.

JOINING HARDWOOD-PLYWOOD SHEETS. When working with veneer-core plywood for wall paneling and other purposes, the craftsman will have his choice of the following methods of joining:

1. V joint
2. Butt joint
3. Block-treatment joint
4. Wood-faced extruded moldings
5. Tongue-and-groove joint
6. Open recessed joint
7. Splined joint
8. Mitered joint
9. Battens of wood, plastic, or metal

The butt joint, or merely fitting two pieces together on the same stud with a flush surface, is the simplest method. Planing the edges of the two panels along the joint to form a slight "V" adds appeal. For protection against movement of the solid wood stud, which may open the joint, nail ¼-inch-thick plywood strips to the studs and apply the plywood panels to the plywood strips.

CORNER TREATMENT. Although corners may be finished without the use of moldings, they are usually preferable because they simplify the work and, in most cases, give a more professional look to the completed job. Moldings can be made in the workshop or purchased at a lumberyard in a number of different types.

For exterior corners fill in with a quarter round of the same thickness

as the panels. A different effect can be obtained by using a quarter round
of a slightly larger size and sanding its edges.

For interior corners, use cove molding. In order to guard against possible later damage due to movement of the studs, it is wise to employ a
"floating" corner. One of the two panels which meet to form the corner
should not be nailed to a stud at the corner but should be left free in
order to provide a safety valve against movement.

FINISHING HARDWOOD PLYWOOD. There are many ways of finishing
plywood projects. Individual preference, the type of wood, and the nature
of the project will determine the kind of finish to be applied.

Paint, of course, will cover the attractive natural grain pattern of the
wood, so that, generally speaking, only projects utilizing Sound Grade
plywood should be painted. Good Grade plywood is usually intended for
natural finishes to enhance the beauty of the grain rather than cover it.

No matter which type of finish is selected, the important first step is
to prepare the wood's surface. The wood should be clean and dry, sanded
smooth, and have all traces of glue removed and dents and cracks filled.
Pressing with a hot iron and damp cloth will often cause small dents to
disappear.

After the finishing procedure has been decided upon, completely finish
a small scrap of the same plywood as was used in the project. This pre-
testing procedure will give the craftsman advance knowledge of the exact
results to expect so that he may make alterations if desired.

Care must be taken with natural finishes to keep them natural. The
trend today is toward lighter application—enough finish to protect the
wood and give it a dull sheen, but not enough to greatly alter the tone
and color.

CLEAR FINISH. Apply prime coat of clear sealer or thin coat of white
shellac mixed with equal portion of denatured alcohol. When dry, fill
nail holes with plastic wood dough or putty tinted the color of the wood
and rub with No. 1 steel wool or No. 00 sandpaper. Apply a second coat
of clear (or pigmented, if desired) sealer or varnish. Apply a third coat
of dull varnish which may be buffed to a velvety sheen when dry. If the
wood is open-pored, such as oak or mahogany, the only difference in the
procedure is to use a white or natural filler for the second coat in order
to fill the pores.

LACQUER FINISH. Apply a coat of lacquer sealer, sand lightly, and follow with several coats of clear lacquer. Buff and wax.

STAINING AND BLEACHING. Stains and bleaches are used to either lighten or darken the natural color of the wood prior to the application of a clear coating. A great variety of stains and bleaches are available, and manufacturer's directions should be followed closely.

WAX. There are wax-finishing systems suitable for hardwood plywood, but the craftsman must bear in mind that paint or varnish cannot be used later because the wax enters the wood fibers and will soften paint and varnish.

ENAMELING AND PAINTING. With no grain raise, hardwood plywood provides an excellent surface for enameling or painting. The use of a filler is not required for close-grained woods such as birch and maple.

ECONOMICAL USE OF PLYWOOD

The use of plywood should be planned so as to minimize waste. Such planning can be done to advantage by drawing sketches of floors or walls to scale and then making two or more trials to see how panels of a given size can be fitted into the areas.

CHAPTER TWO

Fasteners

The stiffness of houses, whether they include all or partial wood framing, depends to an important extent on how well the various structural details, parts, and elements are fastened together. When sufficient fasteners of the correct kind and placement are used, a high degree of stiffness is assured. On the other hand, when improper and too few fasteners are used, stiffness is lacking.

Without a high degree of stiffness, houses are subject to many troublesome and costly defects, some of which are described in Chapters 4, 5, and 6. Other defects include sticking doors and windows, annoying vibrations, out-of-plumb walls, and sagging floors.

In remodeling work where structural details, parts, and elements are moved or new ones added, proper fasteners are more important than when entirely new houses are being built. Unless fasteners are used in ample quantities and according to proper sizes and placement, serious cracks and other difficulties will occur.

Even though correct fastening is so highly important, the literature of house construction and remodeling has previously contained little, if any, instruction in connection with fasteners. As a result, there is much difference of opinion as to what constitutes proper fastening, and, consequently, a large variation in practice. Such practice—usually a matter of precedent, tradition, or individual judgment—does not take into account the forces which fasteners must resist. The purpose of this chapter is to explain commonly required fasteners and to set up general specifications for fastening, in the hope that they will help to replace haphazard practices with sound and efficient ones.

NAIL-HOLDING POWER

In most joints of the types commonly encountered in remodeling work, one piece of material tends to slide on or along an adjacent one, owing to the weights supported or other forces which act on the joint. In some instances, the joints are not subject to analysis with respect to the forces that they must resist and, consequently, cannot be designed on an engineering basis. A good example of this has to do with the joint between the lower end of a stud and a sill. The fastening for such joints is therefore based entirely on experiments carried on by many mechanics over long periods of time. The force that fasteners are required to resist in some other types of joints can be computed and the size, quantity, and placement of fasteners accurately determined.

When joints are subject to the sliding previously mentioned, the fasteners must supply what is known as *lateral resistance*. For example, the lateral resistance of fasteners attaching sheathing to studs comes into action in resisting forces that tend to rack the wall and in carrying the weights of such materials.

The other way in which fasteners are stressed is in direct pull or withdrawal. Fasteners attaching covering materials to the lower edges of joists or rafters are stressed in direct pull by the weights of the materials. Similar stress is induced when fasteners must resist warping, vibration, and wind or earthquake tremors. When fasteners are sufficient in size, quantity, and placement to accomplish the necessary resistance, houses are stiff and the defects previously mentioned cannot occur.

Nails are important fasteners and are used to stiffen many of the structural details, parts, and elements of houses. If we assume that they are used in sufficient size, quantity, and placement, the resistance which is offered by wood to their withdrawal, under stress, is of importance. Usually, the denser and harder the wood, the greater the inherent nail-holding power.

In the following, several common woods are classified according to their nail-holding power:

HIGH HOLDING POWER

Ash	Elm	Maple
Beech	Larch	Oak
Birch		Pine

MEDIUM HOLDING POWER

Chestnut	Gum	Poplar
Cypress	Hemlock	Redwood
Douglas fir		Spruce

LOW HOLDING POWER

Basswood	Cottonwood
Cedar	Fir

The size, quantity, and placement of nails have a marked effect on the strength of a joint. Thus, more nails are required in woods of medium holding power than in woods of high holding power.

The resistance to withdrawal of nails increases almost directly with the diameter of shank; that is, if the diameter of a nail is doubled, the holding power is almost doubled, provided the nail does not split the wood when it is driven. The lateral resistance of nails is also practically doubled if their diameter is doubled.

The moisture content of the wood at the time of nailing is extremely important in terms of good nail holding. If nails are driven into wet wood, they will lose about 75 per cent of their full holding power when the wood becomes dry. Then, shrinking and warping are not resisted and the defects previously mentioned occur.

As previously stated, the splitting of wood by nails reduces their holding power. Even if the wood is split only slightly around a nail, there is considerable loss in holding power. Because of hardness and texture characteristics some woods split more in nailing than do others. The heavy, dense woods, such as maple and oak, split more in nailing than do the lightweight woods, such as basswood and spruce. Woods such as pine and Douglas fir split more than northern white pine. The most common means taken to reduce splitting is the use of smaller nails. The number of such nails must be increased, of course, to maintain the same gross holding power.

Nail Shanks. Continuous research tends to indicate that the holding power of nails depends to an appreciable amount upon their shanks. Chemical etching of shank surfaces constitutes one effort to increase holding power; the use of various coatings is another. Barbing of shanks

TABLE 1. Commonly used nails, their size, gage, and number per pound

Common		Box		Finish		
Penny size	Length, inches, for common, box, and finish*	Common nails			Box and finish nails		
		Gage	Thickness, thousandths	Number per pound	Gage	Thickness, thousandths	Number per pound
2d	1	15	0.072	876	15½	0.069	1,010
3d	1¼	14	0.083	568	14½	0.078	635
4d	1½	12½	0.102	316	14	0.083	473
5d	1¾	12½	0.102	271	14	0.083	406
6d	2	11½	0.115	181	12½	0.102	236
7d	2¼	11½	0.115	161	12½	0.102	210
8d	2½	10¼	0.131	106	11½	0.115	145
9d	2¾	10¼	0.131	96	11½	0.115	132
10d	3	9	0.148	69	10½	0.127	94
12d	3¼	9	0.148	63	10½	0.127	88
16d	3½	8	0.165	49	10	0.134	71
20d	4	6	0.203	31	9	0.148	52
30d	4½	5	0.220	24	9	0.148	46
40d	5	4	0.238	18	8	0.165	35
50d	5½	3	0.259	14			
60d	6	2	0.284	11			

* Coated nails are ⅛ inch shorter.

Note: Flooring nails are similar in appearance to the finish nail but are about 1½ gage thicker for each size. They are made in sizes from 6d to 20d. Wire nails are gaged by the old standard Birmingham wire gage.

also increases holding power, especially if wet lumber must be used. Various other shank treatments, such as grooves and spirals, also tend to increase holding power. Readers may secure manufacturers' literature and study the advantages of one or another form of shank.

NAIL SIZES

The nail industry still clings to the *penny system* to indicate the length of the most commonly used nails, ranging in length from 1 to 6 inches. The symbol for penny is d. Table 1 shows several of the most commonly used nails in terms of penny and inch sizes.

RULE FOR LENGTH OF NAILS

There is a simple rule to follow when selecting nail lengths for both rough (framing) and finish (trim, cabinets, etc.) carpentry work. The rule applies to hardwoods and softwoods. Figure 1 shows the rule graphically. Suppose that pieces A and B are to be nailed together. In the case of hardwoods, the nail penetration, X, into the bottom piece should be one-half the length of the nail. For softwoods, the penetration, Y, into the bottom piece should be two-thirds the length of the nail. Thus, the thickness of the top piece determines the required nail length.

FIGURE 1. Nail penetration into hardwood and softwood.

TYPICAL NAIL DATA

Table 2 shows interesting and useful data in connection with the types of nails to use for various purposes.

TABLE 2. Typical nail data

Size and kind of material	Board measure in feet	Trade name	Nails required, lb			Length of nails	No. of nails to each bearing
			12" centers	16" centers	24" centers		
1 × 4 boards and shiplap	1,000	8d common	60	48	30	2½"	2
1 × 6 boards and shiplap	1,000	8d common	40	32	20	2½"	2
1 × 8 boards and shiplap	1,000	8d common	31	27	16	2½"	2
1 × 10 boards and shiplap	1,000	8d common	25	20	13	2½"	2
1 × 12 boards and shiplap	1,000	8d common	31	24	16	2½"	3
1 × 4 Dressed and Matched blind nailed	1,000	8d common	30	24	15	2½"	1
1 × 6 D&M blind nailed	1,000	8d common	20	16	10	2½"	1
1 × 8 D&M blind nailed and 1 face nail	1,000	8d common	31	27	16	2½"	2
1 × 10 D&M blind nailed and 1 face nail	1,000	8d common	25	20	13	2½"	2
1 × 12 D&M blind nailed and 1 face nail	1,000	8d common	21	16	11	2½"	2
2 × 4 to 2 × 16 framing	1,000	20d common	20	16	10	4 "	2
		16d common	10	10	6	3½"	
		10d common	8	6	4	3 "	
3 × 4 to 3 × 14 framing	1,000	60d common	30	25	15	6 "	1
2 × 6 D&M flooring	1,000	20d common	35	27	18	4 "	1
2 × 8 D&M flooring	1,000	20d common	27	20	14	4 "	1
1 × 4 drop siding	1,000	7d siding	45	35		2¼"	2
1 × 6 drop siding	1,000	7d siding	30	25		2¼"	2
1 × 8 drop siding	1,000	7d siding	23	18		2¼"	2
½ × 4 beveled siding	1,000	6d siding	23	18		2 "	1
½ × 6 bev. siding	1,000	6d siding	15	13		2 "	1
½ × 8 bev. siding	1,000	6d siding	12	10		2 "	1

¾ × 10 bev. siding	1,000	45	35		7d siding	2¼″	2
¾ × 12 bev. siding	1,000	60	50		7d siding	2¼″	3
¾ × 4 ceiling	1,000	18	14	9	8d finish	2½″	1
½ to ⅝″ ceiling	-,000	11	8	6	6d finish	2 ″	1
⅞″ finish lumber	1,000	25	12	13	8d finish	2½″	2
1⅛″ finish lumber	1,000	12	10	6	10d finish	3 ″	2
1 × 3 flooring, softwood	1,000	42	32	21	8d floor brads	2½″	1
1 × 4 flooring, softwood	1,000	32	26	16	8d floor brads	2½″	1
1 × 6 flooring, softwood	1,000	22	18	11	8d floor brads	2½″	1
⅜ × 1½ flooring, hardwood	1,000	13	10		4d casing	1¼″	1
⅜ × 2 flooring, hardwood	1,000	11	8		4d casing	1¼″	1
13⁄16 × 1½ flooring, hardwood	1,000	27	20		7d casing	2¼″	1
13⁄16 × 2¼ flooring, hardwood	1,000	20	14		7d casing	2¼″	1

1 × 2 furring on brick walls—100 lineal ft. . 20d cut nails, requires 5¼ lb

Base per 100 lineal ft. . . . . .8d finish, requires 1 lb, 16″ on centers

Sides of trim, per side of inside trim . . . . . . .4d finish ⎫
  6d finish ⎬ requires about ½ lb total
  8d finish ⎭

48″ wood lath, per 1,000 lath . . . . .3d fine, requires 7 lb

Metal lath, per 100 sq yd . . . . .1″ staples, require 12 lb

or metal lath, per 100 sq yd . . . . . .1⅛″ No. 12 hook head nails, require 15 lb

⅜″ gypsum lath, per 100 sq yd . . . .1⅛″ × 13 gage—5⁄16″ heads, require 10 lb
  Smooth diamond points

¼″ plasterboard, per 100 sq yd . . . . .1″ × 13 gage—5⁄16″ heads, require 10 lb
  Smooth diamond points

13⁄16″ wallboard, per 1,000 sq ft . . . . .3d flathead nail, requires 5 lb

¼″ wallboard, per 1,000 sq ft . . . . .4d flathead nail, requires 9 lb

⅜″ wallboard, per 1,000 sq ft . . . . .4d flathead nail, requires 9 lb

NAIL POINTS

Nail points are highly important and should be selected with the greatest of care. The selection depends upon the nail use. The point can influence both the holding power and the splitting resistance of the wood through which the nails are driven.

Diamond Point. Most of the commonly used nails have diamond points. The gradual taper causes nails to hold well without splitting dense woods.

Blunt-tapered Point. This type of point pierces wood fibers instead of spreading them and thus reduces splitting in hardwoods.

Long Diamond and Needle Points. Either of these points may be used when rapid driving is desired. The sharp points allow easy setting (starting), and the nails can be driven without much driving effort.

Chisel Point. This type of point helps to ease nails through exceptionally hard woods.

Duckbill Point. If nails are to be clinched, this point is recommended.

NAIL CLINCHING

In order to increase the holding power of common nails used in rough carpentry work, they should be clinched. In other words, if a portion of a nail extends out beyond the surface of wood, that portion may be bent over. As previously mentioned, nails having duckbill points can be used to advantage for this purpose.

If plain-shanked nails such as shown in Table 1 are clinched, they will have about 45 per cent greater holding power than a corresponding nonclinched nail. The clinched portion of a nail should be at least ¼ inch long. Longer clinched portions do not provide much more holding power. Clinching should be done perpendicular to the grain of wood.

NAILHEADS

The nails used in connection with all rough carpentry work should have flat heads such as shown on the common nail in Table 1. The diameter of the heads should be at least twice the diameter of the shanks. For all finish carpentry work in connection with trim and cabinets, the nailheads should be of the kind shown on the casing nail in Table 1. Some materials require nailheads of a special kind or size. In such cases manufacturers generally offer the necessary information.

GENERAL NAILING SPECIFICATIONS

The structural details shown in Figures 2 through 15 are those most commonly used in ordinary remodeling work. They will serve as a guide when planning and building additions to, or rearrangements of, existing structural details.

FIGURE 2. Two-piece beam.   FIGURE 3. Double sill.

Figures 2 through 15 also indicate the recommended quantities and placement of nails for fastening all structural members together. The kind of wood is not taken into consideration other than to assume high and medium holding power. In the illustrations, toenailing and perpendicular nailing are indicated by small blank and solid circles, respectively. Toenailing applies when nails must be driven at a slant.

Figure 2. Two-piece Beam. Use 10d or 12d nails. Place two nails at *a*. The nails at *b* should be driven every 16 inches. At girder joints, four nails should be driven as shown at *e*. Use two toenails as shown at *c*.

Figure 3. Double Sill. Use 10d or 12d nails as shown at *a* and *b*. The *c* nails should be driven at 24-inch intervals.

FIGURE 4. Joists.   FIGURE 5. Joists bearing on beam.

Figure 4. Joists. Drive 20d nails at *a* and *b*. Drive 10d nails for toenailing, as shown at *c*, and space them about 16 inches apart. The toenailing helps to prevent movement of the headers during times when a house is subjected to high winds or earthquakes.

Figure 5. Joists Bearing on Beam. Drive at least three 10d or 12d nails for the perpendicular fastening and at least one 10d or 12d nail for toenailing.

Figure 6. Subfloor and Sill. Boards 4 inches or less in width should be nailed using two 8d nails, and wider boards with three 8d nails at each crossing of joists and headers. Drive two 8d nails when board ends occur over joists.

The sills should be fastened by means of 16d nails spaced 16 inches apart and so that the nails go through the subflooring and into the headers.

Figure 7. Plywood Subfloor. Drive 8d nails spaced not more than 6 inches apart along all edges and 12 inches apart along intermediate members.

FIGURE 6. Subfloor and sill.

FIGURE 7. Plywood subfloor.

Figure 8. Studs. Drive two 8d or 10d nails on each wide face. The nails should be driven at points about 1 inch above the plate.

Figure 9. Joists Bearing on Ribbon. Drive at least five 10d or 12d nails to fasten each joist to a stud.

FIGURE 8. Studs.   FIGURE 9. Joists bearing on ribbon.

Figure 10. Rafter Ends. Drive four 12d nails as indicated.

Figure 11. Porch Connections. Drive five 12d nails for fastening ceiling joists and rafters to the studs.

FIGURE 10. Rafter ends.   FIGURE 11. Porch connections.

Figure 12. Diagonal Wall Sheathing. Use 8d nails. For boards 8 inches or less in width, drive two nails at each end of each board, two nails through each board into studs, and three nails through each board into the corner-post assembly. For wider boards drive an additional nail at each of these points. Joints in adjacent runs of boards should be separated by at least two stud spaces. The fastening of sheathing boards is extremely important and adds greatly to the stiffness of a house.

Figure 13. Plywood Wall Sheathing. Plywood less than ½ inch thick should be nailed using 6d nails spaced 5 inches apart along edges and 10 inches apart on intermediate framing members. Plywood ½ or more inches thick should be nailed using 8d nails at the same spacings. Vertical

FIGURE 12. Diagonal wall sheathing.   FIGURE 13. Plywood wall sheathing.

joints between plywood panels should not be on the same stud in succeeding rows of sheathing. For the horizontal joints, nailing strips should be set between the studs and nailed to them.

Figure 14. Shingles. Nail 1 inch above exposure line and ¾ inch from edge of shingles using rust-resisting nails long enough to penetrate through the roof boards. Shingles wider than 8 or 9 inches should be split and nailed as two shingles.

Figure 15. Rafter and Ceiling Joists Supported by Wall Plate. Drive four 10d nails through joist into rafter. Overlap the joists over bearing partition and drive five 10d nails. Toenail the joist and rafter to plate using two 10d nails on each side of assembly.

FIGURE 14. Shingles.

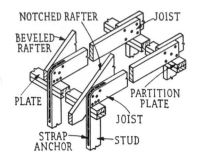

FIGURE 15. Rafter and ceiling joists supported by wall plate.

Additional security against uplift is afforded by metal straps placed as shown and nailed with four 8d nails to studs and with two 8d nails to upper edges of joists.

FASTENING DECORATIVE PLYWOOD

Nails or adhesives may be used in fastening plywoods. Often, a mechanic will want to use both nails and glue. One of the big advantages in working with plywood is that it is splitproof; thus, nails may be used close to edges, and outside fastenings or clamps may be used without fear of damage to the plywood.

For best appearance, nails should be countersunk, and the depressions filled with wood filler or plugs.

The following nailing schedule is suggested for wall paneling and other hardwood plywood projects:

Panel thickness	*Nail size*
¼ inch	4d finish nails (1-inch brads are used over firm backing)
⅜ inch	4d finish nails
½ inch	6d finish nails
¾ inch	6d or 8d finish nails

Several adhesives of the urea-formaldehyde type are available for use with plywood projects. They are water-resistant, easy to work with, simple to prepare, and they do not stain. In addition, casein types and vinyl glue, all with excellent properties, are being used widely. In all cases, the glues should be mixed according to manufacturer's instructions. The following simple instructions have proved practical for urea glues:

1. Place the amount of glue required in an enamel, iron, or glass mixing pot and add water slowly. The right consistency is reached when the glue just drips from the end of the brush. The glue remains usable for as long as it is spreadable, usually about four hours. Apply the glue with a brush.

2. Put the parts together and make sure that all joints fit properly and line up squarely. Mark the parts so that they can be identified quickly when the point of assembly is reached. Not more than 15 minutes should elapse between the time of applying the glue and the time of applying pressure to the assembled joints.

3. Apply plenty of glue to one of the two surfaces at each point of joining. Adjust hand screws and clamps to hold the work firmly together until the glue is hard. Drying takes from 4 to 12 hours depending on the temperature and type of wood. For best curing the room temperature should be approximately 70°F.

4. Following application of the clamps, test again for alignment. Scrape off excess glue as it oozes from the joints. A helpful hint is to dust the excess glue with sawdust, which absorbs the moisture and makes the glue easier to remove. Avoid using water or a moist rag in removing the excess glue. This will only spread the glue around in a thin layer, which will show on the finished product.

5. When the glue is dry, remove the clamps and carefully remove excess glue. Sand before finishing.

FASTENING FURRING STRIPS TO MASONRY

The remodeling of basements frequently poses the problem of fastening wood furring strips to either concrete block or concrete foundations.

Concrete Block. A simple method consists of drilling holes in the block and driving wood pegs tightly into the holes. Furring strips can be nailed directly to the pegs. Star drills may be used for drilling the holes. Or, if available, electric drills with masonry bits speed up the work.

Concrete. Where solid concrete is concerned, Rawlplugs or iron expansion anchors constitute simple and sure methods of fastening furring strips to concrete.

Holes of sufficient depth and diameter to admit the plugs or anchors must first be drilled by means of a star drill. In the case of Rawlplugs,

ANCHOR NAIL

FURRING STRIP

ANCHOR NAIL

CONCRETE BLOCK FOUNDATION

FIGURE 16. Anchor bolt for sill.

lead cores are driven into the holes. Screws can then be used to fasten furring strips to the cores at the surface of the concrete. In the case of iron expansion anchors, expansion pieces are driven into the holes and bolts used to fasten furring strips to the expansion pieces at the surface of the concrete.

In addition to the foregoing methods, the use of hardened-steel nails sometimes works out satisfactorily if they can be driven into mortar joints between concrete blocks.

Another and quite different method of fastening furring strips to masonry consists of using adhesive anchors, as indicated in Figure 16. The furring strips must be softwood, such as white pine.

To attach the anchor nails, spread enough adhesive on the anchor base with a putty knife to ensure a film of adhesive approximately $\frac{1}{16}$ inch thick after the anchor has been firmly pressed against the masonry. Allow 48 hours for the adhesive to set. Hold furring strips against the attached anchor nails and tap lightly with a hammer. Use the resulting indentations as centers for holes to be drilled through the furring strips. Press the furring strips over the anchor nails. If the masonry is uneven, insert wood shims between the anchor nails and the furring strips. Finally, plumb the furring strips and clinch the nails.

FASTENING SILLS TO FOUNDATIONS

As shown in Figures 3, 4, and 17, single or double sills are used as a base for headers and joists. The sills are securely fastened together and the headers are toenailed to the sills. All this fastening would be of little good, so far as stiffness is concerned, unless the sills are fastened to the foundations by means of anchor bolts, as shown in Figure 17. Such bolts

FIGURE 17. Adhesive anchor nails.

must be set in the concrete while it is still plastic and should be spaced 4′ 0″ apart.

When sills are to be supported somewhat as shown in Figure 18, powder-actuated fasteners may be employed. The fasteners are shot into place by a gunlike mechanism. This procedure saves considerable cost and time.

FIGURE 18. Powder-actuated fasteners for sills.

MITER STIFFENERS

When joints in frames of any kind tend to be loose, a miter stiffener, such as shown in Figure 19, can be used to advantage. The miter fits into a single saw cut making an interlocking and tight joint.

FIGURE 19. Miter stiffener.

JOIST HANGERS

In remodeling work, we are apt to encounter several situations where joists cannot be supported in the conventional manner. In such cases, steel joist hangers, such as shown in Figure 20, may be used to great advantage.

The *A* part of the illustration shows a hanger for fastening ceiling joists to beams. This hanger is especially helpful when it is impossible to put the joists on top of the beam.

The *B* part of the illustration shows how hangers may be used to fasten floor joists to beams.

FIGURE 20. Joist hangers.

The *C* part of the illustration shows how hangers may be used to fasten new posts or columns to beams where added support is required. Also shown are somewhat different types of hangers for fastening smaller joists to beams.

CHAPTER THREE

Insulation

Authoritative tests have shown that there is a 50 per cent heat *loss* through the structural details of an *uninsulated* house during *cold* weather. In other words, *half* of the heat produced by the heating system in an uninsulated house is actually *wasted*. This means that *half* of the money spent for fuel is also wasted. In addition, such houses are subject to drafts, unequal temperatures, vapor condensation, and many other uncomfortable or unhealthy conditions.

Authoritative tests have also shown that there is a 50 per cent heat *gain* through the exposed structural details of an *uninsulated* house during *hot* weather. In other words, the interior of an uninsulated house often becomes so warm, both day and night, that it is uncomfortable to live in. If an uninsulated house is cooled by mechanical means, the required equipment is excessively expensive from the standpoints of initial cost and operating power.

In order to visualize where heat losses and gains occur in an uninsulated house, let us study Figure 1.

The X part of the illustration shows the percentage of heat *loss* through each of the important structural details. For example, 32.9 per cent of the total heat loss occurs through the exterior walls. In terms of the whole house, the *total* heat loss depends upon wind conditions, method of construction, and the difference between interior and exterior temperatures. But, whatever the total is, 32.9 per cent of it is lost through the exterior walls. The percentages of heat loss through other structural details are as indicated.

FIGURE 1. Distribution of heat losses and gains in a typical house.

The *Y* part of the illustration shows the percentage of heat *gain* through each of the important structural details. For example, 24.2 per cent of the *total* heat gain occurs because the roof and top-floor ceiling are not insulated. The *total* heat gain depends upon wind conditions, exposure to the sun, and the temperature of the exterior air. But, whatever the total is, 24.2 per cent of it comes in through the roof and top-floor ceiling.

All heat-loss and heat-gain percentages shown in Figure 1 are based upon two-story houses. The percentages are approximations and will vary, for example, with the ratio of roof area to wall area. In a one-story house, the percentage is likely to be much greater for the roof and correspondingly less for the walls. Otherwise, the values shown are reasonably typical.

Old or relatively new houses may be insulated in any one or more of several ways to give them more resistance to heat losses and gains. Such work can be done as separate projects or at the time other remodeling work is being carried on. The purpose of this chapter is to describe the kinds of insulation generally used, to explain several important aspects of its application and benefits, to suggest several effective remodeling projects, and to show how to plan and do typical installation work.

WHAT IS INSULATION?

When we start to think about insulation it is only natural that our first question should have to do with the material itself. What is it? Once we have satisfactorily answered this question, we will have something definite upon which subsequent discussions can be based.

When a material or substance possesses such special qualities that it can resist, or tend to resist, the flow of heat through its bulk, it may be called *insulation* or an *insulating material*. At this point we should understand that no known material or substance is able completely to stop the flow of heat through its bulk. So long as there is a difference in temperature between the two sides of a material, some heat will flow through its bulk.

Any solid building material will resist the flow of heat to some extent.

For example, frame and masonry walls or floors reduce the flow of heat to a slight degree. Because of its internal structure, wood is a better insulating material than any of the denser materials such as concrete or metal. However, none of the ordinary building materials, in the thicknesses generally used, are able to retard the flow of heat to any appreciable degree.

In order to qualify as an insulating material, a substance must be lightweight and contain a high percentage of air spaces or voids. Some natural substances, such as cork, fur, cotton, wool, and straw, are thus endowed and have long been used as insulating materials. However, such substances are not suitable for modern construction. Therefore, new insulating materials (substances) have had to be developed and manufactured. Such materials possess what is known as *concentrated resistance to the flow of heat*.

KINDS OF INSULATION

So far as trade names are concerned, there are many varieties of insulating materials available. However, all varieties may be grouped into six basic kinds.

Loose Fill. This kind is bulk in nature and is sold in bags. Three types are available: fibrous, powdered, and granular.

Blanket. This kind is manufactured in strips and is sold in rolls or packs. It is flexible and may be obtained in several widths and thicknesses. Two types are available: those encased in plain kraft paper, and those encased in aluminum foil.

Batt. This kind is similar to blankets except that the batts are produced in small units usually about 15 inches wide and 8 to 48 inches long.

Structural Insulating Board. Produced in large units, this kind, as the name implies, is a synthetic or manufactured insulating lumber, commonly known as *rigid boards*. It can be obtained 4 or more feet in width, 8 or more feet in length, and in ½- and 1-inch thicknesses.

Slab. Slab insulation is generally composed of small, rigid units which are 1 or more inches thick and up to 24 by 48 inches long. This insulation is especially made for use in connection with flat or nearly flat roofs.

Reflective. Reflective insulations are distinguished from all other kinds by the fact that they depend solely upon surface characteristics for their resistance to the flow of heat. While other insulations resist the flow of heat by means of air spaces and voids, this kind actually *reflects* heat. Therefore, and in order that they be effective, reflective insulations must always be so placed that their reflective surfaces face air spaces.

All the basic kinds of insulation are used in the manufacture of various and sundry products for use by the building industry. A visit to a lumberyard or to a building-material dealer's showroom will prove of great interest and help in the selection of insulation for any building purpose. Inexperienced mechanics will find that the blanket kind is easy to install and that it can be used to advantage, except as explained in connection with Figure 6.

BENEFITS OF INSULATION

Now that we have defined insulation and have reviewed the basic kinds, we can think about some of the important benefits it makes possible in any house regardless of geographic location.

At this point we should understand that insulating materials are not always *extra* or added structural costs. In many instances, they can replace or be used instead of traditional materials. For example, rigid boards can be used in place of wood sheathing and in place of traditional lathing.

The following general benefits are important considerations so far as remodeling plans are concerned:

Less Costly Heating System. Because insulating greatly reduces heat loss, new heating systems can be of small capacity and thus less costly.

Less Costly Cooling Systems. Insulation greatly reduces the amount of heat gain during hot weather. Thus, cooling equipment can be of small capacity and therefore less costly.

Fuel Savings. As indicated at the beginning of this chapter uninsulated houses waste 50 per cent of the heat supplied by heating systems. As such waste is reduced by means of insulation, fuel consumption is also reduced. Within a reasonably short time, the fuel savings pay for the insulation. After that time, the insulation constitutes a profitable investment.

Power Savings. With less heating or cooling required, fan and burner motors do not operate as long or as often.

Decorating Savings. In older houses, where wood lath were used, ceilings generally develop light and dark streaks, known as *ghost marks.* Such marks become noticeable long before a heating season is over and make frequent cleaning and redecorating necessary. Proper use of ceiling insulations prevents such undesirable conditions. In fact, well-insulated houses are much easier to keep clean and require redecorating much less often.

Protection against Vermin. Many forms of insulation, especially the loose-fill kinds, protect houses against all kinds of vermin.

Comfort. Perhaps the greatest and most appreciated benefit of insulation has to do with the living comfort it makes possible. A well-insulated house makes "climate-conditioning" a reality.

INSULATION PRINCIPLES

In order better to understand how insulation functions and the benefits it makes possible, we shall review a few simple principles, all of which are nothing more than basic laws of nature.

Heat Flow. Heat has a natural tendency to flow from a high temperature level to a low temperature level. This constitutes an unchangeable law. In other words, if the temperature of the air within a house is 70°F at a time when the temperature of the outdoor air is only 40°, the heat within the house will tend to flow in the direction of the colder air. Or, if the temperature at the interior surface of a wall is 70°, while the temperature at the exterior surface is only 40°, heat will flow from the warm to the cold surface. The purpose of insulation is to resist such flow.

How Heat Flow Takes Place. There are three ways in which heat flow takes place through a wall or other structural detail: conduction, convection, and radiation. All three ways of heat flow are in operation so far as heat loss or gain is concerned.

CONDUCTION. As an example of heat flow by conduction, suppose that we put one end of an iron bar into a fire. Before long, the other end will become too hot to handle. The heat will have traveled from one end of the bar to the other. In like manner, if one side of an ordinary building material is hot or cold, heat will travel to the opposite side by conduction. Or, if one piece of cold building material touches another piece which is warm, heat will flow from the warm piece to the cold piece. In like manner, if cold air comes in contact with warm air, heat will flow from the warm to the cold air.

CONVECTION. When warm air, from a radiator or other source, comes in contact with colder air in a room, heat flow takes place, as previously explained. Also, the warm air rises and creates a circulation. The circulation carries warm air to the cold surfaces of exterior walls (the surfaces became cold because heat flowed to the opposite and colder surfaces), where it loses heat to the walls by conduction. This process of heat flow is known as *convection*.

RADIATION. Heat is radiated from the sun to the earth. In like manner, heat is radiated from any warm object or material to a nearby colder object or material. In other words, warm plaster radiates heat to the exterior surface materials in a wall.

How Heat Flows through a Wall. Figure 2 illustrates the manner in which heat flows (or is transferred) to, through, and away from an exterior wall. The source of heat in a room can be a radiator or hot-air outlet of any kind. As indicated in the illustration, the heat flows from its source to the interior surface of the exterior wall by means of conduction, convection, and radiation. It flows through the wall by means of conduction and radiation. From the outside surface, the flow away from the wall is by means of conduction, convection, and radiation.

During hot weather, the flow of heat is reversed.

FIGURE 2. Heat transfer or flow to, through, and from a wall.

HOW INSULATION FUNCTIONS

We can safely classify most kinds of insulation into two general classes: *mass* and *reflective*. The mass class includes all kinds which have appreciable thickness or bulk, such as loose fill, blankets, bats, and rigid sheets or boards. The reflective class includes only those kinds which have little or no bulk.

When mass insulations are placed in walls or other structural details, they effectively resist the flow of heat because they have low conductivity (concentrated resistance) and because very little convection or radiation is possible. When reflective insulations are placed in walls or other structural details, they resist the flow of heat effectively because the heat is reflected back whence it came. Such insulations also retard radiation, as from plaster to exterior-surface materials, and do not have enough bulk for conduction to take place.

HOW MUCH INSULATION TO USE

It might be natural to conclude that the more the insulation used in structural details, the more the insulation value obtained. Such a conclusion is not logical because of the law of diminishing returns. Generally speaking, the first inch of insulation thickness is the most effective and each successive layer of the same thickness is less and less effective. For example, a single thickness of rigid insulation in a flat roof might save about 2¼ tons of coal per heating season per 1,000 square feet of insulated area. Adding a second layer of the same thickness might save about 1 ton more. Adding a third layer might save only ½ ton more. Thus, there is a point where additional thicknesses serve to little advantage but add considerable cost.

The law of diminishing returns does not apply to insulating materials which are available in only one thickness. For example, blankets, bats, and rigid sheets or boards are manufactured in certain thicknesses which, for them, is the most effective thickness to use. There must be successive thicknesses to result in diminishing returns. However, the law does apply to insulations of the reflective kinds, which can be used in one or more curtains or sheets.

CONDENSATION

The air around us always contains some moisture in the form of invisible vapor. The amount of such moisture in the air at any given time generally depends upon the temperature of the air. Under ordinary conditions, warm air is able to hold more moisture than cold air. In fact, the warmer the air, the more moisture it is able to hold. Conversely, the colder the air, the less moisture it is able to hold.

The percentage of moisture actually held, in relation to the total amount that air is able to hold, at any given temperature, is called the *relative humidity*. In other words, when warm summer air feels wet, its relative humidity is high.

The temperature at which the air is no longer able to hold all the moisture it contains is called the *dew point*. At this point of temperature, the moisture condenses out of the air. This is what happens when warm air surrounding a glass containing an ice-cold liquid is chilled by the glass to a temperature below its dew point. Moisture from the warm air condenses on the glass, which then appears to "sweat."

These facts are important because vapor moisture, in uncondensed form, can pass through most building materials—lath, plaster, wood, even masonry. And in winter, outdoor temperatures are usually far below the dew point of the warm air inside a home. Such moisture can cause many troubles within frame walls and to the siding and paint at the exterior surface of them.

It is recommended that a vapor barrier be placed in walls, top-floor ceilings, and in floors over unheated areas to prevent penetration of vapor moisture, from the warm interior, into parts of structural details where

FIGURE 3. Attic ventilation.

the temperature may be below the dew point. Most kinds of mass insulations are provided with a moisture barrier on one surface. The reflective insulations, being made of metal, are natural moisture barriers.

Ventilation is another important aid to condensation control. It should be provided above insulation installed in attics. So placed, it permits the escape of vapor moisture, that in winter may find its way to the attic area. In summer, it reduces the head load on the attic insulation. All this will seem more important when we realize that an average family creates about 26 pounds of water vapor per day when bathing, doing laundry work, cooking, etc.

Attic Ventilation. When top-floor ceilings under unused attics are insulated, vents should be placed at the gables and at the cornices, as shown in the *A* and *B* parts of Figure 3. The gable vents, which are generally known as *louvers,* exhaust the air that comes in through the cornice vents. The total area of the cornice vents should be in the proportion of 1 square foot per 300 square feet of ceiling area. This proportion should be doubled for roofs having little pitch.

Where hip roofs are involved, the louvers can be cut into the roofs at points as near to their highest points as possible.

Crawl-space Ventilation. Such spaces should be ventilated by means of vents cut into the side walls. The total area of such vents should be in the proportion of 2 square feet of vent area per 100 lineal feet of enclosed wall, plus ⅓₀₀ of the area enclosed by the wall.

SUGGESTED REMODELING PROJECTS

The following suggestions include only such insulating work as can be accomplished without having to tear out or otherwise disturb existing structural details. However, each and every one of the projects suggested has definite merit in terms of fuel savings and added living comforts.

Top-floor Ceilings. In cases where attic spaces are too small for use or where homeowners do not plan to create living areas in them, insulation can be placed between the joists which support the floor and ceiling, as a means of insulating the rooms below.

Ceiling insulation is of value in any climate because it reduces heat loss during the winter or cool seasons and heat gain during hot seasons. Thus the insulation will help to reduce fuel bills and make rooms much more comfortable during all seasons of the year.

INSULATING MATERIALS. Any one of the three kinds of insulation shown in Figure 4 may be used.

BLANKET OR BATT. The *A* part of the illustration shows such insulation applied between joists. Both kinds are generally placed so that their moisture barriers are in contact with the ceiling lath. For the purpose of ceiling insulation, thickness of 3 or 4 inches is sufficient. Tacks or staples can be used to fasten the nailing flanges to the joists.

LOOSE FILL. The *B* part of the illustration shows such insulation after being poured between the joists. Some form of moisture barrier should be placed in contact with the plaster.

REFLECTIVE. The *C* part of the illustration shows the insulation applied between joists. Such insulation is fragile and should not be used in top-floor ceilings unless there is a floor to protect it. Note that air spaces are

FIGURE 4. Top-floor ceiling insulation.

required both above and below it. Tacks or staples may be used to fasten the nailing flanges to the joists.

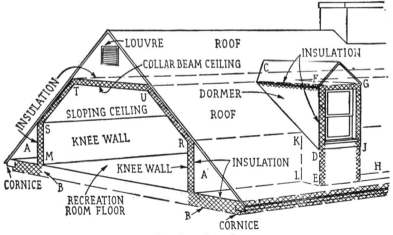

FIGURE 5. Knee-wall and roof insulation in attic space.

Attic Knee Walls and Roof. When attic spaces are being remodeled, the areas near the meeting places of roofs and floors, as shown at *A* in Figure 5, are generally too low and cramped for any good use. For this reason knee walls, also shown in the illustration, are usually constructed.

The ceilings of attic spaces are always lowered by means of collar beams. Insulation can be installed in the knee walls, the sloping ceilings, the collar-beam ceiling, and at the locations marked *B*.

INSULATING MATERIALS. Any one of several kinds of insulation can be used, depending upon the type of ceiling and wall-surface materials (see Chapters 4 and 5) being employed.

PLASTER. If plaster is to be applied to the walls and ceilings, a rigid insulating material 1 inch thick can be used in place of noninsulating lathing. In such cases, the areas marked *B* can be insulated by means of blanket, batt, or reflective insulating materials.

PLANKS, ETC. If planks, block, board, tile, or panel surfaces are to be used, the walls, ceilings, and areas marked *B* can be insulated by means of blanket, batt, or reflective insulating materials in much the same manner as shown in Figure 4. One-inch thick rigid panels or boards could also be used, in which case they would serve as backing for the surface materials and instead of the furring strips which would otherwise be necessary.

Dormers. In order to provide more light and better natural ventilation in remodeled attic spaces, dormers such as shown in Figure 5 are frequently constructed. Insulation is necessary in the two side walls, such as *CFD*; in the ceiling, such as *CFG*; in the front walls, such as *DJHE*; and in such areas as *KDEL*.

INSULATING MATERIALS. The same kind of insulation as used for knee walls and ceilings should be installed in the dormer details. However, where so many irregularly shaped areas are involved, the flexible blankets and batts are much easier to install.

Roofs. In many houses of recent design and construction, the attic spaces are not high enough for use except as possible storage areas. In such cases, the ceilings of rooms under the attic spaces are subject to great heat losses and gains. The heat losses are serious in terms of winter fuel bills, and the heat gains are apt to make the rooms almost unbearable, both day and night, during the summer. Insulation can be installed in either the ceilings or the roofs.

INSULATING MATERIALS. Any kind of insulation, placed in either the roofs or ceilings, would definitely help to reduce heat losses. However, a particular kind of insulation should be used as a means of avoiding the uncomfortable heat gains. This holds true only so far as roofs are concerned and when attic spaces are empty.

Empty attic spaces would be the best kind of insulation against the hot summer sun, were it not for radiation. When no insulation is used, as indicated at *A* in Figure 6, the roof absorbs great quantities of heat from the sun and radiates all of it to the ceilings of the rooms below attic

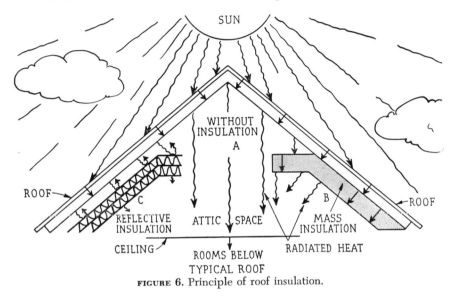

FIGURE 6. Principle of roof insulation.

spaces. Mass insulations, such as shown at *B*, may retard heat flow for a short time, but in doing so they absorb heat which is eventually radiated to the ceilings. The radiation process is apt to continue long after sunset time with the result that rooms are uncomfortably warm both day and night. Reflective insulations, such as shown at *C*, have very little mass. Thus, they cannot store much heat or emit appreciable amounts of radiation. In addition, reflective insulations tend to reflect the sun's heat away from attic spaces.

Foundations. When basements are remodeled, some form of insulation is generally required in connection with the interior surfaces of concrete or concrete-block foundations. Any one or more of several conditions may be encountered. For example, in climates where freezing temperatures occur the foundations may be cold. This would constitute a serious source of heat loss and cause the radiation of cold drafts into the living areas. In climates where a great deal of rain occurs, the surfaces of foundations may be cool and slightly damp. In other cases, foundations may sweat to the extent that water runs down their surfaces.

INSULATING MATERIALS. All of the conditions mentioned in the foregoing paragraph can be corrected or remedied by means of insulation.

Cold Surfaces. The *A* part of Figure 7 shows panels of decorative insulation applied to furring strips on a concrete-block wall. The *B*, *C*, and

FIGURE 7. Decorative insulation for basement walls.

D parts of the illustration indicate typical patterns which can be employed. The *B* pattern may be used to create a feeling of more space in a small recreation room while the *C* and *D* patterns may be employed to make a long room appear to better advantage. The material can be secured in various colors and textures and in many sizes and thicknesses. Some brands are manufactured in neutral tones which may be painted or otherwise decorated. Colored nails to match the insulation are available.

Cool and Damp Surfaces. Masonry foundations can be insulated against cool and damp surfaces by means of reflective insulation, as shown in Figure 8. The insulation is ½ inch thick and of a width suitable for installation between 1- by 3-inch furring strips spaced 16 inches on centers. It should be fastened in place by means of laths. After the insulation has been installed, any desired surface material may be applied over the laths.

SWEATING. Sweating occurs during warm weather when the surface temperatures of foundations are below the dew-point temperatures of the air. The kind of insulation shown in Figure 7 may be used to prevent sweating.

ANY SURFACE MATERIAL— SEE CHAPTER 5

FURRING STRIP

LATH

CONCRETE BLOCK OR CONCRETE

REFLECTIVE INSULATION

TACK

PLASTER

FIGURE 8. Reflective insulation applied to masonry wall.

Basement Floors. Concrete floors may be cold and damp for the same reasons explained in connection with foundations. See Figure 8 in Chapter 6.

Floor Slabs. In some unfortunate instances, concrete floor slabs for basementless houses have been placed directly on the ground, as shown in Figure 9, without insulation under them or around the foundations. In such cases, areas of the floors, such as between *A* and *B*, are apt to be especially cold. The heavy dashed line shows the path taken by low temperatures as they travel from the outside soil through the foundations and into the floors. Such conditions can be remedied by insulation.

INSULATING MATERIALS. By means of some simple excavating, 2-inch waterproof insulation can be applied to the exteriors of the foundations, as shown at *E*. Even more insulating effect can be obtained by removing only parts of the floors and installing more waterproof insulation around the interior surface of the foundations, as shown at *F*. Hot asphaltum can be used to cement the insulation to the foundations.

Crawl Spaces. Unless crawl spaces are well vented, as previously explained, and unless the floors above them and the soil surface are insulated, low temperatures and dampness, especially in cold or damp climates, will flow up through the floor and cause discomfort.

INSULATING MATERIALS. Figure 10 shows a pictorial view of a typical crawl space along with the usual floor construction and other structural details. Either blanket or rigid insulation can be used between the floor

FIGURE 9. How to insulate floor slab on ground.

joists as a protection against low temperatures and dampness. As a further and also important means of protection, especially against dampness, soil surfaces can be covered using heavy, waterproof paper somewhat as shown in Figure 10. All joints between strips of the paper should be lapped 6 inches and cemented together by means of hot asphaltum. The ends of the strips should be bent up 6 inches and cemented to the foundation also by means of hot asphaltum.

Added Rooms. Major remodeling projects often consist of adding new rooms to existing houses. Such rooms, often similar to the room shown in Figure 11, generally have shed-type roofs and only crawl spaces under

FIGURE 10. Crawl-space insulation.

FIGURE 11. How to insulate added rooms.

them. The following insulation suggestions are presented in the order of their importance:

Ceilings. Ceiling areas, such as the one shown at *ABCD* in Figure 11, may be insulated using blankets, batts, rigid, loose-fill, or reflective insulation. Blankets, batts, and loose fill could be placed between ceiling joists, and rigid panels could be used in place of traditional lathing. However, because there is so little space between shed roofs and ceilings, especially in terms of heat gain, reflective insulation between roof joists is recommended.

Floors. Floor areas, as *EFGH* of Figure 11, can be insulated as shown in Figure 10, using either blankets or rigid panels.

Walls. While walls are being built, and at times immediately after the exterior wood sheathing has been applied, blanket, batt, loose-fill, or reflective insulation could be placed between studs. Figure 12 shows how

FIGURE 12. Details of wall insulation.

blankets are used in walls. (NOTE: As shown at *X*, the insulation should be placed between the 2 by 4 and 2 by 6 sills.) Rigid insulation could also be used as wall sheathing and as plaster backing.

DOUBLE GLAZING. As indicated in Figure 1, windows and doors account for almost one-third of the heat losses and more than one-fourth of the heat gains in average houses. The total window area is always much greater than the total door area. Thus, it is wise to consider any possible means of giving windows more resistance to heat flow.

INSULATING MATERIALS. There are no insulating materials, as such, that can be applied to windows. However, it is possible to install sash which have two panes of glass separated by an air space. Such sash are available in all standard sizes and can be depended upon to reduce heat flow by as much as 50 per cent. As shown in Figure 13, existing windows can be given the benefits of double glazing by means of an added pane of glass that can be removed at will.

ORIGINAL GLASS

ADDED GLASS

SCREEN

FIGURE 13. Double glazing.

Infiltration. As indicated in Figure 1, infiltration (cracks around windows and doors) accounts for about one-seventh of the heat losses and for about one-eighth of the heat gains in average houses. The *A* part of Figure 14 shows how cold and hot air flows through such cracks. In masonry walls, cracks often occur between the window frames and the surrounding masonry units. Such cracks should be filled with caulking compound.

INSULATING MATERIALS. Heat losses and gains through the window cracks shown in the *A* part of Figure 14 can be prevented by means of the typical weatherstripping shown in the *B* part of the same illustration. In order to install such weatherstripping, the sash must be grooved as shown. Woodworking mills have the equipment for cutting the grooves. Other types of weatherstripping are also available, but they do not have the finished appearance of those shown in Figure 14.

STORM SASH. Storm sash accomplish about the same resistance to heat flow as double glazing.

Figure 15 illustrates a typical application of wood-frame storm sash to the type of windows found in most old houses. Such sash create an air space between themselves and the prime windows. The air space acts as insulation and the two panes of glass reduce heat loss by conduction. In

FIGURE 14. Details of typical weatherstripping.

addition, infiltration losses are reduced and less sweating occurs. However, in order for storm sash to be effective, they must be *tightly* fitted at such places as indicated at *B*. Unless tight fits are assured, storm sash have little value. This fact should be kept in mind.

Metal-frame storm sash are more effective than the old-style wood-frame varieties, provided that they are properly fitted.

If storm sash are employed, they should be fitted to *all* windows in houses—not confined to the sides facing prevailing winter winds.

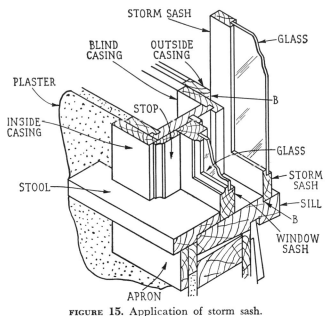

FIGURE 15. Application of storm sash.

Existing Walls. As indicated in Figure 1, walls account for more heat losses and gains than any of the other structural details in average houses. Thus, it is wise to give careful attention to ways and means of applying insulation to them. The following suggestions constitute several economical ways of providing effective insulation against excessive heat losses and gains.

Frame Walls. There are two logical ways of insulating existing frame walls. One way has to do with the application of loose-fill insulation between studs. The other way has to do with the application of rigid insulation to surfaces. Both ways avoid excessive cost.

Pneumatic Application. The application of fill insulation between studs of existing walls is somewhat difficult, owing to lack of access to such areas; but, if small areas of siding and sheathing are temporarily removed, loose-fill insulation can be blown in by means of a hose under pneumatic pressure. Such installation work must be done by professional applicators equipped with the necessary apparatus. This process works out to advantage only when no headers or fire stops, such as shown in Figure 12, are present.

The necessary vapor barriers can be provided by applying two or more coats of an efficient vapor-resistant paint, such as aluminum, to plaster surfaces, or other interior finish, prior to the time decorating work is started.

Application of Rigid Insulation. See Chapter 5.

Masonry Walls. See previous explanation in connection with Figure 7. Also see Chapter 5.

Flat Roofs. Some form of built-up roofing, consisting of waterproof paper, asphaltum, and fine gravel, is generally used on flat or nearly flat roofs. In such cases, insulation can be applied in either of two ways.

FIGURE 16. Insulation on flat roof.

INSULATING MATERIALS. As shown in Figure 16, 2-inch slab insulation may be laid on the decks of such roofs; or reflective insulation can be applied between the rafters in such a manner that air spaces above and below it are assured.

Sound Transmission. Sound actually travels through wood structural details. In other words, such materials convey sound from one location to another. For example, sounds originating in basement recreation rooms are transmitted through the floors to areas above the recreation rooms. In like manner, sounds originating in kitchens are transmitted through the walls to adjacent areas. There are several ways of controlling or reducing such sound transmission.

New Construction. If major remodeling projects include new frame walls, the studs can be staggered and blanket insulation placed between them as indicated in the *A* part of Figure 17. Note that separate studs are required for each wall surface. This arrangement of studs separates the two surfaces so that there is not a continuous material between them through which sound can be transmitted. The insulation tends to reduce the passage of sound between the studs and through the walls.

FIGURE 17. Insulation against sound transmission.

If new floors are being constructed, dual joists can be installed and blanket insulation placed between them as indicated in the *B* part of the illustration. This joist arrangement separates the ceiling and floor surfaces so that transmission of sound is greatly reduced.

Existing Floors. In cases where new hardwood finish floors are going to be laid, rigid or thin blanket insulation can be installed as indicated in the *C* part of the illustration.

Existing Walls and Ceilings. See Chapters 4 and 5.

HOW TO PLAN AND DO
TYPICAL REMODELING PROJECTS

The following projects constitute typical examples of the insulation problems most generally encountered and are set forth in keeping with approved planning and installation procedures. Only a few of the previously suggested remodeling projects are included because some of them have already been sufficiently explained and because all such work follows about the same pattern. Blanket insulation is herein used because of its popularity and simplicity.

TOP-FLOOR CEILING

This project is typical of any and all cases where top-floor ceilings, under empty attic spaces, are to be insulated against heat losses and gains.

PROBLEM 1: ANY TOP-FLOOR CEILING. For the purpose of this problem, we can assume that the attic space does not have a floor and that blankets of the double-thick variety 16 inches wide are to be used. The problem is to install the insulation between the joists.

SOLUTION. As indicated in Figure 18, a convenient length of 2 by 10 plank can be placed across the tops of the joists and used for body support during the installation work.

Unfold the blankets and cut them to approximate length by means of a saw or tin snips. Lay the strips between the joists, as shown in the picture, so that their moisture barriers are down.

The ends of the strips should be prepared as shown in the *A* part of Figure 19 and then sealed to the plates as indicated in the *B* part of the illustration. Heavy tacks or an automatic stapler may be used. In Figure 18 the mechanic is shown sealing a strip end to a plate.

Unfold the nailing flanges on the blankets and bend them over the top edges of the joists, as shown in Figure 18. Space the tacks or staples about 6 inches apart.

Any tears in the liners (casings) can be repaired by brushing the torn area with hot asphaltum and then covering the area with a piece of the liner.

FIGURE 18. Application of blanket insulation between ceiling joists.

FIGURE 19. Sealing insulation to plate.

When insulating between joists, it may at some time be necessary to join two strips of blanket. This is easily accomplished by placing a 2 by 4 header between the joists and forming flanges, such as shown in the *A* part of Figure 19, at the strip ends which are tacked or stapled to the header.

In the Condensation section of this chapter we learned that when top-floor ceilings under unused attics are insulated, gable and cornice vents, such as shown in Figure 3, are necessary. Such vents are available at all lumberyards and should be installed before the advent of cold weather and the heating season. Without them, condensation in troublesome amounts is likely to occur.

KNEE WALLS

This project is typical of any and all cases where attic knee walls are to be insulated against heat losses and gains.

PROBLEM 2: KNEE WALLS IN FIGURE 5. For the purpose of this problem, we can assume that the attic space is being remodeled to create a recreation room and that the knee walls were erected to give the room a better appearance.

SOLUTION. In this solution we shall be concerned with the knee wall marked *SM* and the area under it marked *B*.

The *B* area, between the joists, should be insulated before the knee wall. Cut strips or blankets to approximate length, as shown at *X* in Figure 20, and then prepare their ends as shown in the *A* part of Figure 19. Make sure the moisture-barrier sides are down. Seal the ends of the *X* strips at points *a* and *b*, as shown in Figure 20, by means of tacks or staples. Fasten the nailing flanges to the joists.

For the knee wall, cut strips of blankets to the length shown at *Y* in Figure 20. Prepare their ends and then place them between the studs, as shown in Figure 21, so that the moisture-barrier sides face the room. Make the seals *c* and *d*, as shown in Figure 20, and fasten the nailing flanges, as shown in Figure 21. Space the tacks or staples about 6 inches apart.

FIGURE 20. Application of blanket insulation to knee walls.

FIGURE 21. Application of blanket insulation to knee-wall studs.

COLLAR-BEAM CEILING

This project is typical of any and all cases where collar-beam ceilings are to be insulated against heat losses and gains.

PROBLEM 3: COLLAR-BEAM CEILING IN FIGURE 5. For the purpose of this problem we can make the same assumption as set forth in Problem 2, except that a collar-beam ceiling was erected as a further aid to the appearance and comfort of the recreation room.

SOLUTION. The areas marked $STUR$ should be insulated using continuous strips of blankets, as indicated in Figure 22. Cut the strips of blanket to approximate length and prepare their ends. Make the seals at e and then draw the strips along ST, TU, and UR so that seals can be made at the knee-wall plate at R. Make sure that the moisture-barrier sides face the room.

FIGURE 22. Application of blanket insulation to sloping-ceiling and collar beams.

In order to prevent any possibility of condensation in the recreation room, ample ventilation must be provided for. This can be accomplished by installing cornice vents and louvers, as shown in Figure 3 and as explained in the condensation section of this chapter. Referring to Figure 5, we can see that when the cornice vents and the louvers have been installed, air will enter the A areas, pass between the insulation and the roof in areas ST and UR, and enter the open space over the collar beams. From there it will be exhausted through the louvers.

CRAWL SPACES

This project is typical of any and all cases where floors above crawl spaces are to be insulated against heat losses and dampness.

PROBLEM 4: ANY CRAWL SPACE. For the purpose of this problem it can be assumed that a typical crawl space, such as shown in Figure 10, is involved. The problem is to apply insulation between the joists and to seal the surface of the soil.

SOLUTION. When new floors, such as shown in Figures 10 and 23, are being constructed, the blanket insulation can be applied in the following manner:

FIGURE 23. Blanket insulation between joists above a crawl space.

By means of lath, as indicated in the illustrations, fasten galvanized-wire mesh to the bottom edges of the joists. Lay the blankets on the wire so that their moisture-barrier sides are up. Use tacks or staples, spaced about 8 inches apart, to fasten the nailing flanges to the sides of the joists.

When existing floors are to be insulated, the blankets can be applied in the following manner:

Tuck the blankets up between the joists so that the moisture-barrier sides are up. Fasten wire mesh to the bottoms of the joists as previously explained.

If pipes, ducts, or other obstructions exist, shape the insulation to fit snugly around them. If necessary as a means of assuring a tight fit, cement the liners of the blankets to the obstructions by means of hot asphaltum.

COMMON CONDENSATION TROUBLES

In climates where freezing winter weather occurs, many condensation troubles are apt to cause discomfort and even damage to interior trim and decorations. Generally, such troubles can be avoided or controlled by simple means. For the purpose of this discussion, we shall pose window sweating as a typical condensation trouble.

What causes window sweating? The principles of such condensation are explained in the Condensation section of this chapter. During cold

FIGURE 24. Attic fans for summer cooling and all-year ventilation.

weather, the interiors of houses are warm and the air generally has a high relative humidity. In other words, the air is warm and contains a great deal of moisture vapor. The surfaces of window glass are cold because they are in direct contact with exterior air. When the warm and humid interior air comes in contact with the cold window glass, the air is chilled below its dew point and it cannot hold as much moisture. The excess moisture is deposited on the window glass. Unless storm sash are tightly fitted, they do little to prevent such condensation.

Why is interior air humid? The excess moisture comes from cooking, bathing, the laundry where clothes are washed and dried, from occupants, from gas-fired heating equipment, from gas refrigerators, and many other sources.

How can condensation be controlled or avoided? The only remedy consists of ventilation. When cooking is in progress, kitchens should be ventilated by means of exhaust fans or open windows. The same holds true in connection with bathrooms and laundries. Enough ventilation to avoid condensation will be at the expense of some heat loss, but such losses are not serious.

Figure 24 shows typical installations of attic exhaust fans. During the winter, such fans can be used, as required, to ventilate houses—draw out humid air. Such fans also aid in the ventilation of attic spaces. During the summer months, such fans help materially to keep a house cooler, especially after sunset.

CHAPTER FOUR

Ceilings

Ceiling-surface materials often fall heir to any one or more of several natural and unfortunate defects. Natural defects are unavoidable even in the best of construction. They are caused by various changes in structural details. Unfortunate defects are caused by poor materials and by careless workmanship at the time houses are built.

Natural defects occur in the form of cracks. They are likely to appear in old houses and are actually the marks of time. Unfortunate defects, such as crumbling or roughness, are apt to appear in new houses within a year or two after construction is complete.

Defects of any kind are objectionable, because they mar or completely ruin the otherwise beautiful effects of modern decorating materials. Where defects exist, any attempt to accomplish satisfactory decorating constitutes useless expense and effort.

New structural materials, which can be used satisfactorily to repair ceilings or to give them entirely new and beautiful surfaces, are now available. The new materials are easy to apply and some of them accomplish soundproofing and insulating effects along with their highly desirable remodeling benefits. For example, previously unfinished basement and attic spaces can be transformed into attractive and usable living areas. See Chapters 7 and 9. The ceilings in such areas can be erected so that they are beautiful examples of modern materials, so that they are practically soundproof, and so that they have a high degree of insulating effect.

In this chapter we shall become acquainted with the most commonly encountered ceiling defects and learn how to judge them in terms of necessary repair or improvement. We shall also examine some typical remodeling suggestions, any one of which may be applied to any room in a house. Finally, we shall learn how to repair ceilings and how to plan and install new surface materials.

PLASTER DEFECTS

By means of the following explanations, we shall learn a great deal about the most commonly encountered ceiling defects so far as plaster on lath is involved. We shall also learn how to recognize and judge them in terms of recommended repair work and the application of new surface materials.

Cracks. As previously mentioned, cracks occur because of natural or unfortunate conditions. In some instances, both conditions are at fault.

Natural Conditions. There are several more or less natural conditions which are apt to cause plaster cracks, even though the best materials and excellent workmanship are used and exercised at the time a house is being built. In terms of practical and economical construction, such conditions cannot be avoided. They are almost sure to occur, especially as the years pass.

Lumber Shrinkage. As indicated by the typical structural details shown in Figure 1, the framing members of most houses are made entirely of wood. One wood detail supports another wood detail. All details are dependent upon each other. If something happens to one detail, one or more other details will be affected.

The best structural lumber, even when carefully kiln-dried or allowed to dry naturally over a long period of time, still contains some moisture at the time it is used to build structural details for a house. After a house has been subjected to one or more winters during which artificial heat is provided, the wood structural members lose moisture through the drying process and, at the same time, shrink in proportion to the amount of drying. Most of the shrinkage occurs across the grain. For example, the 2 by 8 joists shown in Figure 1 shrink along the 2- and 8-inch dimensions.

As shrinkage takes place in various structural members, especially in joists, plates, and sills, the supported members change positions. The plaster, being hard and brittle, cannot change its position. Therefore it cracks.

ALL DETAILS MADE OF WOOD

FIGURE 1. Typical structural details.

Settlement. Unless broad footings are provided under foundations, especially in soft soils such as clay, the foundations are apt to settle down into the soil to a variable degree. If such settlement is equal, all around a foundation, no plaster cracking is apt to happen. On the other hand, unequal settlement causes various structural members to shift positions. This invariably causes plaster cracking.

Expansion and Contraction. In climates which are subject to considerable and sudden changes in temperature, the resultant expansion and contraction in structural details causes some shifting of their positions. Such shifting is quite likely to crack nearby plaster.

Weight Shifts. Wood structural members actually bend when heavy weights or loads are applied to them. As they bend, they affect other supported members. Thus several members are apt to shift their positions. If a piano is moved from one side of a room to another side, the transfer of its weight could cause several structural members to shift their positions. Plaster cracks may be the result.

Wind Force. Severe windstorms exert a terrific pressure on one or more sides of a house. In some extreme instances, the pressure can be as much as 20 pounds per square foot. Such pressure causes various structural details to bend or to shift their positions. Plaster cracks are the inevitable result. Earthquakes also cause structural details to bend and to shift their positions. Again, plaster cracks are sure to follow.

Unfortunate Conditions. There are many more unfortunate than natural conditions which cause plaster to crack. While such conditions are deplorable, they must be recognized and understood.

POOR MATERIALS. In all too many cases, poor materials are the cause of severe and widespread plaster cracks in ceilings all through a house.

OVERSANDING. The use of too much sand in a plaster mix is a common evil often carried on as a means of reducing the amounts of more expensive cementitious materials. Such plaster is weak and is sure to crack shortly after being applied. To test for this condition, scratch the surface. If the quantity of sand used was too great, the surface will scratch deeply and the plaster is apt to crumble.

TOO LITTLE THICKNESS. Another common evil consists of applying the base coat of plaster about $\frac{1}{4}$ inch thick, whereas it should be at least $\frac{1}{2}$ inch thick. In the plastering trade, this is known as *paperhanging*. Plaster cracking is almost inevitable.

IMPROPER APPLICATION. If the finish (white) coat of plaster is applied over an exceptionally dry base (brown) coat, there will be too much suction and the finish coat is apt to crack in the form of what is known as *chip cracking*. Chip cracks are short and take various directions. They form a spidery pattern all over a ceiling.

FAULTY CONSTRUCTION. The greatest cause for plaster cracking, especially in a new house, is faulty construction. Some of these causes are similar to natural conditions previously explained. However, where faulty construction exists, the cracks are larger and more frequent.

If a foundation is faulty or lacks adequate footing support, severe settlement is likely. As the settlement occurs, structural details are pulled away from their normal positions. This causes out-of-plumb conditions which crack ceiling plaster.

Poor carpentry work, probably more than any other factor, is responsible for unsightly plaster cracks. Improper bracing, poor corner construction, weak framing around windows and doors, joists too small or spaced too far apart, careless nailing, etc., all contribute to the causes for plaster cracks. Even the best job of plastering cannot stand up under such faults and the resulting strains.

GREEN LUMBER. As previously explained, even kiln-dried lumber will shrink to some extent after a year or two. However, when green lumber (see Chapter 1) is used, the resultant shrinkage is great enough to cause severe and even dangerous plaster defects.

Judging Defects. The causes of plaster cracks have a great deal to do with our judgment of them and what should be done to repair or otherwise improve the appearance of ceilings.

Cracks caused by shrinkage, settlement, faulty construction, and green lumber will eventually reach their maximum and are not likely to change thereafter. In old houses, they are at their maximums. In new houses, the maximums come after about two years. Such cracks generally run diagonally across ceilings or occur at the corners where walls and ceilings meet. They extend all the way through the plaster and are apt to be $\frac{1}{16}$ inch or more in width. They can be repaired without fear that they will reopen. Where many of them occur in a ceiling, an entirely new surface material should be used as a means of creating satisfactory appearance.

Cracks caused by expansion and contraction, weight shifts, winds, and earthquakes are generally very narrow and are likely to reoccur after being repaired. They are likely to appear near the centers of ceilings and where walls and ceilings meet. Repairing them is a gamble. Where there are enough of them to constitute an eyesore, an entirely new surface material should be used.

Defects caused by poor materials or oversanding are apt to be a combination of peeling and cracks. In other words, wherever a crack occurs some of the plaster peels off on both sides of it. Such plaster is unsound. A new and strong surface material should be applied by means of nails which are long enough to be driven through the plaster and into the ceiling joists.

When ceiling plaster is too thin, cracks will appear more or less at random or in long lines, especially along lath joints. In such cases, and as previously explained, a new and strong surface material should be applied.

As noted earlier in this discussion, cracks caused by the improper application of plaster are of short lengths and extend in all directions. Such cracks cannot be repaired. Therefore, a new surface material should be applied.

DAMAGE DUE TO WATER. A single wetting, of the kind sometimes caused by a sudden roof or water-pipe leak, is not likely to harm plaster, especially if it was in a sound condition prior to the wetting and if quick drying is possible. However, repeated wettings are apt to cause rotting and unsound conditions. To test suspected plaster, scratch it with a putty knife or other sharp tool. If the scratching causes crumbling, the plaster is beyond repair and a new surface material should be applied.

BLISTERS. If the finish coat of plaster is subjected to excessive humidity or other dampness, the formation of large blisters is likely. The blisters are caused by a particular type of lime which contains a high percentage of unhydrated magnesium. The humidity or dampness causes the magnesium to expand and the blisters are thus formed. If the blisters occur over a large area, satisfactory repair work is impossible and a new surface material should be applied.

FROZEN PLASTER. If plaster is applied during a time when it is subjected to a freezing temperature, it is apt to be permanently damaged. Unfortunately, the results of such damage are not always visible at the time the freezing takes place. Months or years may pass before the finish coat starts to peel. In such a case, no repair work is possible. A strong new surface material should be applied by means of nails which are long enough to be driven through the plaster and into the ceiling joists.

DRYOUTS. This condition is apt to occur when plastering is done during hot summer weather or when a dry wind is blowing. The wind enters through window and door openings and evaporates water from the new plaster. Unless corrected immediately, dryouts form rough areas which cannot be successfully painted or otherwise decorated except with ceiling paper. A new surface material should be applied.

OVERLY RETARDED PLASTER. Sometimes plaster contains too much of an ingredient known as a retarder. When this happens, the plaster becomes soft and powdery after it is applied. To correct such a condition, plasterers spray the plaster with alum and water or zinc sulfate and water. Lumps of the retarder often form on the surface of the plaster. If they are not removed, they will burn through the finish coat and any paint or other decorations applied to the ceiling. There is no easy or satisfactory method of repair. Therefore, a new surface material should be applied.

PLASTERBOARD DEFECTS

In a great many modern houses, various forms of dry plasterboard are used as ceiling surfaces instead of the traditional plaster. When properly installed, such ceilings are excellent and can be decorated the same as plaster. By means of the following explanations, we shall learn something about the most commonly encountered ceiling defects. We shall also learn how to recognize and judge them in terms of recommended repair work and the application of new surface materials.

Poor Joists. Most of the plasterboards can be joined, one to another, in such a manner that the joints are not visible after painting or other decorating is completed. However, if the joints are carelessly made, using improper materials, they are apt to buckle a little, open up, or in other ways become unsatisfactory in appearance. If the condition is not severe, repair work can be done. Otherwise, a new surface material should be applied.

Cracks. Sometimes because of extreme settlement, shrinkage, or excessive shifting of structural details, plasterboards may crack. Because of the surface materials such boards are made of, crack repairing seldom proves successful. A new surface material should be applied.

Damage Due to Water. Excessive wetting is quite likely to make most plasterboards unsatisfactory. Sometimes their surface materials peel. In other instances, they warp or buckle. When any such defects are present, repair work is difficult and seldom satisfactory. A new surface material should be applied.

Nail Holes. Plasterboards are generally fastened to ceiling joists by means of nails. The nailheads should be driven just below the surface and the resulting dents filled with a mortar supplied by manufacturers. Now and then, because of careless workmanship, such patches can be seen under decorations. Here again, repair work is seldom satisfactory. A new surface material should be applied.

SUGGESTED REMODELING PROJECTS

Whether a house is large or small, comparatively new or old, the ceilings can be restored to their first or even greater beauty. This promise holds true regardless of how badly cracked or otherwise marred the ceilings may have become. Years of extensive research among building-material manufacturers, plus a great deal of experience, have developed scientific and practical materials and methods for creating beautiful ceilings. The costs are low and the methods have been simplified. Any of the following suggestions can be applied to ceilings under any and all conditions:

Repairing Cracked Plaster. In cases where cracks are not large, not extensive, not in prominent locations, and not likely to reoccur, repair work is the easiest and most economical improvement method. For example, suppose that we are concerned with a medium-sized crack along one side of a room where the wall and ceiling meet. Further suppose that we have observed the crack and are convinced that it is of shrinkage origin and therefore not likely to reoccur. Such a crack can be repaired with little difficulty and in such a manner as to make the ceiling look like new.

New Surfaces over Sound Plaster. There are many cases where ceiling plaster is sound—holds tightly to the lathing—but where cracks, of one kind or another, make the plaster unsightly and not suited to modern painting or other decorations. Also, we may want to give one or more rooms the benefit of soundproofing or cut down the amount of sound transmitted to rooms above. Finally, we may want to enjoy the beauty that only new ceiling-surface materials provide.

Surface Materials. There are many types and kinds of new surface materials available. A visit to a lumberyard or to a building-material dealer's showroom will prove to be interesting and helpful when deciding which materials we may want to use. The following materials are typical:

ACOUSTICAL TILE. Both soundproofing and insulating qualities are included in this tile. When it is applied to a ceiling, the following benefits are assured:

1. The room will be much more quiet.

2. Less sound will be transmitted to rooms above.

3. The amount of heat loss and heat gain through the ceiling will be appreciably reduced.

As shown in Figure 2, this tile can be cemented to existing plaster.

KINDS. The kind illustrated in Figure 2 is known as *perforated* tile. Note that the surface contains many small holes. A *plain* tile without holes is also available.

SIZES. Most manufacturers produce such tile in 12- by 12-, 12- by 24-, 16- by 16-, and 16- by 32-inch sizes and in thicknesses which range from ½ to 1 inch.

COLORS. Both kinds of this tile can be secured in a wide range of colors. Or, as indicated in Figure 3, both kinds can be painted.

FASTENING. As shown in Figure 4, the tile can be fastened to existing plaster by means of cement. It can also be nailed to furring strips.

PATTERNS. By use of the tile sizes previously mentioned, any of the typical ceiling patterns shown in Figure 5 may be obtained. Generally, the 12- by 12- or 12- by 16-inch sizes are used on small ceilings and the 12- by 24- or 16- by 32-inch sizes on large ceilings.

TILE EDGES. Acoustical tile are provided with tongued-and-grooved edges of the type shown in Figures 8 and 9. Narrow and extra-wide flanges are also available. The extra-wide flanges are desirable when the tile is fastened by means of nails.

FIGURE 2. Typical perforated acoustical ceiling tile for application on old plaster.

FIGURE 3. Acoustical ceiling tile may be painted any desired color.

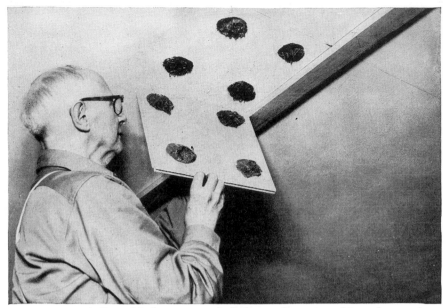

FIGURE 4. Over old plaster, acoustical tile may be cemented into place.

DIAMOND PATTERN- THIS STRIK-
ING DESIGN CAN BE CREATED
WITH SQUARE-SHAPED TILE UNITS

SQUARE DESIGN- EASIEST TO PLAN.
ANY SQUARE TILE CAN BE USED.

COMBINATION ASHLAR **PATTERN-**
USE BOTH SQUARE **AND RECT-**
ANGULAR TILE.

TWIN-RECTANGLE DESIGN–
FOR RECTANGULAR TILE ONLY.

HERRINGBONE DESIGN – FOR
RECTANGULAR TILE ONLY.

ASHLAR PATTERN – USE
EITHER SQUARE OR RECTANG-
ULAR TILE UNITS.

FIGURE 5. Typical tile patterns for ceilings.

PREFINISHED CEILING TILE. Other kinds of tile, which can be applied to existing plaster, are available in a wide range of colors. Some of them have factory-finished surfaces and other qualities which include square edges, high light reflection, high insulating value, and waterproof texture. However, such tile do not reduce noise in a room.

New Surfaces over Unsound Plaster. When plaster is not sound, furring strips should be used (see Figure 6). The furring strips should be nailed to the ceiling, using nails which are long enough to go through the plaster and lath and into the joists. This procedure creates a firm base for tile and holds the plaster firmly in place.

FIGURE 6. Acoustical tile being applied over unsound plaster.

SURFACE MATERIALS. Same as mentioned in connection with New Surfaces over Sound Plaster.

ACOUSTICAL TILE. Same as mentioned in connection with New Surfaces over Sound Plaster, except that the tile must be fastened to furring strips.

KINDS, SIZES, COLORS, AND PATTERNS. Same as mentioned in connection with New Surfaces over Sound Plaster.

FASTENING FURRING STRIPS. As previously mentioned and as shown in Figure 6, the furring strips must be nailed over the plaster so that the nails penetrate into the joists. The nails should be at least 3 inches long.

CLIP
(A)

FITS TONGUE
(B)

FITS GROOVE
(C)

FIGURE 7. Clip used to fasten tile to furring strip.

FIGURE 8. How clips are nailed to furring strips.

1x3 FURRING
STRIP

NAIL

TONGUED AND
GROOVED TILE

CLIP

FIGURE 9. Section view showing how clip is nailed to furring strip and how tile fits into clip.

Fastening Tile. There are three methods of fastening tile to the furring strips. Any one of them may be employed.

CLIPS. The use of clips constitutes a sure way of fastening the tile and at the same time allows a floating surface which compensates for irregularities in the level of the plaster and furring strips. The *A* part of Figure 7 shows a typical clip. The *B* and *C* parts of the same illustration show how the clip fits the tongues and grooves at the edges of the tile. Figure 8 indicates how the clips are nailed to furring strips as a ceiling project is in progress. Figure 9 is a section view that illustrates how clips are fastened to furring strips and how the tile fits into the clips. Figure 10 indicates the recommended number of clips for the different sizes of tile. Note that the furring strips should be spaced on 8-inch centers where 16-inch tile are involved.

STAPLES AND NAILS. Either staples or nails can also be used for fastening tile to furring strips. Figure 11 shows the use of wide-flange tile and how staples or nails can be employed. Staples and nails should be rust-proof and no longer than $\frac{9}{16}$ inch. The recommended number of staples or nails per tile is set forth in Figure 12.

Prefinished Ceiling Tile. Same as explained under New Surfaces over Sound Plaster, except that the tile must be nailed to furring strips.

New Surfaces over Plasterboard. When plasterboard ceilings contain one or more such defects as previously explained, the same general plan as set forth under New Surfaces over Unsound Plaster can be employed. The old plasterboard must be securely renailed before furring strips are applied.

New Surfaces without Plaster. When basement and attic spaces are being remodeled as a means of providing additional living space in a house, it is probable that unfinished ceiling surfaces will be involved and that new surface materials will have to be applied directly to ceiling joists or rafters. In other cases, old lath and plaster may be in such poor condition that they must be entirely removed. In still other cases, sound-proofing and insulation may be desired.

FIGURE 10. Recommended number of clips for the different sizes of tile.

FIGURE 11. Tile having extra-wide flanges should be used when they are to be fastened with staples or nails.

PUT STAPLE IN INTERMEDIATE STRIP

FIGURE 12. Recommended number of staples or nails per tile.

SURFACE MATERIALS. Same as explained under New Surfaces over Unsound Plaster.

INSULATION. In order greatly to reduce the transmission of sound from a basement recreation room to the rooms above it, blanket-type wool insulation (see Chapter 3) can be stuffed between the ceiling joists prior to the time furring strips are applied (see Figure 13). The benefits thus obtained are worth the added cost of the insulation. Attic spaces can be insulated as set forth in Chapter 3.

FIGURE 13. Blanket insulation being applied between joists in a basement ceiling.

ACOUSTICAL TILE. Same as mentioned in connection with New Surfaces over Sound Plaster, except that the tile must be fastened to furring strips.

KINDS, SIZES, COLORS, AND PATTERNS. Same as mentioned in connection with New Surfaces over Sound Plaster.

Fastening Furring Strips and Tile. Same as mentioned in connection with New Surfaces over Unsound Plaster.

PLASTERBOARD. This type of surface material is manufactured in large sheets whose dimensions are multiples of 16 inches so that the sheets can be applied to joists or rafters which are spaced 16 inches on centers. All joints and nail dents can be finished so that they are not visible under paint or other decorating materials. This material is particularly well suited to attic remodeling.

KINDS. The various manufacturers of this material employ their own trade names to identify their products. *Sheetrock* is one example. Generally, the material is manufactured in ⅜- and ½-inch thicknesses. The two surfaces are composed of heavy cardboard, and the core is made from gypsum or an insulating substance. Some manufacturers offer wood-grained textures which are factory-prefinished.

SIZES. Most manufacturers produce plasterboard in 4-foot widths and in various lengths, all of which are multiples of 16.

FASTENING. In all cases, plasterboard is fastened by means of nails. Some manufacturers suggest special kinds and sizes of nails but, in general, 4d nails should be employed for board thicknesses of less than ½ inch and 5d nails for boards which are a full ½ inch thick. The nails should be placed at least ⅜ inch from the edges of boards and spaced no more than 7 inches apart.

EDGES. For remodeling work, where painted surfaces are required, the plasterboard should have tapered edges so that the joints can be reinforced and filled according to manufacturers' directions.

NEW LOWERED CEILINGS. As discussed in Chapter 9, thousands of old houses, while being structurally sound and valuable, were built in keeping with living and utility standards of a past era. Such houses can be remodeled, following any one or more of several possible plans, to make them comply with modern living requirements and tastes. For example, the ceilings in old houses are often from 10 to 12 or more feet above the floors. Based on our present-day ideas of beauty, comfort, and utility, such ceiling heights increase decorating costs, add to heating and cooling expense, and do not blend with such equipment as kitchen cabinets or other new and desirable items of modern living. High ceilings can be lowered and new surfaces applied, all at reasonable cost.

To lower a ceiling it is only necessary to add new and generally lightweight framing which can be suspended from the old ceiling and attached to the walls. Then, any of the new surface materials previously discussed can be applied. The results, especially in kitchens and in utility rooms, are exceptionally worthwhile.

MAKING CEILINGS SEEM LOWER. If ceilings are only 1 or 2 feet higher than the now common height of 8 feet, the impression of too much height can be relieved by using a horizontal decorative scheme, such as a wide border below the ceiling.

MAKING CEILINGS SEEM HIGHER. There may be cases where ceilings are too low rather than too high. In such cases, the rather oppressive feeling conveyed by a low ceiling can be overcome by introducing vertical lines into wall decorating schemes. Borders and other horizontal trim should be eliminated.

HOW TO PLAN AND DO TYPICAL REMODELING PROJECTS

As repeatedly stressed all through this book, any and all remodeling projects should be carefully planned and laid out prior to the time materials are purchased and the actual work is started. Careful planning will prevent undue expense and avoid unnecessary labor and other difficulties. Any well-planned project will progress much faster and yield the desired results. The following typical ceiling projects are presented in such a manner as to exhibit proper planning and to provide helpful how-to-do-it instructions:

REPAIRING PLASTER CRACKS

In previous discussions we have learned that some types of plaster cracks are due to natural shrinkage and settlement and that once such conditions have reached their maximums, after a house is about two years old, the cracks can be repaired with reasonable assurance that they will not reoccur. We also learned that other types of plaster cracks occur because of unfortunate conditions which are apt to be repeated and that there is no assurance that such cracks will not reoccur after being repaired. Thus the first planning procedure consists of studying cracks—watching them—in an effort to determine their cause and to decide if we want to chance reoccurrence possibilities.

Large Cracks. If a large crack, ⅟₁₆ to ¼ inch in width, seems to be stable and not likely to reoccur, the following procedure is recommended:

PREPARATION. For cracks which are from ⅟₁₆ to ¼ inch wide, and where the plaster on either side of the cracks is sound and not loose, use a chisel or sharp screwdriver to remove all bits of loose plaster and to create an inverted V, as shown in the *A* part of Figure 14. Dig out the inverted V to the lathing.

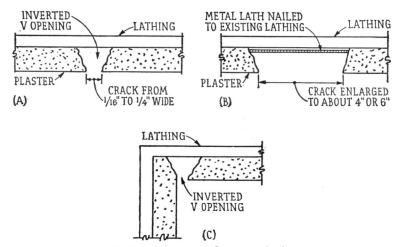

FIGURE 14. How to prepare plaster cracks for repair.

PATCHING MATERIAL. Use any plaster-patching material such as obtainable at hardware stores or from building-material dealers.

PATCHING. The first step in the patching process is to wet the interior of the crack and the exposed lath two or three times about an hour before applying the patching material. A paint brush can be used to make sure the water reaches all areas of the crack.

Mix the patching material as per the directions on its container. Add just enough water to make the material plastic and easy to spread. Use a putty knife to force the material into the crack and to ⅟₁₆ inch of the surface of the surrounding plaster.

Allow the patch to dry for at least 24 hours. Then mix fresh patching material and completely fill the crack. This procedure avoids any chance of a slightly concave surface on the patch due to shrinkage. Smooth the surface of the patch flush with the edges of the surrounding plaster and remove any excess patching material.

When the patching material has thoroughly dried, after two or three days, apply a liberal coat of shellac or other sealer to it.

If a crack is more than ¼ inch wide and if there seems to be some possibility that it will reoccur, the following procedure is recommended:

PREPARATION. Use a chisel and a hammer to deliberately increase the width of the crack to 4 or 6 inches, as shown in the *B* part of Figure 14. Create the inverted V as previously explained. Next, nail a piece of metal lath securely to the existing lathing. Drive the nails at an angle.

PATCHING MATERIAL. For a patch of such width and where metal lath is involved, it is best to use a regular brown coat plaster mix to fill most of the crack and a regular white coat mix for the surface. Both materials are available at lumberyards.

PATCHING. Using the brown coat mix, fill the crack just enough to cover the metal lath. Allow this to dry for a day or two. Then, using the same mix, fill the crack to within 1⁄16 inch of the surface of the surrounding old plaster. Allow this part of the patch two days for drying. Finally, use the white coat mix to finish the patch flush with the old plaster.

Allow the white coat to dry for two weeks, and then apply a liberal coat of shellac or other sealer to the general area of the patch.

Corner Cracks. When cracks are at the line where a ceiling and wall meet, dig out an inverted V, as shown in the *C* part of Figure 14, and apply patching material as explained in connection with cracks from 1⁄16 to ¼ inch wide. Seal as previously recommended.

Small Cracks. If cracks are less than 1⁄16 inch wide, the following procedure is recommended:

PREPARATION. Clean out all visible dirt or bits of plaster by means of a stiff brush.

PATCHING MATERIAL. Same as recommended for 1⁄16-inch cracks.

PATCHING. Wet the cracks about an hour before applying patching. Apply the patching material by means of a putty knife. Force the material into the cracks and trim the surface flush with the surface of surrounding plaster. Seal as previously recommended.

Conclusion. Where cracks are numerous and when they are likely to reoccur, repairing is seldom worthwhile, especially if painted decorations are desired.

NEW SURFACES OVER SOUND PLASTER

The following project is typical of any and all cases where ceiling tile is to be applied over old but sound plaster. The project is presented in terms of a typical problem and its solution.

PROBLEM 1. KITCHEN CEILING. For the purpose of this problem we shall assume that Plates I through VI, which are at the back of this book, show the plans for an *old* house. We can further assume that the kitchen-ceiling plaster, while still sound, contains a great many small cracks which are sure to reoccur and which create a poor appearance. The problem is to remodel the ceiling so that its appearance will be in keeping with new cabinets and other equipment we plan to install.

SOLUTION. First, it can be assumed that we would like to apply acoustical tile directly to the old plaster. Such tile will create a new and beautiful appearance, reduce noise in the kitchen, and add some insulating effect to the ceiling. The insulating effect will be worthwhile because the ceiling is under attic space which is cold during winter and hot during summer.

PLANNING. The first planning item consists of checking the ceiling to see if it is level enough for the application of tile. The checking can be done with a long and straight piece of 1 by 3 or 2 by 4. Hold this straightedge at various locations against the ceiling. If the surface of the plaster touches the straightedge at all points along the length, the ceiling is level or flat enough for tile. We can assume that it is and that cemented tiling is therefore possible.

The next item of planning has to do with the size and pattern of tile. Since the kitchen is only 10' 0" by 11' 6", the small or 12- by 12-inch tile size will create the best appearance. And, because the room is almost square, the square design shown in Figure 5, without a border, is in keeping with good taste.

LAYOUT. What is commonly called layout work is actually part of the planning. In this solution, the purpose of layout is to locate the center point of the ceiling and to determine by sketch trials the best position for the first piece of tile.

The X part of Figure 15 shows what constitutes the center point of the ceiling. The dashed line is located by four dimensions: G and H near one end of the room and J and M near the opposite end. The center point is located by two dimensions, such as N and P, near each side of the room. Locating the center point of a room in this manner compensates for any minor irregularities in the dimensions of the room.

FIGURE 15. How to find center point of a ceiling.

The Y part of Figure 15 is an outline of the kitchen shown in Plate I and illustrates how the foregoing procedure, explained in connection with the X part of the illustration, is put to actual use. Dimensions A and B, along with dimensions C and D, locate the dashed line. Such a line can be made on a ceiling by means of a chalk string. To establish the center point of the ceiling, dimensions E and F should be exactly the same.

Once the center point of a ceiling has been established and marked, the next logical step is to plan the tile positions or layout. The best procedure is to plan the exact position of the first piece of tile to be applied. Then, all other pieces will follow the established pattern.

The W part of Figure 16 shows four center points at A, B, C, and D. The letter L indicates the center points and the letter K indicates the first pieces of tile. The first piece of tile may be applied in any one of the four positions shown relative to the center point. However, we cannot be sure which position to use in this solution until we draw a few sketches accurately to scale.

NOTE: When the sketches are drawn accurately to scale, they represent the actual ceiling. This may be visualized if we imagine that the sketches indicate what we would see if we looked up at the ceiling. Once the sketches are complete, we can use chalk or a chalk string to create lines on the ceiling which are similar to the lines on the sketches. Thus, the

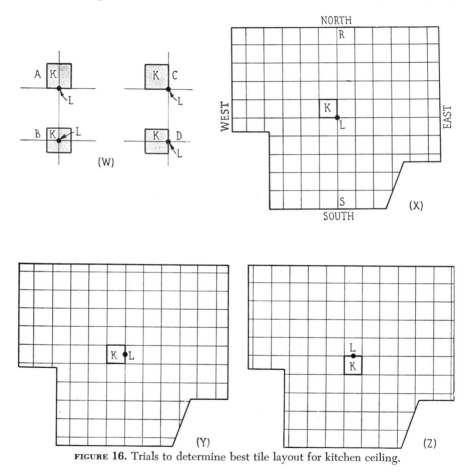

FIGURE 16. Trials to determine best tile layout for kitchen ceiling.

sketches constitute the means by which layout can be planned. This fact will be emphasized in the following explanations:

The X part of Figure 16 shows the outline of the kitchen, the center point L, a trial position for the first piece of tile K, and how all other pieces of tile will appear if we imagine that we are looking up at the ceiling. This arrangement is good, owing to the fact that the north and south borders consist of full pieces of tile and because the west and east borders will not require much tile cutting. The sketches shown in the Y and Z parts of Figure 16, where the first pieces of tile are shown in different positions, are not good because of the irregular borders. Therefore, the arrangement shown in the X part of the illustration should be employed, NOTE: Accurately scaled sketches should always be drawn as part of the layout work in connection with tile surfaces.

The tile should be unpacked so that all pieces can adjust themselves to temperature and humidity conditions. Finally, and as indicated in the X part of Figure 16, nail a straightedge next to line RS. The first row of tile should be applied using the straightedge as a guide.

APPLICATION OF TILE. All manufacturers of ceiling tile make specific recommendations in connection with the adhesive (cement) to use with their tile. Generally, such adhesive has the consistency of putty and can be handled by means of a putty knife. NOTE: All wallpaper or calcimine must be removed from the ceiling before applying tile.

As shown in Figure 4, four dabs of the adhesive should be placed on each piece of tile. In the illustration, the dark spots on the ceiling indicate the approximate positions of the four dabs on the tile. Each dab of adhesive should be about the size of a walnut. The amount of adhesive may be increased or decreased to compensate for low or high places in the ceiling.

In Figure 17 the straightedge and the first row of tile are shown in proper positions. Tile 1 is the same as tile K in X part of Figure 16.

Start with tile 1. Apply the four dabs of adhesive. Then, as indicated in Figure 2, press the tile against the ceiling. The grooved side of the tile must touch the straightedge. Apply uniform pressure and a slight weaving motion. As shown in the illustration, one corner of the tile must touch the corner point L. Be sure that the grooved edge is snug against the straightedge.

Next, apply tile 2. Be sure that the surface of this piece is at the same level as the level of tile 1, so that the tongued-and-grooved joints can interlock properly. If tile 2 has been pressed too much, remove it and add a little more adhesive at all four points.

In like manner, apply tiles 3, 4, 5, 6, 7, 8, 9, and 10 in the order indicated. Tiles 8 and 10 must be about $\frac{1}{16}$ inch away from the walls to allow for expansion. If necessary, these pieces can be sawed to make them fit.

When the first row of tile has been applied, remove the straightedge and apply the second row. All other rows are applied in the same manner. Be sure that all joints and bevels match. The slightest variation would cause undesirable appearance.

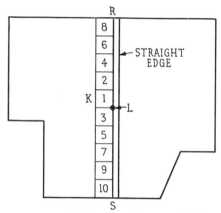

FIGURE 17. Applying first row of tile.

Finally, nail a cove molding all around the wall next to the tile.

PAINTING. The manufacturers of acoustical tile recommend paints which have oil, rubber, or water bases. Such paints will not decrease the sound absorption of the tile. Paint small areas at a time and follow joint lines to avoid undesirable laps in the paint.

NEW SURFACES OVER UNSOUND PLASTER

The following project is typical of any and all cases where tile is to be applied over unsound plaster. The project is presented in terms of a typical problem and its solution.

PROBLEM 2. KITCHEN CEILING. We can assume that the ceiling plaster in the kitchen specified for Problem 1 is badly cracked, impossible to decorate, and probably unsound. The problem is to remodel it and for the same reason set forth in Problem 1.

SOLUTION. First, it can be assumed that we have decided to use acoustical tile and for the same reason as outlined in Problem 1.

PLANNING. The first step consists of checking the old plaster. This can be done by pressing it with our hands. Considerable looseness is indicative of an unsound condition. We shall assume the unsound condition. Therefore, 1- by 3-inch furring strips must be nailed to the joists, as explained in connection with Figure 6. The distance between furring-strip center lines must be the same as the width of the tile.

We shall again assume the use of 12- by 12-inch tile and the square design explained in the solution to Problem 1. We shall also assume that the tile is to be fastened to the furring strips by means of nails.

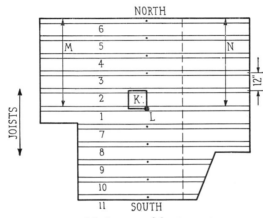

FIGURE 18. Layout of furring strips.

LAYOUT. The center point of the ceiling can be found as explained in the solution to Problem 1.

In order to plan the layout of furring strips, we must draw the outline of the kitchen to scale. Figure 18 shows the required drawing. Furring strip 1 should be directly over the center point L and at right angles to the joists. The tile positions can be planned as explained in the solution to Problem 1. The first piece of tile should be applied in the position indicated by the illustration.

APPLICATION OF FURRING STRIPS. Place furring strip 1 so that its center line is directly over the center point L. Drive one nail near the center of the furring strip to hold it in place. Then adjust it until dimensions M and N are the same. This procedure makes sure that the furring strip is square with the room. Use two nails at each joist location. The joist locations can be determined by tapping the plaster with a hammer. The hammer taps sound solid at joist locations. Fasten furring strips 2, 3, 4, 5, 6, 7, 8, 9, and 10. Make sure that their center lines are exactly 12 inches apart. If spots of plaster fall, use shims as indicated in Figure 6. Furring strips 6 and 11 should be snug against the wall, even if the distances between 6 and 5 and 11 and 10 are not exactly 12 inches.

Check the level of the furring strips by pressing a straightedge up against them. See dashed line in Figure 18. If one or more of them do not touch the straightedge, drive shims between them and the plaster.

APPLICATION OF STARTER STRIP. In order to apply the first row of tile in a straight line, a starter strip is required. See Figure 19. It should be nailed along the center line of furring strip 1. Starter strips can be obtained where the tile is purchased.

FURRING STRIP NUMBER 1 SEE FIGURE 18 — NAIL

TILE   STARTER STRIP   TILE
FIGURE 19. Starter strip details.

APPLICATION OF TILE. Place the first piece of tile (see *K* in Figure 18) so that its groove engages the tongue of the starter strip. See Figure 19. Make sure that the corner of the tile touches the furring strip above the point *L*. See Figure 18. As recommended in the *A* part of Figure 12, use four nails. Apply the first row of tile as indicated in the *A* part of Figure 20. Install the second row so that the flanges lead in the opposite direction. After two rows have been applied, adjacent rows should be applied beginning at the ends of the already applied rows and across the ceiling. This procedure allows nailing at the corner of each tile. It is important to line up the joints, so that they are straight, before nailing since adjustment of tile is difficult once the nails have been driven. This is shown graphically in the *B* part of Figure 20. A $\frac{1}{16}$-inch expansion space must be provided between the tile and the walls.

Finally, nail a cove in place as explained in the solution to Problem 1.

PAINTING. Same as explained in solution to Problem 1.

NOTE. Some mechanics and homeowners prefer to use plasterboard instead of furring strips when unsound plaster is involved. In such cases, the plasterboard should be applied to the ceiling by means of nails which

FIGURE 20. Tile application to furring strips.

are long enough to go through the plasterboard and plaster and penetrate firmly into the joists. The tile is planned, laid out, and applied as explained in the solution to Problem 1.

NEW SURFACES WITHOUT PLASTER

The following project is typical of any and all cases where ceiling tile is to be applied directly to ceiling joists or rafters. The project is presented in terms of a typical problem and its solution.

PROBLEM 3. BASEMENT CEILING. For the purpose of this problem, we can assume that part of the basement space shown in Plate II is to be transformed into a recreation room. The problem is to create a beautiful ceiling which will soundproof the area and reduce the transmission of sound to the first-floor rooms above.

SOLUTION. First, it can be assumed that we have decided to apply acoustical ceiling tile as surface material, and wool blankets between the joists as insulation to prevent sound transmission.

PLANNING. The first step of the planning consists of selecting the insulation. We shall assume the use of wool blankets (see Chapter 3) because they can be stuffed between the joists and fastened to the bottom edges of them by means of laths and nailing flanges.

FIGURE 21. Tile layout for recreation-room ceiling.

The next item of planning has to do with the size and pattern of tile. As indicated in Plate II, and as suggested in Chapter 7, one possible plan for the recreation room could be 19′ 2″ long and 11′ 10″ wide. Ordinarily, we would plan to use either 12- by 24- or 16- by 32-inch tile for an area of such size. However, in this solution we shall assume the use of 12- by 12-inch tile in order to take advantage of explanations given in previous problem solutions. We shall also assume the square pattern and that the tile will be fastened by means of nails.

Plate II indicates that the ceiling joists above the recreation room are supported by means of an I-beam. We can assume that the joists are set between the flanges of the beam so that the beam does not extend below the bottoms of the joists.

LAYOUT. In this problem the layout must be planned in a different manner, owing to the fact that the ceiling is not plastered and there is therefore no surface on which we can mark the center point of the room. The following procedure will be helpful to inexperienced installers:

Use the concrete floor instead of the ceiling as a surface on which to indicate the center point of the room. A plumb bob can be used to transfer the center point to the ceiling when the first furring strip is being applied.

Here again it is necessary to draw a sketch accurately to scale. Figure 21 shows the type of sketch required when planning the tile layout. The center point of the room is indicated at L. The position of the first piece

FIGURE 22. How blanket insulation is applied between joists.

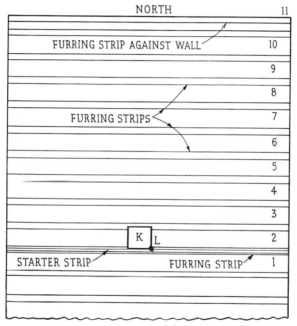

FIGURE 23. Layout of furring strips.

of tile K was determined following the same trial procedure as was explained in the solution to Problem 1.

Application of Insulation. Figure 13 shows how the blanket insulation should be stuffed between the joists. The tool shown in the picture is an automatic stapler used to fasten the insulation.

Figure 22 shows how wood laths are used to fasten the blanket nailing flanges to the bottom edges of the joists.

Application of Furring Strips. Figure 23 shows the furring strips for one half of the recreation-room ceiling. They are nailed over the wood laths shown in Figures 8 and 22. Place furring strip 1 so that its center line is directly over the center point *L* indicated in Figure 23. Adjust this furring strip as explained in the solution to Problem 2. Next fasten furring strips 2, 3, 4, 5, 6, 7, 8, 9, and 10 so that their center lines are all exactly 12 inches apart. Strip 11 must be snug against the wall. Test the level of the strips as explained in the solution to Problem 2.

Application of Starter Strip. Apply the starter strip as shown in Figure 23 using the procedure set forth in the solution to Problem 2.

Application of Tile. The tile is applied as explained in the solution to Problem 2. Sawing and trimming will have to be done where the tile meets all four walls of the room. See Figure 21. When fastening trimmed tile at the north and south walls, the sides of the tile against the walls should be nailed to the furring strips by means of 1½-inch nails driven from the face of the tile. The cove molding will hide the nail heads.

Painting. See solution to Problem 2.

SLOPING ATTIC CEILINGS

When attic spaces (see Chapter 9) are remodeled to create living areas, part of the ceilings in such areas generally slope. In other words, ceiling-surface materials must be applied to the bottom edges of the rafters. Various kinds of tile may be applied to such ceilings in much the same manner as it is applied to horizontal ceilings.

Figure 24 illustrates the application of acoustical tile to a sloping ceiling. Note that wood laths are not used to fasten the blanket insulation to the rafters. However, the usual furring strips are required. Note, too, that a border composed of 12- by 24-inch plain tile is part of the design. The walls may be surfaced as explained in Chapter 5.

Except for the omission of wood laths, the planning, layout, and application procedures for a ceiling of this type are the same as explained in the solution to Problem 3.

FIGURE 24. Tile being applied to sloping attic ceiling.

LOWERED CEILING

The following project is typical of any and all cases where ceilings are to be lowered:

PROBLEM 4. KITCHEN CEILING. For the purpose of this problem, we can assume that the ceiling height of the kitchen indicated in Plate I is 12′ 0″. The problem is to plan and erect a new ceiling which will be 8′ 0″ above the floor.

SOLUTION. Figure 25 will be helpful in visualizing the required framing for the lowered ceiling. The walls, the original ceiling, and the floor are named. The 2 by 4 pieces at *E* should be fastened to the walls by nails which are long enough to go through the lath and plaster and into the studs. The 2 by 4 ceiling joists should be nailed to the *E* pieces.

The *X* part of Figure 26 may be visualized as though we were directly above the new framing and were looking straight down at it. All framing members are composed of 2 by 4 pieces. The pieces marked *E* correspond to those marked *E* in Figure 25. Eleven joists are required.

FIGURE 25. How to visualize frame for lowered ceiling.

Installation of E Pieces. First, cut a 2 by 4 to a length of 11′ 6″. This is for the *MN* wall shown in the *X* part of Figure 26. See dimensions in Plate I. Measure a distance of 8′ 0″ up from the floor and draw a line on the *MN* wall. Use a carpenter's level to make sure this line is horizontal. Place the *MN* 2 by 4 so that its bottom edge coincides with the line. The long side of the 2 by 4 should be flat against the wall. Drive one nail at each end of the 2 by 4. Use 3½-inch nails and make sure that they enter studs in the wall. Test the level again. Then drive at least one nail at each stud location.

Fasten the 2 by 4 pieces on walls *TS, PR, WR, SW, NR, RT,* and

PM in the order named. Make sure that each piece is horizontal and that bottom edges are exactly 8′ 0″ above the floor.

Installation of 2 by 4 Joists. The joists should be 12 inches on centers. Use a measuring tape to determine the exact length required for each. They should fit snugly against the *E* pieces. Toenail them to the *E* pieces. Use 2½-inch nails.

FIGURE 26. Details of frame for lowered ceiling.

In order to stiffen the framing, install 1- by 4-inch pieces as shown at *G, F,* and *H*. Nail these stiffeners securely to the joists.

Joists 3, 4, 5, 6, 7, 8, and 9 are long and should therefore be provided with some support from the original ceiling. The *Y* part of Figure 26 shows how such support can be accomplished.

Nail a 2 by 4 to the ceiling, above the position of stiffener *F*. Make sure that the nails penetrate into the joists of the original ceiling. The 2 by 2 hangers should be nailed to the ceiling 2 by 4 and to the 2 by 4 joists.

Application of Furring Strips. The furring strips must be nailed to the joists and at right angles to them. The procedure is the same as explained in the solutions to Problems 2 and 3.

Application of Tile. This is the same as explained in the solution to Problem 3.

LADDERS AND SCAFFOLD PLANKS

Where ceiling work is concerned, the use of both ladders and scaffold planks is recommended as a means of providing more convenience and greater safety. If only a ladder is used, it will have to be frequently moved. This slows the work and makes for unhandy and tiring working conditions.

Types of Ladders Recommended. For most ceiling work, household safety stepladders may be used. They should include full-rodded steps and double top irons, 5- or 6-foot heights serve the purpose.

Safety Hints. When working on a ladder without scaffolds, always face the ladder when ascending or descending. Make sure the ladder is fully spread and locked with all four legs resting on the floor. Never stand on the top of a ladder or try to reach more than 2 feet to either side of one.

CHAPTER FIVE

Walls

Good taste in home decoration is evidenced by many items which combine to make a harmonious whole. The choice of colors, the pictures, and the furnishings all contribute to the general effect. But, more than any other item, attractive and defect-free walls are the foundation of successful interior decoration.

Nearly every old house has at least one room that is a source of constant disappointment and embarrassment because of unsightly defects in wall surface materials. As explained in Chapter 4, such defects can be classified as *natural* and *unfortunate*.

Natural defects generally occur above or around window and door openings, in the form of thin cracks which resemble spider webs. Unfortunate defects are apt to occur more or less at random, in the form of large cracks which are jagged and deep.

Unsightly walls can be repaired or remodeled to create greatly improved appearance or entirely new and beautiful surfaces. This chapter proposes to suggest typical repairing and remodeling projects and to explain how such work can be planned and accomplished.

PLASTER AND PLASTERBOARD DEFECTS

The defects most generally found in ceiling-surface materials are explained in Chapter 4. The same explanations apply to the defects most generally found in wall-surface materials. However, the defects in wall-surface materials are usually more pronounced and are therefore more unsightly.

JUDGING WALL DEFECTS

Before deciding whether to repair or to remodel wall surfaces, we should consider the types of defects involved and exercise some judgment in connection with reoccurrence possibilities.

Natural defects, such as spider-web cracks above or around window and door openings, generally reach their maximum extent by the time houses are two or three years old. After that time, such defects can be repaired without much chance that they will reoccur. Wallpaper or any of the fabric wall coverings can be applied over the repaired areas.

Unfortunate defects, such as large and jagged cracks, are unstable and likely to reoccur. Thus, their repair constitutes a gamble even if one of the previously mentioned fabric wall coverings are applied over the repaired areas.

Extensive repair work is never completely satisfactory unless wall surfaces are covered with paper or fabric decorating materials.

In general, except where *natural* defects are confined to small areas and where a paper or fabric covering is to be applied, the repair of wall defects is not feasible owing to the fact that they are much more noticeable than similar defects in ceilings and because the best of repair work is seldom satisfactory.

SUGGESTED REMODELING PROJECTS

Whether a house is old or relatively new, the walls in it can be restored to their original or even more desirable beauty. This promise holds true regardless of how badly cracked or otherwise marred the walls may have become. After many years of extensive research and a great deal of experience, building-material manufacturers have created new, beautiful, and enduring wall-surface materials. The costs are low and the installation procedures have been simplified. Any of the following suggestions can be applied to walls under any and all conditions.

Repairing Cracked Plaster. In cases where the cracks are above or around window and door openings, or at a corner where two walls meet, repair work constitutes the easiest and most economical improvement method.

MATERIALS. Any regular plaster-patching mix, such as sold by hardware and paint stores, can be used. Various patching "pencils" are also available for use in connection with hairline cracks.

Repairing Holes in Plaster. In houses which have been occupied at various times by several different families, and in some cases where only one family has been involved, the plaster or plasterboard may have been injured in many locations by hangers, nails, or screws used to hang mirrors, pictures, shelves, etc. Such injuries are generally in the form of holes. They can be repaired in such a manner as to leave no trace of them.

MATERIAL. Any plaster-patching mix.

Plastic Wall Coverings. Several such coverings, under various trade names, are available at paint and hardware stores. In most cases, the coverings look like thick paint and may be applied by means of a paint brush. In theory, the coverings fill cracks and other irregularities and at the same time create new surfaces which will not crack even when used in connection with unstable defects. The new surfaces are washable.

MATERIAL. The coverings may be obtained in cans ready for application. Several colors are available.

Fabric Wall Coverings. Several such coverings, under various trade names, are available. They are applied like wallpaper. In theory, the coverings will not crack or even tear when used in connection with unstable defects. The new surfaces are washable.

MATERIAL. The coverings can be obtained in rolls and are applied by means of a paste. Generally, several patterns and colors are available.

New Surfaces over Sound Plaster. As previously mentioned, nearly every old house is likely to have one or more wall surfaces which are not suitable for modern decoration. Sometimes the defects do not affect the soundness of the plaster. In such cases, the problem is to select new surface materials which can be applied *over* the plaster. Any one of the following materials can be depended upon to provide new and enduring beauty:

SURFACE MATERIALS. Many types and kinds of new surface materials are available. A visit to a lumberyard or to a building-material dealer's

FIGURE 1. Typical planks and blocks for walls.

showroom will prove to be interesting and helpful in deciding which materials to use for various rooms.

Planks. The *A* part of Figure 1 shows typical wall planks being applied over old but sound plaster. Figure 2 illustrates the use of such planks in a remodeled kitchen and dining-room area. Planks are easy to install, and as indicated in the illustration, create beautiful surfaces.

KINDS. Generally speaking, planks are manufactured in two basic kinds. One kind, such as shown in Figure 2, has a hard-baked surface that is soilproof and suitable for use in kitchens and bathrooms where cooking and bathing activities create greasy smoke or high humidity. The other kind has a soft surface which provides soundproofing and insulation effects. It is suitable for use in living rooms or basement recreation areas.

SIZES. Hard-baked varieties are generally 8' 0" long, 1' 4" wide, and $\frac{3}{16}$" thick. The soft-surface varieties have the same length and width

FIGURE 2. Remodeled kitchen showing use of planks on walls.

but may be $\frac{1}{2}$" or $\frac{3}{4}$" thick. All such wall-surface materials are meant for 8' 0" ceiling heights. Where higher ceilings exist, special arrangements with suppliers must be made. Or, as explained in Chapter 4, ceilings can be lowered to the modern 8' 0" dimension.

COLORS. The hard-baked varieties can be secured in many colors to suit any decorating scheme. The soft-surface varieties are limited to tones of gray or tan.

PATTERNS. The hard-baked varieties can be secured in many patterns so far as the texture of their surfaces is concerned. For example, striped or golden mahogany and natural or silver walnut patterns are available.

FASTENING. Most planks are fastened by nails and clips. However, they can also be cemented to old plaster.

EDGES. All planks are provided with tongued-and-grooved edges for easy installation and as a means of making better joints between them.

Blocks. The *B* part of Figure 1 shows typical wall blocks being applied over old but sound plaster. Figure 3 illustrates how blocks may be combined with planks in a remodeled attic space. Like planks, the blocks are easy to install and create beautiful and durable surfaces.

FIGURE 3. Remodeled attic space showing use of blocks.

KINDS. As explained in connection with planks, two basic kinds are available: hard-baked and soft surfaces.

SIZES. The hard-baked varieties are generally 16 inches square and $\frac{3}{16}$ inch thick. The soft-surface kinds are manufactured in several sizes ranging from 12 by 12 inches to 16 by 32 inches. The thicknesses vary from $\frac{1}{2}$ to 1 inch.

COLOR. Same as for planks.

PATTERNS. Same as for planks.

FASTENING. Same as for planks.

EDGES. Same as for planks.

BOARDS. The difference between planks and boards lies in their sizes and intended uses. Planks are intended for use where high-class interior finishes are required, whereas boards are generally used in cottages or farm buildings where only a medium-grade finish and insulating effects are necessary.

KINDS. Most boards are manufactured from materials which have insulating qualities. Thus, their surfaces are more or less soft. There is some variation in board materials, but for the most part they are lightweight and similar to the acoustical tile described in Chapter 4.

SIZES. Several sizes are available. Widths range from 1' 0" to 4' 0" and the lengths range from 6' 0" to 12' 0". Thicknesses vary between ½" and 1".

COLORS. In general, the colors range from gray to shades of tan. However, some manufacturers offer special-order selections of color.

PATTERNS. Little, if any, pattern is available. For the most part, the boards all have a resinlike finish. However, there is often some unavoidable color variation which can be used to advantage in creating a slight color pattern. A borderlike pattern may be worked out by means of wood or metal moldings, inserts, overlays, bevels, and inlays, all of which should be placed at joints.

FASTENING. All fastening should be done by means of nails. When nailheads are to be covered by moldings, 1½-inch common or large-head nails serve the purpose. When nails will not be covered, 1½-inch finish nails should be used.

EDGES. Several different edges are available. Some are tongued and grooved. Others are square, bevel-lapped, or rabbeted, depending on the type of joint desired.

Corrugated and Grooved Boards. Figure 4 shows typical corrugated boards on the walls of a breakfast nook. Grooved boards are similar, except that instead of being corrugated, their surfaces are composed of thin and closely spaced parallel grooves which are $\frac{1}{32}$ or $\frac{1}{16}$ inch deep.

KINDS. Both corrugated and grooved boards are manufactured from wood but are tempered so that they have the qualities of hardboard.

They are weather- and moisture-resistant and may be painted like ordinary wood trim.

SIZES. Both boards are manufactured in various sizes which can be used with little waste for most remodeling work. They are generally ⅛ inch thick.

COLORS. Most manufacturers produce the boards in the natural colors of wood. In other words, several colors may be available. However, color

FIGURE 4. Typical application of corrugated boards to a breakfast-nook area.

is of little importance owing to the fact that the boards can be painted to suit any requirement.

PATTERN. No pattern, as such, is available. However, the corrugations and grooves tend to create a three-dimensional effect.

FASTENING. All fastening should be done by means of finish nails, the same as for ordinary interior trim.

EDGES. Square.

Panels. As their name implies, panels are generally manufactured in the form of large sheets which can be applied to walls. Figure 5 illustrates the use of typical panels in a remodeled bathroom.

KINDS. Two basic kinds are available. One kind, such as shown in Figure 5, has a hard-baked surface which is soilproof and suitable for kitchens and bathrooms where greasy smoke or high humidity must be considered. The other kind has a soft surface which provides sound-proofing and insulating effects. It is suitable for living and recreation rooms.

FIGURE 5. Typical panels used in remodeling a bathroom.

SIZES. Panel sizes range from 2′ 0″ by 4′ 0″ to 4′ 0″ by 8′ 0″ and are generally $\frac{5}{32}″$ thick. Care should be exercised to select the size which assures the least waste.

COLORS. Plain and combinations of colors are available. In all cases, the panels are factory-finished and ready for application.

PATTERNS. A great variety of patterns which look like mahogany, birch, limed oak, prima vera, and walnut are available. For example, the pattern shown in Figure 5 is silver walnut. Some panels are scored to make them look like tile.

FASTENING AND EDGES. Same as planks.

FIGURE 6. Typical installation of perforated hardboard in a kitchen.

FIGURE 7. Typical hanging fixtures for use in kitchen.

Perforated Panels. One of the newer and interesting wall-surface materials consists of perforated panels. The perforations are generally $\frac{3}{16}$ inch in diameter and are spaced 1 inch apart throughout the panels.

Figure 6 shows a typical application of such panels to the walls of a kitchen. Note that all sorts of objects may be hung in any desired positions by means of the hangers illustrated in Figure 7. A great variety of such hangers is available. They lock on the panels or lift off without the use of tools of any kind.

The panels offer a unique opportunity for personality expression with an almost endless variety of potential arrangement of pictures and wall decorations. In children's rooms, recreation rooms, garages, living rooms, and workshops the panels may serve a multitude of uses.

Because many of their characteristics are similar to wood, the panels will tend to change slightly in dimension when exposed to fluctuations in humidity conditions.

The panels can be fastened directly to studs, furring strips, joists, or other framing members spaced not more than 16 inches on centers, or over a solid backing of wood, plasterboard, or plaster.

SIZES. Several sizes are available in thicknesses of ⅛ and ¼ inch. In most cases, panel sizes can be selected to fit specific wall areas with little or no waste. The ⅛-inch thickness is used where the load on the hangers is not great. The ¼-inch thickness is a heavy-duty panel which should be used in places where the load on the hangers is exceptionally high.

COLORS. Tan and brown.

PATTERNS. Smooth or leatherlike.

FASTENING. Nails, screws, or glue.

EDGES. Square.

New Surfaces without Plaster. When basement and attic spaces are being remodeled, as a means of providing recreation areas and bedrooms, it is likely that wall-surface materials are not present and that new surface materials must be applied to masonry foundations or to rough framing. In other cases, old lath and plaster may be in such bad condition that they must be removed.

SURFACE MATERIALS. All of the previously described surface materials can be applied to foundations or to rough framing by means of furring strips. Therefore, their descriptions are not repeated here.

Plywood. Chapter 1 contains a great deal of information about plywood, none of which is repeated here. What is discussed in the following relates to plywood paneling and planks made especially for wall surfaces:

KINDS. Two general kinds are available. One kind is manufactured in panel form and must be finished after application. Another kind is manufactured in plank form but is factory-finished.

SIZES. Panels are 4 feet wide and can be obtained in lengths of 6, 7, and 8 feet. The most commonly used thicknesses are $\frac{1}{4}$ and $\frac{3}{4}$ inches. The $\frac{1}{4}$-inch panels are generally used for wall surfaces except in basements where the $\frac{3}{4}$-inch thickness is recommended. Planks are manufactured $16\frac{1}{4}$ inches wide, from 6 to 8 feet long, and $\frac{1}{4}$ inch thick.

COLORS. The colors of panels and planks are determined by the kind of wood selected.

PATTERNS. The pattern of plywood panels and planks, like their colors, is determined by the kind of wood selected. Panels can be obtained in mahogany, birch, knotty pine, walnut, elm, oak, and many other woods, all of which have their own particular patterns. Planks can be obtained only in oak, walnut, birch, and mahogany woods.

FASTENING. Both panels and planks can be fastened by means of adhesives, nails, and screws.

EDGES. All plywood products are manufactured with square edges. However, various kinds of joints can be obtained by means of beveling, rabbeting, etc.

Panel Sheet Rock over Plasterboard. In cases where existing plasterboard (dry-built wall surfacing) is in bad condition, as explained in Chapter 4, new sheet-rock paneling can be applied directly to it as a means of creating new and handsome surfaces.

KINDS. Three surface finishes are available: calendered manila paper suitable for any decoration, high-quality paper printed to look like knotty pine, and striated (lengthwise ridges of various widths).

SIZES. All three finishes are manufactured in lengths ranging from 8 to 10 feet, 16 inches wide, and $\frac{3}{8}$ inch thick.

COLORS. The manila-paper finish is a light tan but can be painted or papered to suit decorating schemes. The knotty pine has the natural color of wood. The striated is a light tan or gray.

FASTENING. All fastening is done by means of adhesives.

EDGES. The edges are slightly rounded so that each piece has the appearance of real-wood planks.

HOW TO PLAN AND DO TYPICAL REMODELING PROJECTS

As repeatedly mentioned in connection with all of the projects explained in this book, remodeling work should be carefully planned and laid out prior to the time materials are purchased and actual work is started. Such procedure will prevent material waste, cut down the amount of labor, and assure much better final results. The following wall projects are presented in such a manner as to exhibit proper planning and to provide helpful how-to-do-it instructions:

REPAIRING PLASTER CRACKS

As previously mentioned, wall cracks are much more objectionable than similar cracks in ceilings. This is because the wall cracks are at a level where they are more likely to be seen. Another important consideration relates to the fact that wall cracks are apt to reoccur. Thus, the repair of them constitutes a gamble in terms of appearance and decorating expense. With this fact in mind, such repair work should be done with the greatest possible care.

Large Cracks. When cracks are more than ⅛ inch wide, regardless of their probable cause, they should be enlarged and some reinforcement installed before the patching material is applied.

PREPARATION. The dashed lines in the X part of Figure 8 indicate the original position of a large crack. In order that reinforcement can be installed and the benefits of keyed patching assured, the crack should be enlarged, in the form of an inverted V, so that its opening is at least 4 inches wide and so that it extends to the face of the lathing. This part of the work can be accomplished using a chisel and a hammer, being careful not to strike heavy blows. Use a stiff brush to clean all plaster dust out of the enlarged crack.

PATCHING. Thin metal lath can be used for reinforcement. Short pieces of it can be cut to the lineal shape of the enlarged crack and to a width that will make a snug fit against the face of the original lathing, all as shown in the *Y* part of Figure 8. Use 1-inch brads, spaced about 2 inches apart, to nail the reinforcement securely in place.

For a patch of such width and where metal lath is involved, it is best to use a regular plaster mix for the patching shown in the *A* part and a regular white coat mix for the *B* part. Use a brush to wet thoroughly the interior of the crack prior to the time patching is started. Then, using regular plaster, fill the *A* part of the crack. Force the new plaster against the metal lath and make sure that it is in firm contact with the sides of the crack. Where wall cracks are concerned, the *A* part of the patch should constitute about two-thirds the depth of the crack. Allow this part

FIGURE 8. Repair of large wall cracks.

of the patch to dry for a day or two and then apply the white coat in enough quantity to create a $\frac{1}{32}$-inch ridge, as shown in the illustration. The ridge allows possible white-coat shrinkage without fear that its final surface will be lower than the surface of the original plaster. After a day or two, what is left of the ridge can be sandpapered down so that it is flush with the original plaster.

When the white coat is thoroughly dry, after about two weeks, apply a liberal coat of shellac, or some other sealer, to the patch.

Small Cracks. Where cracks are only about $\frac{1}{16}$ inch wide, the patching procedure set forth in Chapter 4, in connection with cracks $\frac{1}{16}$ to $\frac{1}{4}$ inch wide, may be employed.

HAIRLINE CRACKS. Where very small cracks of hairline width are involved, any of the patching pencils available at hardware and paint stores may be used to fill them. Follow directions which accompany such pencils.

CRACKS IN THIN PLASTER

It is hoped that not many readers will be confronted with what was previously (see Chapter 5) described as *paperhanging*. Large cracks in thin plaster cannot be repaired. In such cases, the only alternative is to apply furring strips as a base for planks, blocks, or panels.

REPAIRING HOLES IN PLASTER

In newer houses, lathing is likely to be in the form of a plasterboard that has heavy paper surfaces and a gypsum core. In old houses, lathing is likely to be in the form of small wood strips. Holes in plaster vary from those made by nails or screws to those made in connection with toggle bolts and other fasteners.

Small Holes. If holes are no more than $\frac{1}{16}$ inch in diameter, their repair is quite simple.

PATCHING. Use a nail to dig out all loose plaster, dirt, or dust. Wet the hole and then force the patching mix into it. Leave a small ridge. After a day or two, the ridge can be sandpapered flush with the surrounding plaster and sealed by means of shellac or other sealers.

Large Holes. If holes are $\frac{1}{4}$ inch or larger in diameter, their repair demands somewhat more work and care.

PREPARATION. If the lathing is plasterboard, use an ice pick or an awl to enlarge the hole near the surface of the lathing. This is the same inverted-V principle previously explained. Clean out all plaster particles, dust, and dirt.

PATCHING. Wet the interior of the hole. Then mix the plaster-patching material into a stiff but plastic state. Force the mix into the hole by means of a small trowel or an old pencil. Enough of the mix should be used to create the anchor shown in the *X* part of Figure 9. To prevent surface shrinkage, leave a little ridge at the surface of the old plaster. When the ridge is sandpapered flush and a sealer has been applied, the patch will not be noticeable under paint.

FIGURE 9. Repairing holes in plaster.

If a large hole extends through plaster and wood lath, the same procedure is recommended.

If the holes do not extend through the lathing, the procedure indicated in the *Y* part of Figure 9 is recommended. In such cases, the lathing serves as the anchor.

NEW SURFACES OVER SOUND PLASTER

The following projects are typical of all cases where plank and block surfaces are to be applied over old but sound plaster. The projects are presented in terms of typical problems and their solutions:

PROBLEM 1. BEDROOM WALLS. For the purpose of this problem, we can assume that Plates I through VI, which are at the back of this book, show the plans for an *old* house. We can further assume that bedroom 3 is to be converted into a nursery in which soilproof walls are required. The problem is to apply plank surfacing to the walls.

SOLUTION. It can be assumed that soilproof planks, such as shown in the *A* part of Figure 1, are to be used.

PLANNING. When contemplating the use of such planks, the first step consists of checking the walls for level. This can be done by holding a long and straight 1 by 3 or 2 by 4 piece at various locations along the walls. If the surface of the plaster touches the straightedge at all points along its length, and at all locations, the walls are level enough for planks to be applied without furring strips. Level conditions can be assumed.

In order to assure the best and lasting results, we shall use both fastening clips and adhesive. Both of these items are available where the planks are purchased.

LAYOUT. When wall planks are involved, the purpose of layout is to plan their exact locations on the walls so as to create the best appearance. It is not often that wall dimensions are such that whole planks can be used without some cutting. In most cases, two of the planks for each wall must be made narrower. In this solution, we shall do the layout work for a typical wall in bedroom 3.

In order to do the layout work accurately and to the best of advantage, we shall draw a sketch of the wall next to the living room. Our sketch must be drawn to scale.

The X part of Figure 10 illustrates the best type of sketch for inexperienced mechanics to draw. In the sketch, $ABCD$ represents the wall. The center point of the wall is shown at L. The vertical line EF represents a joint between two planks.

Each plank is 16 inches wide. Lines GH, JK, LM, OP, QR, and ST represent joints between other planks. These lines are drawn 16 inches apart. Thus, planks 1, 2, 3, 4, 5, and 6 can be full width, while planks 7 and 8 must be cut to about 10-inch widths. This balances the wall and creates the best appearance.

APPLICATION OF PLANKS. Plank 7, as shown in the X part of Figure 10, should be applied first. In order to be sure that it is plumb, even if the corner AD of the room is not plumb, mark a plumb line from the ceiling as shown in the Y part of the same illustration. However, we must add $\frac{1}{8}$ inch to the 10-inch width of plank 7 for the reason shown at A. The plumb line constitutes a guide for application of the first plank.

Typical clips and how they are used to fasten planks are shown in the A part of Figure 11. They should be spaced about 16 inches apart and nailed by means of lath nails. In order to allow for expansion between planks, a $\frac{1}{32}$-inch space must be provided. It can be measured as shown in the B part of the illustration.

FIGURE 10. Plank layout.

The planks should not touch the floor when applied to the wall. Thus, a temporary 1- by 2-inch level starter strip, as shown in Figure 12, should be nailed to the wall above the floor. The planks should rest on this strip during application.

Cut plank 7 to length and to the exact width of 10½ inches. Saw the plank with the finished surface up. If the corner *AD*, as shown in the *X*

FIGURE 11. Applying first two planks.

parts of Figures 10 and 12, is not plumb, the edge of the plank must be cut to fit and so that its groove edge coincides with the plumb line.

Apply adhesive to the rear face of plank 7 and press it into proper position, as indicated in the *X* part of Figure 12. Quickly attach and nail the clips. Apply adhesive to plank 1 and insert its tongue into the groove of plank 7. See *Y* part of Figure 12. Press planks firmly together but do not force them. See the *A* part of Figure 11 for proper spacing. All other planks are applied in the same manner except the last one (number 8 in the *X* part of Figure 10) which is only cemented into place.

The layout work and installation of planks for other walls is carried on in the same manner. Around windows and doors, the planks should be cut so as to fit snugly against the wood trim.

The *C* and *D* parts of Figure 11 show typical metal corner moldings and how they are installed.

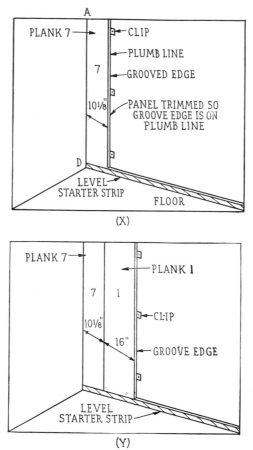

FIGURE 12. Typical clips and plank spacing.

When all planks have been applied, the starter strips can be removed. Figure 13 shows how a piece of scrap plank should be used back of the base and where the nails should be driven.

Cove or other types of moldings can be nailed to the corners where walls and ceiling meet. This will give a finished appearance to the remodeled walls.

PROBLEM 2. BEDROOM WALLS. For the purpose of this problem, we can assume that bedroom 2, as shown in Plate II, is to be remodeled to serve the dual purpose of a den and sewing room. We can further assume that the existing wall decoration consists of several layers of wallpaper and that in one large area the plaster has been damaged. The problem is to remove the old wallpaper, to repair the damaged area, and to apply soilproof blocks (in a basket-weave design) to the walls.

PLANNING. The room has three windows all of which are located at one corner. This situation will require some careful planning in order to place the basket-weave design in such a manner that blocks around the

FIGURE 13. How to apply base.

ceiling, windows, and floor will appear well balanced. We shall use both adhesive and fastening clips.

LAYOUT. As explained in the solution to Problem 1, the purpose of layout is to plan the exact locations of all blocks prior to the time application of them is started. This is highly important because the room dimensions and the window locations are not likely to be such that whole blocks can be used for all areas. In this solution, we shall do the layout work for one typical wall in bedroom 2.

In order to do the layout work accurately, we shall draw some sketches of the rear wall.

The *X* part of Figure 14 illustrates the best type of sketch for inexperienced mechanics to draw. In the sketch, *ABCD* represents the wall.

FIGURE 14. Layout of rear wall of bedroom 2.

The center point is shown at L. The window openings are shown in terms of the edges which the block will contact.

Each block is 16 inches square. Starting at the center point, we can lay out blocks 1 through 10 horizontally in such a manner that blocks 9 and 10 are of equal width and constitute a balanced border. The 8' 0" ceiling height makes six rows of whole blocks possible. However, this layout has two flaws. First, it is not a good policy to place the bottom edges of the first row of blocks at the floor level. Second, the vertical joint between blocks 4 and 5, as indicated at *M*, does not have a balanced appearance.

The *Y* part of the illustration shows a better layout. The first row of blocks has been moved so that their bottom edges are several inches above the floor level. This is in keeping with the recommendation shown in Figure 13. The joint between blocks 4 and 5 has been moved to coincide with the edge of the window trim. Block 9 is a little wider than block 10, but the difference will not be noticeable in the window corner.

The basket-weave design can be created by alternating the horizontal and vertical grains in the blocks.

FIGURE 15. Applying first block.

REMOVING OLD WALLPAPER. Ordinarily, old paper can be soaked with warm water and then scraped off using a wide-blade putty knife. Washing soda may be added if clear water does not loosen the paper.

REPAIRING DAMAGED AREA. The damaged plaster can be removed entirely and in such a manner that the edges of the remaining plaster, around the damaged area, are straight and square. A piece of plasterboard can be nailed to the lathing to take the place of the removed plaster.

APPLICATION OF BLOCK. Nail the started strip to the wall, making sure that it is level regardless of the level of the floor.

Start the installation with block 9 and be sure that the groove edges, as shown in Figure 15, are toward the area to be covered. If necessary, as shown in the *Y* part of Figure 14, cut the first block to size. Trim off the tongue edge. Remember that blocks should be sawed with the finish surface up. As indicated, install the first block in the left-hand corner and others beyond it toward the right-hand side, keeping the groove edges of each block on the top and to the right-hand side. Complete each horizontal row before starting the next. Apply adhesive as explained in connection with planks; and clips as illustrated in Figure 15. Clip application and joint spacing are as illustrated in the *A* and *B* parts of Figure 11. Other application procedures are the same as explained in the solution to Problem 1.

NEW SURFACES OVER FOUNDATIONS

The following project is typical of all cases where decorative plywood is to be applied to the surfaces of concrete-block foundations. The project is presented in terms of a typical problem and its solution.

PROBLEM 3. BASEMENT RECREATION ROOM. For the purpose of this problem, we can assume that the basement space shown in Plate II is to be remodeled to provide a recreation area. The problem is to apply ¼-inch plywood to the surface of the concrete-block foundation. The surface of the foundation is often damp.

SOLUTION. It can be assumed that the west end of the basement, between the pilaster and the chimney, is the area involved. The space is 19′ 2″ long and 11′ 10″ wide.

PLANNING. As indicated in Chapter 7, the east wall of the area will be framed, using 2 by 4 studs. Because the foundation is sometimes damp, the plywood should be protected by means of a thick coat of Medusa white waterproof portland cement paint applied directly to the block. The application can be done with a brush. As an added protection against the transmission of moisture to the plywood, asphalt-saturated and -coated paper should be tacked to the face of the furring. Lap the paper 6 inches at joints. As a further protection, a ¼-inch air space should be left above and below the plywood. This will allow a circulation of air behind it and help to keep the space between it and the foundation dry.

LAYOUT. In this problem the layout consists of planning the most economical size of plywood to use and then to plan the furring strips.

Just as an example of how such layout is done, we shall be concerned with only the west wall where the pilaster is located. As usual, we must draw a sketch, accurately to scale, which will represent the west wall. Figure 16 shows such a sketch.

The area *ABCD* represents the west wall. The wall areas on either side of the pilaster are 8' 11" long and 7' 6" high. Plywood panels 4 feet

FIGURE 16. Layout for west wall of basement recreation room.

FIGURE 17. Details of furring around pilaster.

wide and 9 feet long can be used without too much waste. The *G* and *H* areas are 4' 0" wide and 8' 11" long. Thus, only 1 inch of plywood is wasted. The *E* and *F* areas are only 3' 6" wide; hence 6 inches of plywood will have to be wasted. However, this is a satisfactory layout, and it provides a horizontal joint 4' 0" above the floor. This is a good design where such a long room is involved.

Figure 17 shows the details of furring strips around the pilaster and of the interior and exterior joints, such as at *X* and *Y*.

Figure 18 shows the details of the vertical and horizontal furring strips. The horizontal strip at *P* must be under the joint indicated in Figure 16.

APPLICATION OF FURRING STRIPS. The furring strips shown in Figure 18 constitute the minimum number recommended. A sturdier plywood installation would result if double that number were used.

Apply the vertical pieces first, and then fill in the horizontal pieces, as shown by the details in Figures 17 and 18.

The strips can sometimes be fastened to the block by means of special concrete nails which are available at hardware stores. If such nails do

FIGURE 18. Details of furring strips for west wall of basement recreation room.

not hold the strips firmly in place, a star drill will have to be used to drill holes for wooden plugs or toggle bolts. In most cases, the wooden-plug procedure shown in Figure 19 works out satisfactorily. Enough plugs should be used to hold the strips securely in place. Use a straight-edge and a carpenter's level, at such locations as noted by the dashed lines *MN* and *ST* in Figure 18, to plumb all furring strips. Drive shims as may be required to bring them up to the required level.

APPLICATION OF MOISTUREPROOFING. Paint the spaces between all fur-ring strips with the waterproof cement paint previously mentioned. Then apply the waterproof paper over the furring strips as indicated in Figure 17.

APPLICATION OF PLYWOOD. The back of the plywood can be given a sealer coat of paint as a final precaution against moisture. Apply wood glue to the edges of the plywood which will be in contact with the furring strips. Use 1-inch brads spaced about 6 inches apart on the outer edges of each panel and 12 inches apart at the intermediate furring strips. If glue is not available, use 4d finish nails at the same spacings recommended for brads.

DRILLING HOLE   FILLING HOLE WITH WOOD PLUG   NAILING STRIP TO PLUG

FIGURE 19. How to fasten furring strips to block wall.

The joint indicated in Figure 16 may be made V-shaped by merely sanding off the corners of the two panels to a depth not greater than the thickness of the veneer.

WALL-SURFACE MATERIALS ON FRAMING

When surface materials are to be applied directly to wall or partition framing, the recommended application procedures are the same as explained in the solutions to Problems 1 and 2, except that furring strips are required. The following details are typical:

Blocks on Framing. When blocks are to be applied to wall or partition framing, horizontal furring strips spaced 8 inches on centers must be provided, as shown in the *A* part of Figure 20. The blocks can then be fastened by means of clips.

Planks on Framing. When planks are to be applied to wall or partition framing, the horizontal furring strips should be spaced 16 inches on centers. See the *B* part of Figure 20.

FIGURE 20. Details of block and plank over furring strips.

FIGURE 21. Details of soft-surface plank over furring strips.

FIGURE 22. Details showing how planks 16 inches wide are fastened directly to studs.

Soft-surface Planks or Panels on Framing. When such surface materials are to be applied to wall or partition framing, the horizontal furring strips can be spaced either 8 or 16 inches on centers. For most installations, the 8-inch spacing is recommended. See Figure 21.

Figure 22 shows typical details relating to the method of fastening soft-surface planks or panels directly to framing members.

CHAPTER SIX

Floors

The advantages of well-laid and beautiful floors are familiar to every-one. Good floors are easy to keep clean. They are comfortable to walk on. They constitute important and pleasing aspects of decorating schemes. On the other hand, defective floors catch dust and dirt. They are un-sightly. They are also severe and lasting sources of annoyance and keen disappointment.

Like many other details of houses, floors are subject to many natural and unfortunate defects. Natural defects are unavoidable. The unfortu-nate varieties are the results of poor materials or of careless workmanship at the time houses were built.

Natural defects, such as small cracks between boards or shrinkage, are likely to appear in old houses and are actually the marks of time. Un-fortunate defects, such as large cracks between boards and dished sur-faces, often appear in new houses.

Unsightly or defective floors may be repaired or remodeled to create greatly improved appearance or entirely new surfaces. Many new mate-rials are available for such purposes.

The new materials are easy to use and apply. Some of them provide soundproofing and insulating effects in addition to highly desirable beauty.

For example, when attic spaces are being remodeled to provide new recreation or bedroom areas, the new floors may include soundproofing qualities which prevent the transmission of objectionable noises or sounds to other areas at lower levels. Or, when basement spaces are being remodeled to create new recreation areas, the new floors may include some of the soft qualities of a rug-plus-insulation protection against dampness and chill from the soil underneath the floors.

Previously unfinished spaces, such as basements and attics, may be transformed into living areas as explained in Chapters 7 and 8.

The purpose of this chapter is to explain the important fundamentals of floor defects, to discuss typical repair and remodeling projects, and to show how such projects are planned and accomplished.

FLOOR DEFECTS

By means of the following explanations we shall learn the fundamentals of floor defects, how to recognize such defects, and how to judge them in terms of recommended repair and remodeling work.

Cracks in Wood Floors. When cracks appear in wood floors, the faults generally stem from natural or unfortunate conditions and, in some cases, from a combination of both.

NATURAL CONDITIONS. There are several natural conditions which are apt to cause cracks, even though the best of materials and excellent workmanship are used and exercised at the time houses are being built. Such cracks are not disgraceful. They are almost sure to occur as the years pass.

LUMBER SHRINKAGE. The best of flooring lumber, even when carefully kiln-dried or allowed to dry naturally until its moisture content is low, may eventually shrink across the grain. In the A part of Figure 1, the double-headed arrow at X points across the grain of a typical floor board. When only a small amount of such shrinkage occurs, thin cracks between boards are sometimes visible. Such cracks may appear in isolated locations or they may be quite general.

As explained in Chapter 4, the structural details of houses may shrink and cause some shifting of their positions. If such shifting occurs to any appreciable extent, floor boards may be pulled apart so that cracks appear between them. Or, the boards may be pushed together with enough force to cause them to buckle and form humps in floors.

WETTING. When floors are not well protected by means of varnish or other sealers, frequent wetting may cause the boards to swell beyond their normal widths. In a case of this kind, the boards press against one another. This is apt to cause crushed fibers along their edges. After subsequent drying and shrinkage, there are cracks between the boards, owing to the fact that the crushed fibers do not recover their original shapes.

FIGURE 1. How compression set makes cracks. A, flooring when laid; B, the same flooring after it has absorbed moisture as a result of damp conditions in unfinished house; C, the same flooring after subsequent drying. The inverted-V-shaped joint is permanently deformed and there is a wide crack.

SETTLEMENT. As explained in Chapter 4, settlement often causes shifts in the positions of structural details. When such shifting occurs, floor cracks are likely to occur.

UNFORTUNATE CONDITIONS. Unfortunate conditions are always caused by inferior flooring lumber or by careless carpentry work. Such conditions are beyond logical excuse. Yet, they must be recognized and understood.

EXCESS MOISTURE. When cracks develop in new floors, within a year or two after the floors are laid, the fault can generally be traced to excess moisture in the flooring stock.

Well-informed manufacturers of flooring lumber make every effort to dry flooring stock properly and to keep it dry in their warerooms prior to sale and shipment. However, there are other cases where careless handling and unethical sales of wet stock take place. When wet (green) floor lumber is used, large cracks between boards and most unsightly appearances are sure to occur.

Properly seasoned (dried) lumber can absorb dangerous amounts of moisture if it is stored prior to use in a house where plaster and masonry walls or floors are not dry. Or, if especially humid conditions exist in houses, either before or immediately after floors are laid, the boards will absorb moisture. Whatever the reasons for moisture absorption, cracks are sure to occur. The only remedy consists of keeping lumber dry until completed floors can be sealed by means of shellac, varnish or other finish materials.

COMPRESSION SET. If several days of damp weather occur immediately after a floor is laid (see *A* part of Figure 1) and before the finish, such as varnish, shellac, or other sealers have been applied, the moisture content of the floor is likely to increase greatly. Such moisture can cause floor boards to press against one another as they swell. Heavy pressure of this sort generally results in crushing of wood fiber near the joints between boards. Technically known as *compression set* (see *B* part of Figure 1), this crushing is another common cause for cracks between boards. A relatively narrow margin of each board has to take the brunt of the compression. After boards have once been compressed, they seldom recover. See *C* part of Figure 1.

CROOKED STOCK. Another cause of cracks between floor boards, also aggravated by moisture changes, is the use of crooked boards; that is, boards that have bent edgewise. If a crook is so pronounced that much pressure must be applied to drive a board into place, three cracks are sure to appear, sooner or later—one at each end of the board on one side and another along the middle part of the board on the opposite side.

DISHED BOARDS. Many old houses have softwood floors in which the boards are 3 or more inches wide. Unless such flooring is very well protected by means of paint or varnish, frequent wetting or humid conditions may cause the edges of the boards to warp or curl in such a manner that their centers will be lower than their edges. This condition is unsightly and unsanitary.

DIRTY FLOORS. The best of floors will soon lose most of their original beauty unless they are kept clean and otherwise taken care of as outlined in a subsequent part of this chapter. Dirt ruins finishes! Once this happens, the boards absorb moisture, and cracks appear.

FLOOR SQUEAKS. In most instances, floor squeaks develop because too few nails were originally driven in each of the floor boards. To be effective, the nails should be spaced no more than 10 inches apart. Screw-type nails have more holding power than the plain-shanked varieties and are therefore better suited for application to floors.

JUDGING DEFECTS. The *causes* of floor cracks should have considerable influence on our judgment of what to do so far as repairs and remodeling are concerned.

Natural cracks in the floors of old houses are likely to be at their maximum widths and are not apt to increase in number or extent. If they are not too unsightly, they can be repaired without fear that they will reopen.

Unfortunate cracks are apt to be unstable and cannot be repaired with any assurance that they will not reoccur. Such cracks practically ruin the appearance of floors and they are not sanitary. The only satisfactory remedies consist of wall-to-wall carpeting or the application of new surface materials.

Cracks in Concrete Floors. There are a few natural reasons why cracks appear in concrete floors. However, most such cracks are due to unfortunate conditions.

NATURAL CONDITIONS. The following conditions are classified as *natural* reasons why concrete floors develop cracks. Here, the term *natural* is used to indicate items which are not the fault of poor materials or careless workmanship.

WASHOUTS. Sometimes the soil under concrete floors is partly washed away. In such cases, parts of the floors are left without support, and cracks occur because plain concrete has very little tensile strength.

FOUNDATION SETTLEMENT. If foundations and footings settle, the resulting movement is apt to cause strains which the small tensile strength of plain concrete cannot cope with. Cracks are the result.

FREEZING. If the soil under concrete floors should freeze, the resultant expansion would cause cracks in the concrete.

HEAVY BLOWS. Because plain concrete has so little tensile strength, severe blows from a heavy instrument, or the dropping of a heavy object on it, could cause cracks.

UNFORTUNATE CONDITIONS. All of the unfortunate causes of cracks in concrete floors can be traced to poor proportioning of ingredients, improper mixing, too little thickness, or downright carelessness by mechanics.

PROPORTIONING AND MIXING. Concrete is one of the best and most durable of building materials when correct proportions of portland cement, sand, crushed rock or gravel, and water are used and when mixing is carried on properly. It is only when too little cement, dirty sand, cheap crushed rock or gravel, and too much water are used, together with careless mixing, that concrete floors are subject to undue cracks and poor appearance.

TOO LITTLE THICKNESS. Any concrete floor should have a total thickness, including base and topping, of at least 4 inches. Where thinner floors are placed, even with the best of concrete, cracks are apt to occur.

CARELESSNESS. If mechanics fail to observe the foregoing specifications, allow mixes to reach initial set before being placed, forget to compact the placed concrete, add water after mixing is complete, allow the concrete to freeze, neglect proper curing, etc., the resulting floors will fall heir to cracks, lack of waterproof qualities, and unsightly appearances.

DUSTING. If the surfaces of concrete floors are always "dusty," in spite of frequent sweeping or washing, the fault can be traced to excessive steel troweling at the time the floors were placed. Dusting is also the result of using dry cement to hasten the setting of newly placed floors.

PEELING. Sometimes the surfaces of concrete floors have a tendency to peel or flake off, in spots, leaving unsightly holes or depressions. This happens when topping is placed on bases that are too dry. It also happens if mechanics fail to apply a thin grout coat (cement and water) to bases before topping is placed.

DIRTY FLOORS. The best of concrete is somewhat porous, especially when topping is not used in connection with floors. Grease, dirt, and spilled liquids will penetrate into the pores of concrete unless quickly or frequently removed. Once such penetration has taken place, the stains are impossible to remove.

WET FLOORS. When basement concrete floors are wet most of the time, the cause can be traced to poor concrete or to the fact that a static head of water is present under such floors.

Judging Defects. Natural defects, especially in old houses, are quite likely to be at their maximum. In cases where only a few small cracks are involved, repair work may be carried on without fear that the cracks will reoccur. Where many large cracks are involved, repair work is not feasible. In such cases, a new surface material should be applied.

Unfortunate defects cannot be repaired with any assurance that they will not reoccur. Any repair work constitutes a gamble and there is little chance that repaired floors will be anything but eyesores. In such cases, new surface materials should be planned.

SUGGESTED REMODELING PROJECTS

As mentioned in the first paragraph of this chapter, floors constitute an important aspect of the decorating schemes employed for interiors of houses. In fact, remodeling or modernization plans are not complete unless or until careful attention has been given to existing and proposed new floors. Therefore, the following suggestions are presented as a means of showing some of the projects and materials we can work with to create beautiful and modern floors in many areas of our homes:

Repairing Cracks in Wood Floors. In older houses where natural cracks between boards are not wider than $\frac{1}{16}$ inch, it is safe to fill them and then do some refinishing work. The results are generally satisfactory in terms of beauty and economy. Cracks originally caused by compression set or crooked boards can also be repaired if we are sure they are at their maximum and if they are not wider than $\frac{1}{16}$ inch. The repair of wider cracks, especially where they are likely to reoccur, is a gamble not likely to produce satisfactory or lasting results.

MATERIALS. For the repair of narrow floor cracks only fine sawdust and shellac are required.

Repairing Large Cracks. As previously mentioned, the repair of large cracks, $\frac{1}{8}$ inch or more in width, is a gamble which is not likely to produce satisfactory or lasting results. However, such repair work can be tried before resorting to the more expensive alternative of an entirely new floor. The repair procedure consists of inserting slivers of wood into the cracks.

MATERIALS. Slivers of wood, fine sawdust, and shellac.

Correcting Floor Squeaks. Floors can be tightened by means of nails driven from the surface of the boards into the joists. The nailheads can be driven below the wood surface and the dents filled.

MATERIALS. It is advisable to use special flooring nails of the screw type. Such nails have much greater holding power than ordinary plain-shanked types.

Replacing Damaged Boards. It sometimes happens that one or more boards in a floor become damaged or are otherwise unsightly. Such boards can be replaced by means of a simple procedure. Unless the whole floor is refinished, the new boards are likely to be prominent.

MATERIALS. Only new boards, of the same kind and color as the existing boards, and a few nails of the screw type are required.

New Flooring in Place of Old. If an existing hardwood floor contains so many natural or unfortunate defects that it is beyond repair, it can be torn out and replaced by a new hardwood floor. However, such a procedure is quite expensive and not recommended unless an old house is to be practically rebuilt. The necessary hammering could easily dislodge otherwise sound plaster on ceilings under the floors and cause other difficulties. As a worthy alternative, we can resurface such floors with soft tile. The process is not difficult, it creates new and beautiful surfaces, and the cost is low.

MATERIALS. Many kinds of soft tile are available including plastic, asphalt, cork, and rubber. A visit to any lumberyard or to a building-material dealer's showroom will prove to be interesting and helpful.

SIZES AND COLORS. A great variety of sizes and colors are available. Selection can be based on room sizes and color schemes desired.

FASTENING. Most soft tile are applied or fastened by means of adhesives which manufacturers recommend and supply. However, some of the plastic tile may be applied without the use of adhesives or other fasteners.

PATTERNS. Manufacturers and dealers will supply suggestions which can be used in planning tile patterns for any room.

Repairing Cracks in Concrete Floors. When cracks in concrete floors are not more than 1 inch wide, and when the floors are dry and in otherwise good condition, repair work can be depended upon to produce satisfactory surfaces for paint or stain.

MATERIALS. Medusa portland cement and clean sand. Various prepared compounds are also available at hardware stores.

Soft Recreation-room Floor over Concrete. If an existing concrete floor in a basement recreation room is sound, level, and fairly dry, a luxurious new surface can be applied. It will feel soft when walked on, and as previously explained, will provide insulation against dampness and chill.

MATERIALS. Rigid insulation board or panels 1 inch thick provide the softness and insulating effects. Thin hardboard is required so that table and chair legs will not dent the insulation. Any kind of soft tile can be used for the surface.

Parquet Squares or Blocks over Concrete. If an existing concrete floor is sound, level, and always bone-dry, hardwood parquet squares or blocks can be cemented directly to it. They are easy to lay and the cost is reasonable. They can be finished the same as any other hardwood floor.

MATERIALS. The squares are manufactured from oak, maple, birch, and beech woods. They have tongued-and-grooved edges.

SIZES. The squares are available in sizes ranging from 8 by 8 to 12 by 12 inches square and $2\frac{5}{32}$, $3\frac{3}{32}$, and $\frac{5}{16}$ inch thick.

FASTENING. The squares are fastened to the concrete floor by means of adhesives which the manufacturers recommend and supply.

PATTERNS. There are a great variety of patterns available from the various manufacturers. The pattern shown in Figure 2 is the most popular.

Plank Floors for Remodeled Attic Areas. Colonial-type hardwood plank flooring constitutes an ideal floor surface for bedrooms in remodeled attics. It can be applied over any type of wood subflooring, along with insulation to reduce the transmission of sound to rooms at a lower level.

MATERIALS. Figure 3 shows a section of typical plank flooring in which the edges of the boards are square and therefore create flush joints. If shallow V-joints are desired, boards with beveled edges should be used.

FIGURE 2. Typical parquet squares.

FIGURE 3. Typical pattern for plank floor.

Such flooring must be carefully handled and stored in a dry, well-ventilated place prior to laying. It should not be laid unless or until the interior temperature is at least 70°F.

KINDS. Oak and Maple.

SIZES. The planks are manufactured in random lengths. Widths range from 3 to 8 inches and thicknesses from $25\!/\!32$ to $5\!/\!16$ inch.

FASTENING. Nails and screws.

PATTERN. As indicated in Figure 3, boards of various widths can be employed to create patterns. The numerals in Figure 3 indicate board widths in inches.

Floor-sag Correction. There are many instances, especially in very old houses, where floor joists have suffered permanent deflection. There are other instances where the joists bend under the weight of people or furniture. In either case, the remedy consists of installing one or more screw-type columns as a means of pushing the joists up to a level position and keeping them there.

MATERIALS. Screw-type columns can be obtained in various sizes.

Tile over Plywood in New Attic Rooms. In cases where attic spaces do not have flooring, plywood may be used to excellent advantage. Any of the soft tiles may be applied to it.

MATERIALS. Any good grade of ¾-inch thick softwood plywood. See *tile* in previous explanation.

Tile over Wood Floors in Bad Condition. In very old houses there are many instances where softwood floors are badly dished, worn, and unsanitary. Such floors may be remodeled by means of plywood and soft tile.

MATERIALS. Same as previously explained.

New Board-type Hardwood Floors over Concrete. The traditional or board-type hardwood flooring may be applied over concrete floors. There is a simple and easy way to do it. Wood sleepers can be fastened to the concrete by the methods explained in Chapter 2. The hardwood flooring can be nailed to the sleepers. If hot asphaltum is mopped between the sleepers, the floor will be dampproof.

New Masonry Surfaces for Concrete Floors. There are several kinds of masonry materials which can be applied in thin coats over old concrete floors to create new and desirable surfaces.

MATERIALS. Surco concrete is made using special aggregates and a synthetic rubber liquid in place of much of the water ordinarily used in concrete. The mixture produces a rubberlike surface which is beautiful and durable. Perlite concrete uses a special type of aggregate to produce a coating which has a high degree of insulating ability, as well as a desirable surface.

Refinishing Existing Hardwood Floors. By means of electric sanding machines, hardwood floors which are in sound condition may be given a brand-new surface for refinishing. The final result is equal in quality to a new floor.

New Hardwood Floor over Softwood. In a case where all of the floors in an old house were originally laid using softwood, a new and modern hardwood flooring can be applied directly over the old flooring.

MATERIALS. For this purpose, oak and maple boards from 1 to 1½ inches wide and ⅜ inch thick can be used.

HOW TO PLAN AND DO TYPICAL REMODELING PROJECTS

Following our usual and recommended procedures, we shall study several typical remodeling projects from the planning and installation standpoints. The procedures herein set forth are explained in terms of inexperienced mechanics. No inference is implied that possible other methods would not be as effective.

REPAIRING SMALL CRACKS IN WOOD FLOORS

In previous discussions we learned that small cracks are apt to occur between the boards in wood floors. We concluded that such cracks are at their maximum widths after houses are two years old and that repair work is feasible.

The *A* part of Figure 4 shows a section view of typical hardwood flooring over wood subflooring. The joint between the two boards is tight and flush. The *B* part of the illustration indicates a crack between tongued-and-grooved boards. The *C* part shows a crack between shiplap boards. Shiplap boards are not employed for modern floors, but they may be encountered in old houses. In the illustration, the cracks are exaggerated for visualization purposes.

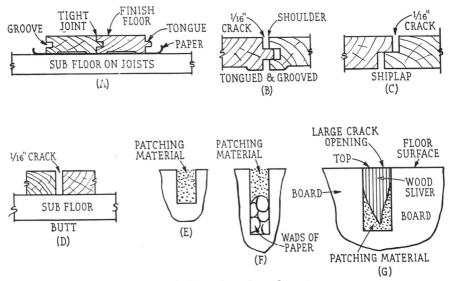

FIGURE 4. Typical cracks and repair.

Preparation. First, use a stiff brush or a small knife blade to clean out the cracks as much as possible. (Care should be exercised not to cut or mar the shoulders. See *B* part of illustration. If the shoulders are cut, crack repair is much more difficult.) Then, wipe the surface of the boards, near the cracks, with a damp cloth to remove particles of dust or dirt. If the floor is in need of a thorough cleaning, such work should be done prior to the repair work. The floor should be dry and the room temperature warm. If repair work is done during extremely cold weather or when the floor is cold, later expansion might squeeze out the patching material.

Patching Materials. If possible, fine sawdust from the same kind of wood as the floor should be obtained by sawing pieces of such a board. A more laborious process, consisting of sandpapering such a board, provides superior dust for the purpose. A small amount of ordinary, fresh shellac is necessary. If the surface of the floor is considerably darker than the sawdust, a little stain can be mixed with the sawdust and shellac until the mixture matches the color of the surface.

PATCHING. Add shellac to small amounts of sawdust until the mixture is plastic and easy to spread. Where tongued-and-grooved and shiplap joints are concerned, use a small putty knife to force the patching mixture into the cracks until, as shown in the *E* part of the illustration, the crack is full. Pull the putty knife along the cracks to make the surface of the patching material flush with the shoulders of the boards. Allow to dry for at least two hours. If the surface of the floor has a natural finish, the patches may be lightly sandpapered using No. 00 sandpaper. When all patching is complete, the floor can be varnished and waxed or just waxed.

The *D* part of Figure 4 indicates a crack between square-edged boards and a butt joint. The patching process is the same as previously explained, except that very small wads of paper, such as facial tissue, should be shoved into the cracks so as to fill them partially, as indicated in the *F* part of the illustration, prior to the time the patching material is applied. The wads of paper are especially useful if such flooring does not have a subflooring under it.

REPAIRING LARGE CRACKS IN WOOD FLOORS

As previously explained, unfortunate and large cracks between floor boards are apt to be unstable. In other words, they are likely to become larger or to open and close with the seasons. Any attempts to repair them constitute rank gambles because the patching materials are apt to be squeezed out at a later time. However, when such gambles are recognized, the following procedures may be tried:

Preparation. Same as in connection with small cracks.

Patching Materials. A mixture of sawdust and shellac, used alone, is not apt to stay in large cracks long enough to merit the time and effort involved. Therefore, slivers of the same kind of wood as the floor boards should be made by means of a knife. Make such slivers so that they have tops, as shown in the *G* part of Figure 4, which are flat and level.

PATCHING. Where tongued-and-grooved or shiplap boards are concerned, force a little of the sawdust-and-shellac mixture down to the bottom of the cracks, as shown in the *G* part of the illustration. Then apply shellac to the slivers and shove them into the cracks, also as shown at *G*. Where butt joints are concerned, use the wads of paper as previously explained, prior to the patching procedures. Pull a putty knife along the cracks to make sure that the tops of the slivers are flush with the shoulders of the boards and to remove excess shellac and sawdust. A cloth soaked with alcohol can be used to clean off any hardened shellac or sawdust mixture. After two hours, the patches may be lightly sandpapered. If the patches are lighter colored than the floor surface, use a little stain to color them as may be necessary.

C O R R E C T I N G   F L O O R   S Q U E A K S

When too few plain-shanked nails are used in laying floors, any one of the natural and unfortunate conditions previously mentioned could exert enough force to pull the boards loose. In fact, ordinary expansion and contraction is apt to, and often does, loosen the nails. Once the nails are the least bit loose, ordinary walking on the floor will further loosen them. Soon thereafter, squeaking is bound to occur.

The *W* part of Figure 5 indicates how most hardwood floors are constructed. The subflooring should be nailed in a diagonal position to the joists. The finish floor boards should be nailed to the subfloor so that they are 90 degrees to the joists. To correct squeaking, the procedure is as follows:

Preparation. Walk around a floor until all areas where squeaking occurs are located. Mark the areas by means of chalk lines. Next, locate the joist positions. This can be done by tapping the floor with a hammer and noting where the tapping sounds solid. When one joist position has been located, we know that all others are probably at 16-inch intervals.

FIGURE 5. Correcting floor squeaks.

Materials. Only nails and some plastic wood are required. The nails should be of the screw type with finishing nailheads. Their length should be at least 2½ inches so that they can go through the finish and subflooring and be firmly embedded in the joists, as shown in the *X* part of the illustration. The plastic wood can be stained to match the floor surface.

NAILING. The dashed line *AB,* in the *W* part of the illustration, indicates a position directly over the joist. Drive one nail through each of the boards in the squeaking area at each joist location. If the nails tend to bend as they are driven, bore a small hole into the boards prior to nailing. The hole should have a smaller diameter than the nails. Use a nail set to drive the heads of the nails slightly below the surface of the boards. Fill the dents above the nailheads with the plastic wood, making sure that the plastic wood is flush with the floor surface.

It is wise to nail the boards, in any squeak area, to at least two joists.

The *Y* part of Figure 5 shows another and less common way in which hardwood floors are constructed. The subflooring should be nailed to the joists. Above each joist furring strips are nailed to the subfloor. The finish floor should be nailed to the furring strips and be at 90 degrees to the joists.

The squeak-correcting procedure is the same as previously explained, except that longer nails must be used. As shown in the *Z* part of the illustration, the nails should go through the finish floor boards, the furring, the subflooring, and well into the joists. It is wise to assume that the furring is at least $1\frac{1}{2}$ inches thick. Therefore, the nails should be at least $3\frac{1}{2}$ inches long.

REPLACING DAMAGED FLOOR BOARDS

If one or more finish floor boards have been damaged, or are unsightly in appearance, new boards can be inserted into the floor as per the following procedures:

Preparation. Let us suppose that we are looking down at a small area of a floor such as shown in the *W* part of Figure 6. Let us further suppose that the dashed-line rectangle, *ABCD,* indicates a damaged place in the floor. Boards *b, c,* and *d* are involved.

Parts of the three boards involved have to be removed so that new parts can be inserted.

First, draw a line on the floor, such as *f* in the *X* part of the illustration, which coincides with the joints marked *m* and *n* in the *W* part of the illustration. In like manner, draw a line on the floor, such as shown at *g,* which coincides with the joint marked *p.* The boards within the area

FIGURE 6. Replacing damaged floor boards.

bounded by lines *f, h, g,* and *j,* as shown in the *X* part of the illustration, must be removed.

Removing Boards. Use a sharp chisel to cut boards *b, c,* and *d* along lines *f* and *g.* Make the cuts at least ¼ inch deep. Then use the chisel to splinter board *c* enough to remove it. Boards *b* and *d* can be removed in much the same manner, being careful not to splinter the boards beyond lines *f* and *g.* When the three boards have been removed, the subflooring will be visible as indicated in the *X* part of the illustration.

Placing New Boards. Cut three new boards, as shown in the *Y* part of the illustration, to the exact length of line *h* in the *X* part of the illustration, so as to make a snug fit. Remove the tongues from the *ends* of the new boards.

Put the new boards in place, as indicated in the Z part of the illustration, so that the side tongues partly engage the grooves. Then stand on the middle board, t, to press the new boards into position.

Nail the ends of the boards as indicated by the dots in the Y part of the illustration. The nails should be 1½ inches long. If the new boards seem loose, add one or more nails along their lengths, as may be required.

Drive the nails slightly below the surface of the boards and fill dents with plastic wood. Stain the new boards to match the floor and finish with varnish or shellac.

If we should find that a floor has furring strips, as shown in the Y part of Figure 5, the cutting lines f and g, as shown in the X part of Figure 6, must be drawn directly over the center lines of the furring. It may be necessary to draw and cut several such lines in order to locate the furring strips. Otherwise, the procedures for inserting new boards are the same as previously explained.

SOFT TILE OVER OLD WOOD FLOOR

The following project is typical of any and all cases where plastic (no adhesive) tile is to be applied directly to old wood floors. The project is presented in terms of a typical problem and its solution:

PROBLEM 1. KITCHEN FLOOR. For the purpose of this problem, we can assume that Plates I through VI, which are at the back of this book, show the plans for an *old* house. We can further assume that the kitchen floor contains a great many cracks and is undesirable in terms of other remodeling plans. The problem is to apply a plastic tile that needs no adhesive.

SOLUTION. First, it can be assumed that the plastic tile is 9½ inches square. Such tile, in any color, will make a beautiful floor and one which will be easy to keep clean.

PLANNING. The first step consists of checking the old floor to make sure that all boards are tightly nailed. If additional nailing is required, use screw-type nails which are 2½ inches long and drive their heads slightly below the surface. It is best if the nails can be driven into joists. If the boards are dished, the edges should be scraped or sanded down until they are flush with other parts of the boards. Apply a generous coat of shellac or other sealer to the wood floor. This will seal the surface so that no moisture can come through the boards.

LAYOUT. The *A* part of Figure 7 shows a scaled sketch of the kitchen indicated in Plate I. In this sketch, we assumed that the first full piece

FIGURE 7. Layout for plastic tile applied over old wood floor.

of tile would be placed at corner *A*. Other such sketches, assuming that the first full piece of tile will be placed at *B, H, E,* and *C*, should also be made as a means of obtaining the best appearance, especially in terms of partial pieces of tile along the walls. Here, we can assume that it is best to place a full piece of tile at corner *A*. The squares represent pieces of tile.

The following layout work should be done on the kitchen floor:

Measure 9½ inches from wall *AB* and draw (or snap a chalk line) line *LM*. Then draw line *JK* so that it is 9½ inches from wall *AC*. Lines *LM* and *JK* must form an angle of 90 degrees at *P*. To test the angle, use the method shown in the *B* part of the illustration. Starting at point *P*, where the lines *LM* and *JK* cross, measure 6 feet to *S* and 8 feet to *T*. If lines *LM* and *JK* meet at 90 degrees, the line *ST* will be exactly 10 feet long. If any error exists, move lines *LM* and *JK* slightly until line *ST* is exactly 10 feet long.

TILE APPLICATION. Unpack the tile and allow several hours of time during which they will accommodate themselves to room-temperature and humidity conditions. Tile should not be laid when room temperatures are less than 70°F.

Start with tile 1, as indicated in the *A* part of Figure 7. Lay it so that its corner is exactly over point *P*. Use three 2d box nails along both the *AJ* and *AL* edges. Place the nails close to the wall, as shown in the *C* part of the illustration. Do not drive the nailheads into the tile as that would distort it.

Lay tile 2 along line *LM* and tightly against tile 1. Use three nails as indicated in the *A* part of the illustration. Next, lay tile 3 through 15 and use three nails in each. Tile 16 will have to be cut to fit and then securely nailed.

Next, lay tile 17 through 22 along line *JK* and nail them as indicated. Tile 23 will have to be cut to fit.

Only tile next to walls should be nailed.

Next, lay tile 24 through 37. Before laying and nailing tile 38, place a little block of wood at the edge of tile 37 and tap it gently to tighten the tile in that row. Make sure all joints coincide with joints in the first row laid.

Lay all other rows alternately, trimming the tile next to walls and making sure that all joint lines coincide.

If any of the tile buckle after a few days, place a heavy weight on them and the buckle will disappear. Place quarter round along the walls to hide the nails. Use metal toe strips at the door where the tile stops.

Wax and clean as recommended by the manufacturer of the tile used.

SOFT RECREATION-ROOM FLOOR

The following project is typical of all cases where insulation, hardboard, and asphalt tile are to be applied over existing concrete floors. The project is presented in terms of a typical problem and its solution.

PROBLEM 2. RECREATION-ROOM FLOOR. For the purpose of this problem, we can assume that part of the basement space indicated in Plate II and set forth in Problem 3 in Chapter 4, is to be remodeled to provide a recreation area. The problem is to install an asphalt-tile floor which will be soft and warm. The tile are 12 inches square.

SOLUTION. It can be assumed that the concrete floor is never wet but that it is damp and cold.

PLANNING. The design shown in Figure 8 will assure ample insulation effectively to reduce dampness and chill. It will create a soft foundation and provide a firm base for the tile. Both the insulation and hardboard should be laid, using hot asphalt emulsion as an adhesive. The tile should be cemented to the hardboard using the kind of adhesive recommended by the manufacturer of the tile.

FIGURE 8. Soft recreation-room floor.

FIGURE 9. Layout of insulation and tile.

LAYOUT. Rigid insulation may be purchased in sheets which are 4 by 8, 4 by 10, or 4 by 12 feet in width and length and $^{25}\!/_{32}$ inch thick. In this case, a size should be used which can be applied easily and with as little waste as possible. As shown in the *A* part of Figure 9 and in Plate II, the recreation room is 11′ 10″ wide and 19′ 2″ long. We can use 4- by 12-foot sheets, as indicated at *A, B, C, D,* and *E,* in such a manner that there is a waste of only 2 inches at the ends of the sheets and 10 inches of waste along the side of sheet *E.*

The hardboard can be planned in the same manner.

In order to plan the position of the first piece of tile, we must make a scaled sketch of the recreation room, such as indicated in the *B* part of Figure 9, and then find the center point *P* by means of lines *HJ* and *FG.* As a trial, we can place the first piece of tile so that its southeast corner is at *P.* The first two rows of tile can then be drawn as shown in the sketch. From this layout it can be seen that only 1 inch will have to be cut from tiles 26 and 31 and that only 5 inches, which is less than half the tile width, will have to be cut from tiles 12 and 21.

Other such layouts may be drawn, but the one shown in the *B* part of the illustration is satisfactory because none of the tile near the walls have to be cut more than half their widths.

By means of chalk, or a chalk line, draw or snap lines *FG* and *HJ* on the concrete floor. Then check the layout by placing uncemented tile on the floor in the same positions as shown in the sketch.

APPLICATION OF TILE. Use a notched trowel (available where the mastic recommended by the manufacturer is sold) to apply a light coat of mastic to the floor area to be covered by the first two rows of tile.

(A)   (B)

FIGURE 10. Cutting and fitting asphalt tile.

Allow the mastic to dry before placing tile on it. To test for drying, press thumb against mastic. If the mastic does not stick, it is ready for tile.

Before placing tile, unpack and stack them so that they are all right side up. The top surface of the tile is smoothest. Tile should always be laid with the marbelized grain of one piece alternating in direction at right angles with the next piece.

Lay two crossrows of tile, as shown in the *B* part of Figure 9, first. Use lines *FG* and *HJ* as guides. Carefully set each piece in position. Do not slide them into place as that may force the mastic up between the pieces. After two rows have been laid, cover one of the remaining quarters of the floor with mastic. When the mastic is dry, place tile in this section, working from center of room to border. Cover one-fourth of the floor at a time until entire floor is laid. Never use a cleaning fluid on asphalt tile. A dull-edged knife or No. 00 steel wool can be used to remove any excess mastic.

When trimming pieces of tile to fit against a wall or around a post where a tight fit is desired, warm the tile enough to make it pliable but not so hot that it cannot be handled with bare hands. The *A* and *B* parts of Figure 10 show how to cut and fit tile.

PARQUET OR BLOCKS OVER CONCRETE

The following project is typical of any and all cases where parquet or block are to be applied over existing sound and dry concrete floors. The project is presented in terms of a typical problem and its solution.

PROBLEM 3. RECREATION-ROOM FLOOR. For the purpose of this problem, we may assume that part of the basement space indicated in Plate II, as explained in the previous problem, is to be converted to a recreation area. The problem is to apply blocks directly to the concrete floor.

SOLUTION. We can assume that the existing concrete floor is sound and that it is always dry.

PLANNING. Because the room is of good size, we can plan to use 12- by 12-inch blocks of the type shown in Figure 2, and the squared pattern illustrated by Figure 5 of Chapter 4.

LAYOUT. As previously explained in connection with layout procedures, the first step consists of making a scaled sketch which can be used to plot the center point of the room and the positions of the first two rows of blocks. Figure 11 shows such a sketch. Lines *AB* and *CD* were drawn from the mid-points of walls *EH* and *FG* and *EF* and *HG* to find the center point *P* of the room. Blocks 1, 2, 3, and 4 were grouped around the center point, and the first and second rows of blocks were indicated. This constitutes a satisfactory layout because blocks 9 and 14 will require little cutting and blocks 26 and 34 will be more than half their original size after cutting.

By the use of chalk or a chalk line, the *AB* and *CD* lines should be drawn or snapped on the floor. Then the layout should be tested by placing uncemented blocks in the positions of the first two rows shown in the sketch.

APPLICATION OF BLOCKS. Using a notched trowel, spread thin coats of the adhesive recommended by the manufacturer on the floor areas to be covered by the first two rows of block. If lines *AB* and *CD* cannot be seen through the adhesive, they should be redrawn or snapped on it. Lay blocks 1, 2, 3, and 4 first. Press them into position, making sure that the tongues engage the grooves enough to make the joints between blocks tight and flush. Next, lay blocks 18 through 25, using line *AP* as a guide. Tap the edge of each block just enough to force its tongue into the groove of the previous block. Block 26 must be cut so as to provide a ½-inch

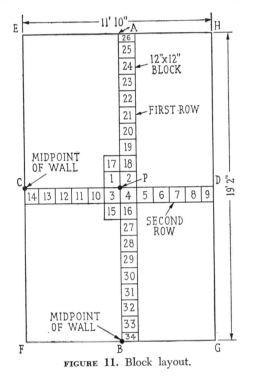

FIGURE 11. Block layout.

expansion space between its edge and the wall. Blocks 16 through 34 should next be laid using line *PB* as a guide. Biock 34 must also be cut so as to provide a ½-inch expansion space. Blocks 10 through 14 and 5 through 9 should be laid along line *CD* to complete the first two rows. Blocks 9 and 14 should also be cut to provide ½-inch expansion spaces. Cover one-fourth of the remaining floor at a time until the whole floor is complete, remembering to provide ½-inch expansion spaces between all blocks next to the walls. The expansion spaces can be covered by a base or other molding.

SANDING. After the blocks have been laid for several days, they must be sanded by means of a heavy electric sanding machine. The finest grit sandpaper obtainable should be used for the last sanding because the smoother the surface, the more beautiful the final finish will be.

PLANK FLOOR OVER WOOD SUBFLOOR

The following project is typical of any and all cases where plank flooring is to be laid on existing subflooring such as in attic spaces. The project is presented in terms of a typical problem and its solution.

PROBLEM 4. ATTIC FLOOR. It can be assumed that an attic space in an old house is being remodeled in order to provide one or more new bedrooms. The problem is to lay plank flooring on the existing subfloor.

SOLUTION. We can assume that the type of flooring shown in Figure 3 is to be used and that both nails and screws must be employed for fastening the plank to the subfloor.

PLANNING. The first step consists of checking the existing subfloor to make sure that all the boards are tightly nailed. If additional nailing is required, use screw-type nails at least 2½ inches long. Their heads should be driven slightly below the surface of the boards. If any of the boards are dished, the edges should be scraped, planed, or sanded flush with other parts of the boards.

If possible, plank flooring should be laid at 90 degrees to the floor joists and in the direction of the longest dimensions of a room but never parallel to the subflooring. If two or more rooms are involved, the planks should, if possible, be laid in the same direction in all of them and extend from one to the other to form a continuous surface. A pattern such as indicated in Figure 3 should be used and end joints should be staggered as shown in the A part of Figure 12. A good grade of heavy waterproof building paper should be laid over the subflooring from wall to wall with joints overlapped at least 6 inches. At the time of laying the planks, the interior temperature must be at least 70°F. This is highly important as a means of preventing shrinkage cracks.

LAYOUT. When laying tongued-and-grooved plank flooring, the first board should be placed at the junction of the side wall and the floor and should be parallel to the side wall with the grooved edge next to the wall. An expansion space of at least ½ inch must be provided between the first board and the wall. However, such a space should not be wider than can be covered by a baseboard or quarter round. As shown in the *B* part of Figure 12, the baseboard or quarter round should be so installed

FIGURE 12. Plank-floor details.

that lower edges are slightly above the finished floor level. Fastening should be done as indicated. Never nail baseboards or quarter rounds to the planks.

APPLICATION OF PLANKS. The first board, next to the wall, should be face-nailed as shown in the *C* part of the illustration. Then the tongue edge should be blind-nailed with the nails driven at an angle of about 50 degrees. When blind-nailing, the head of each nail should be countersunk, using a nail set. Nails should be 8d, of the screw type, and spaced 8 inches apart.

In order to allow for any possible movement or expansion of the planks, a small space (approximately $\frac{1}{32}$ inch) should be left between each board. For this purpose spacer strips, as shown in the D part of the illustration, should be inserted every 8 inches so that the nailing does not draw the planks up too tightly. Do not remove spacers until 6 runs of plank have been laid, then continue in this manner across the room, moving forward the rear row of spacers. Plank flooring is grooved on both ends, and splines are furnished which are to be inserted at the time of installation.

As shown in the A and E parts of the illustration, countersunk screws should be used at each end of every board. Screws can also be used at intervals along the length of boards if they seem necessary as a means of assuring tight fastening. An ordinary brace and bit may be used for drilling the holes for the screws and the plugs. To save time, a counter-bore performing all operations at one time is recommended. The most popular size of plug is $\frac{3}{4}$ inch. A $1\frac{1}{4}$-inch flathead screw is recommended. Oak or walnut plugs may be glued into the holes. Basically, the more nails and screws used, the more satisfactory the results.

SANDING. The finest grit sandpaper obtainable should be used for the last cut. The smoother the floor, the better the finish and final appearance.

TILE OR PLANKS OVER PLYWOOD

The following project is typical of any and all cases where tile or planks are to be applied to plywood.

PROBLEM 5. It can be assumed that an attic space in any house is being remodeled in order to make one or more new bedrooms. It can also be assumed that no subflooring exists in the attic space. The problem is to apply plywood that can be used as a base for tile or planks.

SOLUTION. It can also be assumed that $\frac{3}{4}$-inch plywood is to be fastened directly to the floor joists and that a blanket type of insulation is to be placed between the joists as a means of reducing sound transmission between the new bedrooms and the rooms below them.

FIGURE 13. Details of plywood base for tile and planks.

FIGURE 14. Application of insulation between attic-floor joists.

APPLICATION OF INSULATION. Blanket-type insulation having a thickness of about 4 inches may be installed between the joists as shown in Figures 13 and 14. Both illustrations show the insulation packed just above the lath and plaster of the rooms below. In Figure 14, the mechanic is applying short pieces of the insulation which will serve as a draft stop between the knee-wall plate and the top of the insulation between the joists.

APPLICATION OF PLYWOOD. As indicated in Figure 13, the plywood can be nailed directly to the top edges of the joists. However, it should be noted that wherever plywood joints occur, 2 by 4 blocking must be installed. Use 2½-inch screw-type nails, spaced 8 inches apart, to nail the plywood to all joists and blocking. Countersink the nailheads just below the surface of the plywood. (Also see plywood section in Chapter 1.)

APPLICATION OF TILE. Same as explained in the solution to Problem 1.

APPLICATION OF PLANKS. Same as explained in the solution to Problem 4.

TILE ON PLYWOOD OVER WORN-OUT WOOD FLOORS

The following project is typical of any and all cases where plywood and tile are to be applied over an old single floor.

PROBLEM 6. ANY FLOOR. For the purpose of this problem, we may assume that an old single floor (finish floor without a subfloor) is badly worn and unsightly and that we want to use plywood, over it, as a base for a new tile surface. The problem is to apply the plywood. NOTE: A project of this kind should not be contemplated unless all of the rooms, on a first or second floor of a house, are to be given the same treatment.

SOLUTION. It can also be assumed that ⅝-inch plywood is sufficiently strong for the purpose of this project.

APPLICATION OF PLYWOOD. First, the existing floor should be renailed. This is a precaution against squeaking and other difficulties. Use 2½-inch screw-type nails and drive two of them in every board at all joist locations. Countersink the heads. If the boards are dished, after the renailing, they should be planed or sanded until all edges are flush.

FIGURE 15. Details of plywood and tile over old single flooring.

As indicated in Figure 15, the plywood can be applied directly to the old flooring. Use 2-inch screw-type nails spaced 8 inches apart at all joist locations and along all edges of the plywood. Countersink the nail-heads.

APPLICATION OF TILE. Same as explained in the solution to Problem 1.

HARDWOOD FLOORING ON CONCRETE

The following project is typical of any and all cases where hardwood flooring is to be applied over an existing concrete slab.

PROBLEM 7. BASEMENT-RECREATION-ROOM FLOOR. For the purpose of this problem, we can assume that a basement space is being remodeled to serve as a recreation area. The problem is to apply new hardwood flooring over the existing concrete slab.

SOLUTION. We can also assume that the concrete floor is occasionally damp but never actually wet or cold.

PLANNING. It is best to plan the hardwood flooring so that the boards run in the direction of the longest dimension of the room.

There is definite opportunity for wise economy in using short lengths of either oak or maple flooring. Pieces of short lengths provide the same strength, durability, and smoothness as a floor laid with standard long lengths. For recreation-room requirements, the short lengths are ideal, even if they do require a little more laying time.

There is also definite opportunity for economy in using what is classed as Second Grade flooring. Tests have shown that second-grade flooring is equal in every performance and endurance qualities to first-grade flooring. At times, second-grade lumber is preferred over the first grade because of its pleasingly varied colorations and interesting grain patterns which tend to give a floor more pronounced character. Appearance is by no means sacrificed. Manufacturers give careful attention to selecting only attractive boards.

FIGURE 16. Details of hardwood floor over an old concrete floor.

LAYOUT. Wood sleepers which have dimensions of at least 2 by 2 inches, must be fastened to the concrete at 12-inch intervals, somewhat as shown in the *D* part of Figure 16. The new floor boards must be placed so that they are at 90-degree angles to the sleepers.

APPLICATION OF SLEEPERS. As explained in Chapter 2 and as shown in the *A* part of the illustration, the sleepers can be fastened, as necessary to make them secure, by means of lead shields and screws; or a gun-type fastener can be used to "shoot" nails through the sleepers and into the concrete. Sometimes concrete nails work to advantage. The top surfaces of all sleepers must be at exactly the same level. Where necessary, and as indicated in the *B* part of the illustration, shims may be used to force sleepers up to level.

When the sleepers are all in place, some type of mastic or asphalt should be applied to the concrete between them. This will act as insulation and keep dampness away from the new surface of the floor.

FIGURE 17. Hardwood-floor-nailing details.

APPLICATION OF FLOORING. In order to provide additional insulation, so far as dampness is concerned, Sisalkraft should be spread on the tops of the sleepers and well lapped.

Place and nail the first floor board as explained in the solution to Problem 4 and as shown in the *A* part of Figure 17. Use two 2- or 2½-inch screw-type nails at each sleeper.

After the first board has been nailed, use a scrap piece of flooring, as shown in the *B* part of the illustration, to force grooves over tongues and to make beautiful joints. The *C* and *D* parts of the illustration indicate how nails are to be driven. Use one nail at each sleeper location.

sanding. Most hardwood flooring comes from the mill smoothly surfaced, but in laying any floor, slight inequalities, scratches, and scars are bound to occur. Scraping or sanding removes these. A really smooth sanding is the most important part of a good floor-finishing job. Scrape and sand with the grain lengthwise (see *E* part of Figure 17), using either a cushioned hand-sanding block or a power sander, of the belt or oscillating type—never one of the disk type; No. 2 or 2½ sandpaper is suggested for leveling off high spots and joints, and No. 1 for the second cut. The final step—most important of all—is the finish-sanding with No. 0 or 00 paper (or both, if necessary). Do not be content with anything less than perfect sanding.

HOW TO KEEP HARDWOOD FLOORS BEAUTIFUL

The secret of keeping hardwood floors beautiful is proper care. After they have been newly finished and waxed, it is a simple matter to keep them bright and spotless by daily dusting with an untreated mop and by cleaning and waxing them periodically. Once a floor has been neglected to the point where the finish is worn in spots or dirt has become embedded, nothing short of refinishing will restore its original beauty.

The first rule for proper floor maintenance is: Never use soap and water to clean hardwood floors.

This is highly important because soap and water will injure both the finish and the wood of hardwood floors. Water will sometimes even cause the floor to buckle.

Water spilled on a wood floor should be wiped up and the floor dried immediately. If allowed to remain, it will produce an unsightly white spot which is almost impossible to remove without complete sanding and refinishing.

Several wax cleaning compounds are available which contain no water. They literally dry-clean floor surfaces through the action of solvents which remove the top layer of old wax in which dirt and grime have become embedded, then replace the old wax with a coating of new wax that polishes readily to a lustrous sheen.

SAFETY FEATURES IN CONNECTION WITH THE LAYING OF NEW HARDWOOD FLOORS

Do not:

Lay flooring immediately after its delivery. Store it for a few days in the house where it is to be laid.

Bring flooring into a damp house.

Lay flooring in a damp or cold house. The temperature in the house should be at least 70°F.

Stack bundles of flooring too close together. Do allow ample air circulation between bundles.

Close windows. This is important. Opening windows at tops aids in ventilation.

ASPHALT TILE OVER CONCRETE

The following project is typical of any and all cases where asphalt tile is to be applied over an existing concrete floor, such as in a basement.

PROBLEM 8. BASEMENT-RECREATION-ROOM FLOOR. For the purpose of this problem, we can assume that a basement space is being remodeled to serve as a recreation area. The problem is to apply asphalt tile over the existing concrete.

SOLUTION. PLANNING. Existing concrete floors must be clean and free from all coverings, adhesives, and other surface finishes. All oil, grease, and wax must be removed. Expansion joints, cracks, score marks, and depressions must be filled in to produce a smooth, even surface. The concrete must be thoroughly dry and free from moisture before the asphalt tile is laid. If the floor is unusually porous or dusty, it should be given a coat of hot asphalt before the tile adhesive is spread.

LAYOUT. Few rooms are perfect rectangles. As the field (area within the border) of an asphalt-tile floor must be laid within a perfect rectangle, it is necessary to establish center or guidelines which are at right angles to each other from which tile can be laid. When laying out a room, we should measure only from the principal walls, such as *AB* and *BC* shown in the *A* part of Figure 18. Offsets and other breaks, as shown at

DEF, should be disregarded. In all cases, we must start laying the tile at the center of a floor and work toward the walls, where the width of the border can be adjusted as desired.

To square the area to be covered, first find the center of one end of the floor. Locate the same point at the other-end wall. Snap a chalk line

FIGURE 18. Tile layout.

between these points to mark the center line of the floor. Then measure to find the middle point of the room, as shown in the illustration, on this line. At this middle point, mark off a line across the room at right angles to the first line. This can be done by means of the 3-4-5 triangle method as shown in the illustration.

Measure 4′ 0″ toward each side wall from the center point. Then measure 3′ 0″ from the center point along the longer line. Measure exactly 5′ 0″ from the 3′ 0″ mark on the center line to the 4′ 0″ mark on the crossline. Snap a chalk line across the room between this point and one that is similarly located on the other side of the center line. This line will be at right angles to the first line.

APPLICATION OF TILE. Test the layout by placing tile as shown in the *B* part of the illustration. Another test may be made by placing the first tile so that it straddles the center point. The layout shown is best.

It is wise to use the adhesive recommended by the manufacturer of the tile. The adhesive should be applied to the concrete using a notched trowel having notches $\frac{1}{16}$ inch deep and spaced on $\frac{3}{16}$-inch centers.

Asphalt tile should be laid starting at the center of the floor, working toward the walk, as shown by tiles 1 to 4, 6 to 9, and 11 to 16. Any desired width of border may be obtained by trimming the tile next to the walls. Any asphalt cove base can be cemented to the walls.

CHAPTER SEVEN

Basements

Basements have gone through many years of interesting development.

Some 60 or more years ago, they were practically unknown. There was no need for them, owing to the fact that heating systems consisted of base burners and other stoves which were set up wherever heat was desired. However, small cellars were used for the storage of food. They were located under houses but could only be reached by means of outside entrances.

The advent of hand-fired gravity furnaces, along with hot-water heating systems, brought about the first great improvement in cellars. Such equipment functioned only when located below the floor level of the rooms to be heated. Thus it became necessary to deepen the cellars and otherwise enlarge them, to make room for the equipment and accompanying coalbins. Even in those days families needed more room; so it was only natural that some household activities, such as laundry work, were shifted from kitchens to what soon became known as basements. At best, however, the early basements were dusty and dirty, owing to the use of coal and the removal of ashes.

The arrival of modern heating plants, with automatic fueling, brought about another great improvement. Dust and dirt no longer had to be contended with and basements took on the appearance of the one shown in Figure 1. Such basements could have been remodeled and made into usable living spaces if the old washtubs could have been removed and if clothes could have been dried in ways other than by hanging them on lines.

FIGURE 1. Typical old basement.

FIGURE 2. Same basement after remodeling.

With the coming of automatic clothes washers and dryers, even small basements were suitable for remodeling. Figure 2 shows what was done with the basement illustrated in Figure 1. Such remodeled and attractive space can be used for any number of purposes all in keeping with modern living.

Thousands of homeowners realize the possibilities of their basements and are probably anxious to turn them into attractive and worthwhile living spaces. The purpose of this chapter is to explain important remodeling considerations, to show how many related projects can be accomplished and to illustrate the planning and actual construction work involved in typical remodeling work.

PURPOSE OF REMODELING

Before the actual planning for any basement remodeling begins, we should give a great deal of thought to the following fundamentals:

What is the purpose of the remodeling?
What are the requirements?
Financial considerations.
Will the remodeling be worthwhile?

Ordinarily, remodeling motivation stems from a desire to create additional space or spaces which can be used for one or more of the following typical purposes:

A recreation room	A workbench area
A party room	A darkroom
A new laundry	General storage facilities
Modern storage facilities for food	A workshop

A new bedroom (if 50 per cent of basement is above grade)

Whatever the purpose of remodeling is, it should be firmly established so that the basement can be studied accordingly. No planning can logically be done until or unless the purpose has definitely been set up as a goal. Without a definite purpose, planning would be haphazard and at the risk of disappointing final results.

The requirements of remodeling are closely allied to the purpose. For example, if a recreation area is the purpose, will it satisfy the requirements so far as children or other planned uses are concerned? This aspect also requires careful thought. All requirements of such a space should be written so that they can be studied.

Financial considerations are always important and should be studied. However, this aspect of the remodeling cannot be determined accurately until final plans have been made. In the meantime, we should set up a maximum allowable expenditure to use as a guide.

The question as to whether or not remodeling will be worthwhile should be given careful preliminary consideration. Some of the items to consider are listed in the following:

1. Will the remodeling make a house more desirable from the standpoint of living conditions?

2. Is the general structural condition of a house sound enough to merit the planned remodeling? Unless all other parts of a house are in good condition, the remodeling of any one area might not be a good investment.

3. Will the remodeling add to the value of the house from the standpoint of its possible sale?

4. How much will remodeling increase the real estate taxes?

5. Is the neighborhood such that property values are apt to increase or decrease?

6. Are the prospects for the neighborhood such that continued residence in it is assured?

7. Will the remodeling help to rent a house?

8. Can the cost of remodeling be handled without undue financial strain.

REMODELING PRECAUTION

Inexperienced mechanics and homeowners are apt to do a great deal of preliminary planning without taking into consideration several aspects of the probable cost. This is a common mistake that always leads to unexpected expense or probable disappointment. As a means of helping readers to avoid such a mistake, the following typical remodeling plan is explained.

The *A* part of Figure 3 shows an ordinary basement plan of a type common to many houses. The plan lacks convenience and is poorly

E.M.– ELECTRIC METER   G.M.– GAS METER   TAB.– TABLE
L.C.– LAUNDRY CHUTE   H.P.– HEATING PLANT   W.– WASHER
W.M.– WATER METER   I. – IRONER   W.H.– WATER
D. – DRYER   L.T.– LAUNDRY TUBS
T.– TOILET   • – COLUMN

FIGURE 3. Basement before and after remodeling.

designed. For example, the laundry chute is located far away from the laundry tubs, and the hand-fired gravity furnace is too far from the coal-bin, yet, the design is typical of many basements.

The *B* part of the illustration shows the proposed remodeling plan. At first glance, and without careful thought, this plan seems well designed.

The heating plant, laundry tubs, and other utility equipment are all located in one section of the basement, and the stairway leads directly into the recreation area. However, there are several aspects of the plan which would cost a great deal to accomplish.

Fireplace. The fireplace constitutes a most desirable feature. But, not many existing chimneys, such as shown in the *A* part of the illustration, contain the extra flue necessary for a fireplace. Thus, a great deal of expense would be involved in rebuilding the chimney so as to provide the needed flue. Even if the extra flue is available, the cost of building a fireplace at the base of the chimney is apt to be excessive.

New Heating Plant. A new forced-air heating plant would certainly give added comfort and, unlike the old gravity furnace, could be placed as shown, so as to be out of the way. However, two items of extra expense should be understood. First, the new heating plant would cost several hundred dollars. Second, an entirely new duct system would probably be necessary. That would cost considerably more money. Additional expense would also be involved in patching the floors where the old warm- and cold-air inlets and outlets were located.

New Windows. The windows shown at *A, B,* and *C* would be expensive, especially because of the cost of cutting the solid concrete foundations.

Piping. Moving the gas and water meters would mean expensive pipe relocations.

Water Heater. Moving the water heater would also mean expensive pipe relocations.

Water Closet. Moving the position of this fixture only a few feet would mean relocating both sewer and vent lines.

Washer. New hot- and cold-water pipes, vent and sewer pipes would have to be installed for the new washer. The same is true for the new location of the laundry tubs. In fact, relocating or adding new pipes in connection with any of the plumbing work is very expensive.

Lavatory. The new lavatory would require hot- and cold-water pipes, a vent, and connections to the sewer.

Some of the new ducts, in connection with the new heating plant, would have to be located below the level of the ceiling joists and would be difficult to hide in the recreation area. The same is true for the re-located gas and water pipes.

All of the foregoing items constitute extra expense which could easily amount to a much greater total than a homeowner could or would care to assume in connection with a remodeling project. There are probably few cases where such expense could be justified when only a recreation area results. Most remodeling, so far as basements are concerned, should be planned so that only new walls, ceiling, and floor surfaces, and new partitions are required.

PRELIMINARY CONSIDERATIONS

After the purpose of a basement remodeling project has been definitely established, the next step consists of studying the actual conditions to determine what must be done to make the remodeling possible. Here, we shall discuss some of the most commonly encountered items. In subsequent pages, we shall see how the required work is accomplished.

Ceiling Height. Fortunately, most basements were built to allow at least a distance of 7′ 0″ between floors and ceilings. This distance constituted the lowest ceiling height recommended. Anything lower gives occupants of rooms a cramped feeling and lessens the enjoyment of the new areas. Higher ceilings do not offer much of a problem, except that more wall-surface materials are required. If ceiling heights are more than 9′ 0″, they can be lowered, as explained in Chapter 4.

When ceiling heights are less than 7′ 0″, some excavation can be done. Several methods are explained in subsequent pages.

Columns. Basement columns or posts are for the purpose of supporting walls and floors above them. In most cases, they are located exactly where required. They should not be moved or changed in any way. As shown in Figure 3, remodeling should be planned around them or so that they will be within new partitions.

Bearing Partitions. Sometimes existing basement partitions support floor joists. In such cases, they should not be removed or altered in any way until temporary supports are created. In subsequent pages, such a condition is explained.

Floors. If an old basement does not contain a concrete floor, the remodeling work must include such an allied project.

See Chapter 6 in regard to floor treatment.

Windows. As previously mentioned, the installation of windows in existing concrete foundations is apt to create considerable expense. Power tools are required. In concrete-block walls, the procedure is much easier because blocks can be removed by the process of breaking the thin joints between them.

Basement Water. A *wet* basement is defined as one where water actually flows in through the foundations. A *damp* basement is defined as one where the foundations become damp after hard rains.

WET CONDITIONS. Sometimes basements are built on what appears to be dry ground, but at a later date it is discovered that a static head of water, as shown at *Y* in Figure 4, is present for long periods of time each year. This condition is frequently encountered in basements built on low ground near rivers or other bodies of water. In such cases, the water actually builds up a pressure against foundations and seeps through them. Although masonry foundations are strong and durable, they are somewhat porous and will absorb moisture under pressure. This is especially true as regards concrete block. If the joints between block are carelessly made, the water *runs* through the cracks.

DAMP CONDITIONS. Concrete-block foundations are sometimes subjected to dampness immediately after hard rains. Any one or more of three causes could be at fault. First, downspouts from roofs may dispose of water near the foundations so that the water can soak into the soil, as indicated by the arrows at X in Figure 4, and contact the foundations. Second, the backfill against the foundations may contain old cans, bits of wood, plaster, brick, and other odds and ends of rubbish. If the surrounding soil is hard clay or not easily permeable, the rubbish creates a reservoir of water against foundations and the water will gradually seep through them. Third, the soil may be inherently wet enough to keep water against the foundations.

FIGURE 4. How water and dampness enter a basement.

Ways and means of avoiding wet and damp basement conditions are explained in subsequent pages.

Stairs. Basement stairs are frequently rough in appearance. However, they constitute part of remodeling work and should be improved as explained in subsequent pages.

Wall Surfaces. If foundations are always dry, or if they can be moistureproofed, there are especially made paints which can be used, all as explained in subsequent pages.

See Chapter 5 for new wall surfaces.

Pipes. It is rare, indeed, that ducts or pipes can be moved. Thus, they must be covered as indicated in Figure 2.

Sweating Pipes. During warm weather, one or more of the cold-water pipes in a basement may sweat and drip water. This can be avoided by applying special pipe insulation to them. Such insulation is available at all lumberyards.

Furnace Location. Unless an entirely new heating system is contemplated, remodeling projects should be planned to avoid any changes in furnace locations, pipes, or ducts.

Basement Temperatures. In general, basement temperatures, without artificial heating or cooling, tend to be cooler in summer and warmer in winter than other parts of a house. For example, on a hot summer day the temperature in a first-floor room may be about 86°F, whereas the basement temperature is apt to be about 68 or 72°F. On the other hand, the winter temperature of an unheated first-floor room may be about freezing, whereas the basement temperature may be as high as 40 or 45°F.

From the foregoing it can be seen that basement recreation areas are apt to be quite comfortable during the hottest summer weather. It can also be seen that keeping a recreation area warm during the winter can be accomplished without too much trouble. However, thick masonry walls are apt to radiate a cold sensation during the winter months. How to remedy such a situation is explained in subsequent pages.

Sagging Floors. In some of the older houses the floor joists over the basement areas may have deflected to the extent that the floors they support sag near their mid-points. Such conditions, as explained later in this chapter, should be corrected before basement remodeling is started.

Games. If recreation areas are to include standard pool or billiard tables, the dimensions shown in Figure 5 must be considered. The cues are 57 inches long. Therefore, the tables must be at least 5′ 0″ from the walls, chairs, or other obstructions.

FIGURE 5. Clearance for pool and billiard tables.

Ceilings. Where ordinary wood joists are used in the ceiling above a basement space, any of the surface materials explained in Chapter 4 can be used.

Hot-water Tank. An automatic hot-water tank, containing its own heating mechanism, can be moved to any convenient location at only the cost of additional lengths of pipe. However, a hot-water tank hooked up to a furnace should not be moved away from the furnace.

Electrical Outlets. Lights, switches, and convenience outlets can be moved or added with ease by the use of BX or Romex wire. Local building codes should be studied to ascertain electrical requirements.

RELATED PROJECTS

The following projects are typical examples of commonly encountered preparatory or related work which must be done in connection with most basement remodeling.

Ceiling Height. In many old houses, especially those dating back to the cellar era, basement ceiling heights are apt to be less than 7 feet. Figure 6 shows several suggested ways of lowering floors so that additional ceiling height can be created.

PART *W* OF FIGURE 6. Here, we can assume that the ceiling height, *A*, is only 6′ 6″. We shall also assume that the existing floor and footing are

4 and 8 inches thick, respectively. Four more inches of ceiling height may be obtained by placing a new concrete floor, as shown at *F,* so that its surface is flush with the top of the footing. Or, a total of 12 additional inches can be obtained by placing a new floor, as shown at *H,* so that its surface is even with the bottom of the footing. In this case, the corner of the footing could be furred and trimmed with wood to create an attractive base around the space. When new concrete floors are laid on damp soil, Medusa waterproof cement should be used as part of the concrete mix.

FIGURE 6. Details showing how more ceiling height can be provided in basements.

PART *X* OF FIGURE 6. Some old houses, located in the central regions of the country, have rubblestone foundations, with or without footings, which generally extend to depths far below the earth floor levels. Let us suppose that the existing ceiling height, *D,* is only 6′ 0″. The depth of the foundation can be checked by means of a small excavation in the basement. Depending upon the depth of the foundation, soil can be excavated to a depth G, so as to provide a suitable ceiling height, E.

PART Y OF FIGURE 6. Some old houses, especially in the Eastern regions of the country, have brick foundations without footings. If the soil under the foundation shown at J is a firm clay, the floor can be lowered 12 or 14 inches. A 4-inch retaining wall, as shown at L, should also be placed. The exposed surfaces of the retaining wall can be furred and trimmed with wood to create an attractive base around the space.

PART Z OF FIGURE 6. In some cases, ceiling heights, such as shown at B, are no more than 4 or 5 feet. This poses a much more complicated situation, but there is a way of providing suitable ceiling heights. The necessary work can be done so that a depth of only a few feet of the existing foundation is affected at any one time.

First, excavate down to the level where the new footing is to be placed. Also, excavate under the existing footing to the same depth. Cut off part of the old footing, as shown at O, by means of a cold chisel. Erect form boards, as shown at M and P, and brace them as indicated. The space between M and P is then ready for concrete.

The concrete should consist of 1 part portland cement, 2 parts clean sand, and 4 parts of clean gravel or crushed rock. Use enough water to make the mix free-flowing. Pour the concrete through the opening at O and spade it carefully as a means of making sure that it fills the space, especially under the old footing. Allow the new concrete to cure and harden at least a week before removing the exterior forms.

After the exterior forms have been removed, backfill the soil against the foundation. Be sure to compact the soil as the backfilling is in progress. Such packing will help to avoid dampness on the basement face of the foundation.

When the backfilling has been completed, the interior excavation work can be carried on and the N part of the old footing cut off by means of a cold chisel.

Place the new concrete floor, using a mix composed of 1 part portland cement, 3 parts of sand, and 5 parts of gravel or crushed rock. Use enough water to make the mix plastic but not running-wet.

The basement side or surface of the new foundation, especially the portion between S and T, is likely to be somewhat rough so far as appearance is concerned. However, the whole surface between R and T can be furred and a surface material applied as explained in Chapter 6.

Bearing Partitions. The X part of Figure 7 shows a section view of a basement in which a brick bearing partition is used to divide the space and to support the floor joists. In two-story houses, such bearing partitions also support walls above the first-floor level.

FIGURE 7. Use of I-beam in place of bearing partition.

The Y part of the illustration indicates a plan view of the same basement. The area $ABCD$ is to be turned into a recreation area. To create one large room, the brick partition must be removed between E and F. However, some means must be provided for supporting the joists between E and F when the partition is removed.

The X part of Figure 8 indicates how the brick partition supports the joists and the Y part shows that an I-beam can be substituted for the brick partition.

The first step of such a project consists of measuring the distance GH as shown in the Y part of Figure 7, to determine the required length of the I-beam. When such beams are not more than 12 feet long, an 8-inch

FIGURE 8. Details of joist support.

size is sufficiently strong. When longer lengths are required, local dealers will suggest the sizes to use.

Before the brick partition can be torn out between E and F, the joists must be provided with temporary supports. As indicated in Figure 9, such support can be provided by means of 4- by 4-inch timbers. The A and B horizontal timbers, on both sides of the bearing partition, should be as long as the width of the ceiling. The vertical timbers should be spaced about 4 feet apart.

FIGURE 9. Temporary support for joists.

When the partition between E and F, as shown in the Y part of Figure 7, has been removed, a beam pocket, as shown at G, must be cut into the foundation. This pocket must have a depth equal to the depth of the I-beam. At the H end of the remaining part of the brick partition, a 12-

by 12-inch brick plaster must be laid up as support for the F end of the I-beam. If the beam pocket can be at least 5 inches wide, so as to provide a 5-inch bearing for the I-beam, a brick pilaster at the E end of the I-beam is not necessary. If the pocket is less than 5 inches wide, a 4- by 12-inch pilaster is required.

Before the I-beam is placed into position, the bottom of the beam pocket and the tops of the pilasters should be covered with a bedding of cement and sand mortar. This will assure a firm bed for the I-beam. Make sure that the top flange of the I-beam is snugly fitted to the bottom edges of the joists.

The space left in the floor by the removal of the brick partition can be patched and a new over-all floor covering applied as explained in Chapter 6. The surfaces of the new partition and foundation can be finished as suggested in Chapter 7. The ceiling can be sheathed as set forth in Chapter 4.

Floors. If existing concrete floors are free from cracks and dusting, and are always dry, either paint or stain can be applied in any one of a variety of decorator-styled colors.

Often seemingly dry concrete floors are too damp for good painting results. One method of testing is to lay a rubber mat on the floor and leave it undisturbed for at least two days. If, at the end of that time, moisture shows under the mat, the floor is probably too damp for paint and should be furred as explained in Chapter 6.

PAINT. Concrete floors in a recreation area are often subjected to heavy traffic, especially in connection with pool or billiards, and demand more than ordinary oil paint. Coatings for this type of surface must be extraordinarily adhesive and tough and have the qualities of good aging, rapid drying, and high resistance to soap or other cleaning agents. Paints such as Medusa rubber-base coatings are recommended.

A concrete floor should be thoroughly cleaned of all traces of soap or grease by means of a lye solution. After cleaning, the floor should be etched with a 10 per cent solution of muriatic acid. Pour the solution on the floor, let stand for 10 minutes, rinse, and allow to dry. Hands should be washed in cold water after using the muriatic acid solution.

After the floor is etched, test for porosity by placing a few drops of water on the surface. If the water is readily absorbed, the surface is ready for painting.

Most such paints are applied as they come from the containers, usually in two coats. Three coats are suggested for areas which will be subjected to heavy traffic. When the first coat is dry to touch, apply the second coat. If a third coat is applied, it should be brushed out more than either of the first two coats. Wax will protect the paint and give it more luster.

STAIN. In some instances, stain is a longer-lasting color than paint. Several commercial forms are available, any of which can be applied to concrete that has not been previously painted, oiled, or sealed against penetration.

The floor should be etched as previously explained. The dye should be scrubbed into the surface and forced into the pores. Apply a second coat if the first coat dries without a uniform color. Wax will give the floor added luster, protect the dye, and assure easier cleaning.

Windows. In order to install a window in an existing concrete-block wall, several courses of block must be removed to provide space for the window and so that jamb block, a sill, and a lintel can be laid up around the window opening.

The first step consists of studying the joists over the window location. For example, refer to Section *C-C* in Plate II. This view shows that joist ends are supported by the foundation over the window opening. In a case like this, at least three of the joists on both sides of the window location should be temporarily supported, somewhat as shown in Figure 9, while the window is being installed. If the joists are parallel to the foundations, temporary support for them is not necessary.

The *B* part of Figure 10 shows an elevation view of a typical concrete-block foundation that is similar to the one illustrated in Section *W*-1 of Plate V. It can be assumed that an opening, *ABCD*, in the foundation must be provided for the window. The *A* and *C* parts of the illustration show both wood- and steel-sash windows in a concrete-block wall. We can further assume that steel sash is required.

The next step is to remove the necessary block from the foundation. Joints between block can generally be broken by means of a cold chisel

STEEL SASH
(C)

JAMB BLOCK

LINTEL

SILL

CONCRETE
SLIP SILL

4'0"

SOLID BLOCK

(B)

WOOD SASH
(A)

LINTEL

SILL

5'0"

FIGURE 10. Details of windows in concrete-block foundations.

197

or a steel claw bar. Remove blocks 1, 2, 3, and 4 first. Then remove blocks 5 through 28.

In place of ordinary block, we will need steel-sash jamb block on both sides of the window opening. We will also need a sill and lintel, such as shown at *C* in the illustration.

The mortar for laying block can be composed of 1 part of portland cement and 3 parts of sand. In place of blocks 26 and 28, we will lay the sill and two half jamb blocks. Blocks 22 and 25 should be whole

FIGURE 11. Foundation waterproofing.

jamb block. In place of blocks 19 and 21, we will lay two half jamb blocks, etc. In place of blocks 5, 6, and 7, we will install the lintel. Finally, the solid block, 1, 2, 3, and 4, can be laid above the lintel. This completes the window opening.

Basement Water. As previously explained, basements may be subject to either wet or damp conditions.

WET CONDITIONS. When wet conditions such as caused by severe static pressure exist, a drastic remedy must be applied.

First, excavate a trench all around the foundation somewhat as indicated by the section view in Figure 11. The bottom of the trench should be at the same level as the bottom of the footing. Brush and wash all traces of soil from the foundation.

Second, prepare a mortar composed of 1 part Medusa cement and 3 parts clean sand. A total thickness of 1 inch of mortar should be applied to the foundation in 3 separate coats. Allow 3 days of hardening time between coats. Spray the first and second coats with water before the second and third coats are applied. Use the same mortar mix to build up a slope, as shown in the illustration, between the foundation and the top of the footing.

Third, mop a thick coat of hot asphaltum on the surface of the mortar.

Fourth, lay lines of plain-end drain tile, spaced about ½ inch apart, around the foundation as indicated in the illustration. All lines of tile should have a gradual slope to one location where a connection to a sewer or other means of disposal can be made. Spread heavy roofing paper along the tops of the tile.

Fifth, fill in at least 16 inches of gravel or crushed rock over the tile.

The earth backfill should be free of rubbish and well compacted. The slope of the grade should be as shown in the illustration.

If there is a crack between the floor and the foundation, it should be filled with hot asphaltum.

DAMP CONDITIONS. When damp conditions occur, the remedy is less drastic.

After a hard rain, mark the areas where dampness appears on a foundation.

If the foundation has been painted previously with an oil paint, remove by applying freely a solution of 1½ pounds of caustic soda with hot water. If painted previously with whitewash, calcimine, or cold-water paints, remove by scrubbing surfaces with 1 part muriatic acid and 5 parts water. Clean off loose dirt and dust by means of a stiff wire brush.

On the areas marked, scrub in with a scrubbing brush a coat of Medusa portland-cement paint. Extend paint several feet beyond the marked areas. Work paint into all voids and depressions with a circular motion of the scrub brush.

Wait until the next hard rain to ascertain whether the foundation has been made sufficiently watertight to stop dampness. Then, give the entire surface a first coat of the same paint. Cure by applying a fine spray of water two or three times during the following 18 to 24 hours. Apply a second coat of the paint for thorough protection.

New Foundation Surface. In cases where the basement sides of masonry foundations have poor appearance, in addition to being slightly wet or undesirably damp, new cement plaster surfaces can be applied which will be attractive and waterproof. The following suggestions are typical.

The old surface should be roughened using a stone mason's hammer, drills, or similar tools, exposing a new surface, and leaving ¼- to ⅜-inch-deep holes every 2 or 3 inches, so as to provide a better bond for the cement plaster.

Apply a solution to the wall of 1 part muriatic acid to 10 parts of water, using a fiber or acid brush. Allow the acid solution to exhaust itself, which requires about 10 minutes. Hose off the acid thoroughly with water.

Remove any remaining loose pieces by going over the walls with a wire brush.

If the foundation is made of brick or concrete block, instead of following the foregoing directions, rake out all mortar joints to a depth of ½ to ¾ inch.

Then remove all loose mortar, dirt, grease, paints, and efflorescence. Whitewash, calcimine, cold-water paints, and efflorescence are easily removed by means of a solution composed of 1 part muriatic acid and 5 parts of water. Oil paint can be removed by applying freely a solution composed of 1½ pounds of caustic soda and 1 gallon of water. Rinse with clear water and be sure that all loose particles are removed, preferably by means of a wire brush.

Spray the entire foundation surface with water. Then use a fiber brush to apply a grout coat composed of Medusa waterproof portland cement and water mixed to a creamy consistency. Brush the grout thoroughly into all holes and irregularities in the foundation surface.

The next step consists of applying cement plaster to the surface of the foundation. The plaster should be composed of 1 part Medusa waterproof portland cement and 2½ parts of clean sand. Mix to a stiff workable consistency.

Apply the first coat of cement plaster ⅜ inch thick and be sure to trowel the plaster well into the surface to secure a proper bond. Scratch the first coat with a "scratcher." An old broom or a wire brush can be used. Do not use nails or trowels. The scratches should be about $\frac{1}{16}$ inch deep.

As soon as the first coat has set, spray the surface with water and apply the second coat $\frac{3}{8}$ inch thick. Trowel the plaster with sufficient pressure to obtain a tight, close-grained finish.

FIGURE 12. Basement-stair details.

Care should be exercised not to trowel any more than is absolutely necessary to obtain the proper finish. Excess troweling results in poor plaster.

If there is continual seepage through a foundation, one or more holes should be bored and small pipes inserted to concentrate the flow of water while the plaster is being applied. After the plaster has set, plug the holes with plaster.

Stairs. Many basement stairs, especially in older houses, are rough and unsightly. Such stairs can be given a face lifting at only a fraction of the money new stairs would cost.

Figure 12 shows several details of typical basement stairs. The more common type is shown at *B,* where two or more stringers are notched so treads and risers can be nailed to them. When stairs are against a wall, or between two walls, wallboards may exist as shown at *A*. More economical stairs, as shown at *C,* do not have risers between the treads. Generally, such stairs are nailed together and the wood is not smooth.

Because of ordinary wear, nosings and treads may be rounded and dished to the extent that new paint would not greatly improve their appearance. They should be sanded until the nosings are near their original condition and the treads should be leveled. Sanding will remove old paint. Sanding may be done without removing the old treads by using a small electric hand sander. Some scraping will be necessary with a regular hand scraper.

Better results can be obtained if the treads are removed and taken to a shop where they can be sanded smooth and true with heavy cabinet-maker's equipment.

After the sanding is done, apply a good coat of shellac to the treads before nailing them in place to prevent any tendency to warp. Use finishing nails and a nail set to drive them below the surface.

Risers, stringer, and wallboards can be prepared for new paint by filling all cracks and dents with Spackle or water-base putty. Casein-type cement of the kind used to fill plasterboard joints can also be used. Apply with a wide putty knife. Allow to dry for at least 24 hours. For a good job, apply a primer coat of paint before the undercoater and final coat.

An enamel color may be used. The undercoater can consist of half flat and half enamel paint, but the final coat should be all enamel. When the enamel is dry, nail the treads in place and give them a coat of hard but flexible varnish. For best results, sandpaper lightly on the varnish, wipe away dust, and apply a second varnish coat. A natural finish is achieved with shellac and varnish.

When treads are in so poor a condition that they cannot be repaired, the stairs can be carpeted or new treads added. Lumber dealers can furnish the material, cut it to size, and add the nosing required. Where no risers exist, as shown at *C,* they may be added along with new treads on the old stringers.

Wall Surfaces. If the surfaces of concrete or concrete block are fairly smooth and are otherwise in good condition so far as appearance is concerned, they can be painted any one or combination of several colors using a good grade of cement paint. Such paint creates attractive appearance and also provides a high degree of dampproofing.

If surfaces have been previously painted, paints other than cement paint must be removed. Oil paint, oily stains, soot, grease, shellac, and glue size can be removed by applying caustic soda mixed to the proportion of 1½ pounds with 1 gallon of hot water. Apply freely, wash with water after film softens, and follow with rinsing. Whitewash, calcimine, cold-water paints, and efflorescence (white powdery deposits) may be removed with 1 part muriatic acid mixed with 5 parts of water. Scrub with brush and rinse.

All surfaces should be wire-brushed. Small cracks should be cleaned and filled with a paste made by mixing dry paint and water. Large cracks should be filled with cement mortar.

Before painting, spray the surface with a fine mist of water. Apply first coat of paint with a bristle or calcimine-type brush. Use a horizontal motion, keeping the brush full of paint. Do not brush the paint after application.

Cure the first coat by means of a fine spray of water applied several times during 12 hours. This is important and should not be neglected.

The second coat may be applied on the second day. Cure this coat as previously explained.

See Chapter 6 in connection with new surface materials.

Cutting Structural Details for Pipes and Ducts. In the framing for floors and walls, the joists and studs each support a definite amount of weight and contribute to the stiffness of the framing. Thus we must consider each joist or stud individually and understand that if one of them fails, an undue stress is forced on the others and may cause defects in floors and walls.

PIPES. Sometimes joists have to be notched, somewhat as shown in the *A* part of Figure 13, in order to run pipes to required locations. If a 2 by 10 joist has a notch 5 inches deep in it, the whole joist is no stronger than at the notch. In other words, the strength of the joist is reduced to the strength of a 2 by 5 joist. In order to avoid loss of strength and stiffness, some means of strengthening the joist must be employed. As shown in the *B* part of Figure 13, we can nail 2 by 4 pieces on both sides of the joist to reinforce it. The 2 by 4 pieces should be at least 6 feet long or even the full length of the joist. Use 3½-inch nails and space them not more than 6 inches apart along the length of the reinforcing members.

If, as indicated in the *C* part of Figure 13, holes have to be drilled in studs, they should be reinforced by means of stiff metal straps on both sides of the holes. The straps should be at least 12 inches long and have five or six nail holes.

FIGURE 13. Pipe and duct details.

DUCTS. The ducts used in connection with either gravity or forced-air heating systems are generally run along the under edges of joists or between studs so that notching is not required. However, when notching is required, the same reinforcing as explained in connection with joists should be provided. The *D* part of Figure 13 shows how 2 by 4 furring can be used when a basement forced-air duct is required.

Existing Floor Drains. If existing floor drains are to be covered over with furring and new surface materials, such as suggested in Chapter 6, they must be effectively plugged by means of cement mortar. This is to avoid the entry of sewer gas after the water in the drain seals has evaporated.

Basement Temperature. If there is a possibility of cold drafts being radiated from foundations, especially when parts of them are above grade as indicated in Figure 14, effective insulation can be provided as indicated.

The first step of such a project consists of applying 2 by 2 or 1 by 2 furring strips spaced 16 inches apart. They can be fastened to the foundation and made level as explained in Chapters 2 and 5.

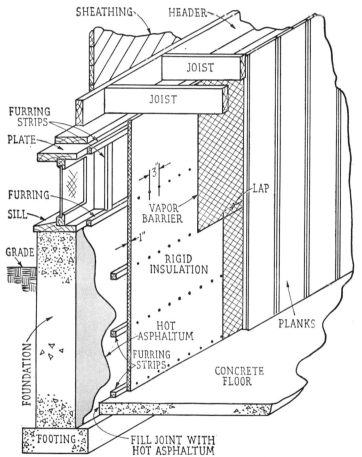

FIGURE 14. Details of insulation against cold drafts from surface of foundation surfaces.

After the furring strips have been applied, the surface of the foundation should be mopped with hot asphaltum. This constitutes effective dampproofing.

Next apply 1-inch thick panels of rigid insulation to the furring strips. Space the nails about 3 inches apart. Then tack well-lapped waterproof

builder paper over the insulation. This constitutes the required moisture barrier.

The interior surface material, such as planks, can be applied as explained in Chapter 5.

Sagging Floors. The *A* part of Figure 15 shows an exaggerated example of deflection (sagging) in a floor joist. Such deflection affects all
joists alike and can cause several troubles including vibration, squeaking,
cracks in surface materials, and out-of-plumb conditions so far as furniture and other household equipment is concerned.

FIGURE 15. How to correct sagging floors.

The *B* and *C* parts of the illustration indicate how a 4 by 4 timber, a
4 by 4 cap, and a screw-type column can be used to correct deflection
and provide permanent support for the weakened joists. If the 4 by 4
timber must be more than 10′ 10″ long, two screw columns should be
used. When only one screw column is necessary, it should be placed at the
mid-point of the timber.

Because of the weight screw columns support, they require a strong
concrete footing of the size suggested in the *D* part of the illustration.

The timber can temporarily be held up against the joists by means of 2 by 4's used somewhat as shown in Figure 9. Then the cap and column can be placed with just enough adjustment of the column to make the whole assembly tight. Screw the column up a little, not more often than once every two or three days, until the floor is level. Such gradual adjustment avoids any chance of cracks in joists or flooring. When the column has been finally adjusted, the cap and joists can be toenailed to the timber.

If a screw-type column must be placed within a recreation area, cartwheel shelving, as shown around the column in Figure 2, can be used to partially hide the column and to provide decorative storage.

TYPICAL REMODELING PROJECTS

For the purpose of the following projects, we shall assume that the house indicated in Plates I through VI actually exists and that the basement is to be remodeled. The projects are presented in the form of problems and their solutions.

PROBLEM 1. We can further assume that the purpose of remodeling is to provide the following items:

1. A large area to be used as a general recreation room

2. A workbench area where the man of the house can engage in a woodworking hobby

3. A general storage area

4. An area for deep-freeze equipment and food storage

The problem is to plan the best use of the basement space.

SOLUTION. From the standpoint of practical expense, we must consider that the boiler and stairs cannot be moved from their original locations.

Our first inclination would be to place the recreation area in the west portion of the basement, as indicated in Figure 16. Partitions on both sides of the chimney would enclose an area 11' 10" wide and 19' 2" long. This plan provides a recreation area of fair size and a well-placed workbench area. However, there are several serious objections:

1. The plan does not provide logical space for general storage.

2. Entrance to the recreation area is through an unfinished part of the basement.

FIGURE 16. Trial remodeling plan.

FIGURE 17. Second trial remodeling plan.

3. The recreation area seems detached because of the distance from the stairs.

4. The width of the recreation area is too narrow as compared to the length. Furniture arrangement and conversation would be difficult.

The plan shown in Figure 17 avoids all of the objections to the plan shown in Figure 16:

1. There is ample and desirable general storage space.

2. The stairs are within the recreation room so that the unfinished part of the basement is not visible.

3. The recreation room does not seem detached.

4. The shape is such that furniture can be arranged to advantage and easy conversation is possible. See Figure 18.

FIGURE 18. Possible furniture arrangement for plan shown in Figure 17.

FIGURE 19. Alternate details.

However, there are two objections to the plan:

1. The new windows add considerably to the cost.

2. Traffic to other parts of the basement must go through one end of the recreation room. This objection could be avoided but only by means of the additional expense items shown in Figure 19.

PART *A* OF FIGURE 19. A hall between the stairs and the recreation area would provide access to the unfinished part of the basement and avoid such traffic through the recreation area. However, considerable additional expense would be involved, all of which seems out of proportion to the advantage gained.

PART *B* OF FIGURE 19. The steps could be rebuilt so as to provide access to both the recreation area and the food-storage area. However, the additional expense involved seems out of proportion to the advantage gained.

We can assume that the plan shown in Figure 17 is acceptable.

PROBLEM 2. The problem consists of erecting 2 by 4 framing for the partition shown between *A* and *B* in Figure 17.

NORTH PARTITION AB

FIGURE 20. Partition framing.

SOLUTION. The first step in the framing is to place the 2 by 4 sill shown between *a* and *b* in the *A* part of Figure 20. Measure the exact distance and cut a piece of 2 by 4 to the length required. Place it on the floor so that it is at 90 degrees to the foundation and flush with the corner of the chimney. Fasten it to the concrete floor by means of powder-actuated nails spaced no more than 16 inches apart.

Next, erect the stud marked *ac*. Its length is $1\frac{5}{8}$ inches less than the distance from the top of the sill to the under edges of the joists. Place it against the foundation and make sure it is plumb. Powder-actuated nails can be used for fastening it to the foundation. Erect stud *bd*, next to the chimney, in the same manner. Place the plate in position and nail it to the under edges of the joists.

Next, cut the studs, such as shown at e, f, and g, to be placed between the sill and plate. Space them 16 inches on centers, starting at the chimney corner. The resulting frame will appear like the framing shown in the B part of the illustration.

PROBLEM 3. The problem consists of erecting 2 by 4 framing for the partition shown between C and D in Figure 17.

SOLUTION. The first step consists of marking the position of corner D on the concrete floor. Also mark the position and width of the door opening. It is helpful to have the door frame at hand so that its width can be measured.

FIGURE 21. Partition framing.

Because of corner D, the sill for partition DE must be placed along with the sill for partition CD.

Place the sills as previously explained except that pieces c and d, shown in Figure 21, are short so as to allow for the door opening.

Erect the stud marked k as previously explained.

Because of the corner D, it is advisable to erect the plate n before any other studs are erected.

Stud m should be placed keeping in mind that it must be part of a three-member corner assembly. Studs e and f should be erected, in the positions indicated, so that studs g and h can be set in at the ends of sill pieces c and d. Piece j should be placed as indicated in the B part of the

FIGURE 22. Framing around I-beam.

VALANCE LIGHTING PLAN
FIGURE 23. Details of valance.

illustration. The framing around the door opening should leave ample room for the door frame to be placed and plumbed by means of shims.

The plate for partition *DE*, shown in Figure 17, should be fastened to headers as indicated in Figure 21.

PROBLEM 4. Plate V specifies that 8-inch I-beams must extend from the chimney to the foundations on the west and east sides of the basement. The two beams are indicated in Figure 17. The problem is to erect framing around the beam in the recreation area so that ceiling-surface material can be applied.

SOLUTION. The *A* and *B* parts of Figure 22 show suggested erection details.

PROBLEM 5. It can be assumed that valance lighting is required along the partition marked *AB* in Figure 17. The problem is to design and erect the valance.

SOLUTION. The details in Figure 23 show design and erection suggestions.

CHAPTER EIGHT

Kitchens

Aside from basements and bathrooms, there is nothing that so definitely dates houses, and nothing that so positively determines their convenience, attractiveness, and general desirability as the design and equipment of their kitchens.

Many exceptionally old houses, especially in rural areas, have kitchens which resemble the one shown in the upper part of Figure 1. Such kitchens date back to the cookstove era and to times before the first useful kitchen equipment was manufactured. Kitchens of such age are dismal places where the work required of housewives actually amounts to hard labor.

With the advent of the first electric refrigerators, improved sinks and cupboards became available and kitchens were somewhat improved. However, the equipment had to be scattered about kitchens wherever floor and wall space existed; this is shown in the upper part of Figure 2. Such kitchens are brighter and more cheery, but they lack convenience and efficiency.

With the coming of improved gas and electric ranges, along with better sinks and cupboards, kitchens like the one shown in the upper part of Figure 3 became possible. More attractive floor and wall surface materials brought about better over-all appearance. Yet, such kitchens are far from efficient. They require a great deal of walking and reaching, retain the feeling of a work area, and are not inviting so far as family activities are concerned.

FIGURE 1

FIGURE 2

FIGURE 3

The remodeled kitchens shown in the lower parts of Figures 1, 2, and 3 prove that any old kitchen can be remodeled and thus transformed into a cheery, beautiful, and efficient area.

For housewives, kitchens are activity centers where they spend a large part of every day. To them, remodeling means a great deal. For example, research has proved that a modern kitchen can reduce walking, movement, and reaching by at least 70, 74, and 60 per cent, respectively. Thus, remodeled kitchens are efficient activity areas where all tasks can be accomplished with much greater ease and in far less time.

For families, remodeled kitchens often become pleasant gathering places both during and between meals. In fact, statistics prove that where such kitchens exist, 85 per cent of the families are eating most of their meals amid such attractive surroundings.

Kitchen remodeling is a fascinating project. This chapter proposes to outline the items relating to such a project which require careful consideration, to call attention to modern equipment, and to show how to go about transforming old-fashioned kitchens into cheery and efficient areas.

BASIC KITCHEN TYPES

After a great deal of research and experimentation, the manufacturers of modern kitchen cabinets were able to design four basic kitchen types which suit the needs of any and all kitchen areas. In other words, no matter what shape or size a kitchen area may be, at least one of the types can be used in connection with it and in such a manner as to ensure convenience, efficiency, and attractiveness.

U Type. See part *A* of Figure 4. In the U-type kitchen, the major appliances and storage work cabinets are arranged on three sides of the area. Figure 5 shows a typical U-type kitchen in a small area.

L Type. See part *B* of Figure 4. In the L-type kitchen, the equipment is located on two adjacent walls. Corner wall and base cabinets are often

FIGURE 4. Basic kitchen patterns.

used in these kitchens so that corner space, which otherwise might be used, becomes usable. Figure 6 shows a typical L-type kitchen in one corner of a large area.

Parallel-wall Type. See part *C* of Figure 4. In the parallel-wall-type kitchen, the arrangement is particularly well adapted to a long, narrow area. This type of kitchen is seldom necessary and is therefore not illustrated by means of a picture.

FIGURE 5. A typical U-type kitchen in a small area.

FIGURE 6. A typical L-type kitchen in one corner of a large area.

<small>FIGURE 7.</small> A typical one-wall kitchen.

One-wall Type. See part *D* of Figure 4. In the one-wall-type kitchen, all equipment is lined up along one wall. This type of installation, somewhat as shown in Figure 7, is often used in small, minimum-cost houses where kitchen areas are only a few feet wide and when doors are necessary in both of the short walls.

Variations. There can be any number of variations from the four basic types, depending upon the sizes and shapes of kitchen areas.

The *E* part of Figure 4 shows the use of an island (sometimes known as a peninsula) in connection with an L-type kitchen in a large area.

The *F* part of Figure 4 shows where automatic laundry appliances and a serving bar (sometimes known as a snack bar) can be placed in a U-type kitchen, where space permits.

(A)

(B)

(C)

(D)

(E)

FIGURE 8. Details of nook plans.

D I N I N G   N O O K S

Built-in dining nooks usually follow three basic plans. The space available generally determines the appropriate type. In many cases, however, the layout is such that there is a choice. It then becomes a matter of selecting the type best suited to the needs.

Standard dimensions are shown in the *A* part of Figure 8. The recommended and standard 36-inch over-all height can be varied to meet particular conditions, such as a low window or other obstructions. However, it is best not to modify this dimension more than 5 or 6 inches.

FIGURE 9. A U-type nook in a variation of a U-type kitchen.

L Type. See part *B* of Figure 8. This type is flexible in that it can be used equally well in large or small corners, such as shown at *E* and *F* in Figure 4. With one side acting as a room divider, an interesting variation is possible. The table used with this nook can be movable or fastened to the floor.

U Type. See part *C* of Figure 8. This type of nook is best suited for large alcoves such as shown in Figure 9. The table should be movable.

Parallel Type. See part *D* of Figure 8. The type of nook can be used in a small alcove or in one corner of a kitchen. It requires a space 5′ 2″ wide and adequately seats four adults. The table should be movable.

As is shown in the *E* part of Figure 8, approximately 18 to 20 inches of table space is needed for a full-service setting. Table tops less than 24 inches wide are too narrow.

All of the foregoing nook equipment may be purchased ready to install.

ADVANTAGES OF REMODELING

The advantages obtainable, even by fairly economical remodeling, are extraordinary. The difference between old and modern kitchens is so great that such projects are the most interesting home-planning activity we can possibly engage in.

Study the top part of Figure 3. Notice in it the items listed in the following summary, keeping in mind that such items are typical of most old kitchens.

1. The sink is old-fashioned and offers little by way of modern conveniences. There is no place for storing cleaning supplies and the exposed plumbing is ugly. The two legs constitute a stumbling hazard. There is no counter space around the sink where soiled dishes, incoming vegetables, or bottles of milk can be placed prior to and immediately after washing.

2. The old-fashioned cupboards require too much reaching and were not designed for convenience or efficiency. Note that many appliances and other kitchen equipment must be stored on the cupboard counter where they constitute an eyesore and are difficult to reach.

3. The table is not shown in the picture. However, it is inconveniently placed in a corner across the kitchen. In preparing a meal, hundreds of steps must be taken from corner to corner because the limited storage space is all on one side of the room.

4. There is no work surface adjoining the range. To transfer cooked foods from cooking utensils to serving dishes, the food must be carried from the range to the table where serving dishes must be placed. Then the utensils must be returned to the range or taken to the sink to be rinsed. This flow of work requires hundreds more steps and unnecessary motions. Such inefficiency makes a housewife's work tedious and tiring.

5. The old tile walls, reaching from the floor level to the window sills, echo every sound and cause the kitchen to be noisy. Also, the tile design and installation are uninteresting.

6. The garbage-can corner is untidy, appears dirty, and certainly is not in keeping with modern standards of cleanliness considering that food is being prepared and served.

7. The window sills are too close to the sink and the height of the windows is out of good proportion.

8. The room lacks cheerfulness and gives the impression of a workshop rather than a pleasant area.

9. The old-fashioned floor covering appears to be worn and lacks any trace of beauty.

10. The ceiling is too high and makes the room look out of proportion.

11. There are no convenient electric outlets to use in connection with modern appliances.

12. There is no toe space under the cupboards.

Other items could be mentioned, but this brief summary shows the inconvenience of preparing, serving, and cleaning up after a meal in this old kitchen.

Now study the bottom part of Figure 3. The advantages of remodeling are immediately apparent. Hundreds of steps are saved as soon as the new cabinet sink (with or without an automatic dishwasher or a food disposer) is made the center of activity. Since its position does not have to be changed, plumbing costs are kept at a minimum. New cabinets, properly located, make the kitchen much more efficient in both storage space and work surface. The sink is flanked by handy wall and base cabinets on either side along with undercabinet storage space.

The refrigerator and range remain in the same position, but now ample counter space is conveniently placed beside each one. The floor covering has been replaced and the windows remodeled.

Note, too, that work has been simplified in this remodeled kitchen. Groceries can now be placed on the cabinet next to the sink. There is no retracing of steps to rinse food, store staples, or put perishables into the refrigerator. Ample work space as well as storage space has been provided.

By reducing steps, the remodeled kitchen cuts down on expenditure of much time and energy. It is much easier to maintain high standards of homemaking in such a kitchen, and the area is a pleasant place to be in.

Figures 1 and 2 can be studied for like contrasts.

WORK CENTERS

In order to accomplish convenience and efficiency, the various appliances and cabinets must be arranged accordingly. In other words, all kitchen items should be grouped so that work can be done to the best of advantage and in a manner somewhat similar to production lines in an industrial plant. For this purpose, the sink and its accompanying cabinets should be grouped into what is called a *work center*. The following centers are typical:

I. Sink center provides space for:

Vegetables	Dishes	Linen

II. Cooking center provides space for:

Pots and pans	Coffee and tea	Toaster
Griddle	Canned goods	Coffeemaker
Cooking cutlery	Dry packaged foods	

III. Food-preparation center provides space for:

Mixing bowls	Mixers	Staples
Baking pans	Spices	Perishables
Cutlery	Canned Goods	

IV. Serving center provides space for:

Dishes	Trays	Glasses
Bowls	Silverware	Island snack bar

V. Planning center provides space for:

Cookbooks	Telephone
Writing materials	Chair or stool

VI. Laundry center provides space for:

Soaps	Bleach
Starch	Irons

Work centers are indicated in the *A* to *F* parts of Figure 4 by means of the same Roman numerals shown in the foregoing lists.

CHOICE OF EQUIPMENT

Cabinet manufacturers offer standardized cabinet sizes in 3-inch multiples. Therefore, cabinets are available to fit almost any wall or floor space. The size and style of kitchens and financial budgets are the chief factors in determining what equipment shall be installed. (NOTE: Planning procedures are explained in subsequent pages.)

Sinks. Modern sinks are shown in Figures 1, 2, 3, 5, 6, and 7. A food-waste disposer is virtually a necessity in modern kitchens. Dishwashers are most convenient but not a necessity. The type of sink is an important factor and should be given special attention in terms of family size and habits.

Ranges. When families already own ranges which are in usable condition, they can be installed in remodeled kitchens. Future replacements and additions should be planned for when new kitchens are being installed.

Refrigerators. Same explanation applies as for ranges.

Base Cabinets. Modern base cabinets are shown in Figures 1, 2, 3, 5, 6, and 7. Ample storage and counterspace are necessities in up-to-date kitchens. Steps and time are saved if small appliances and utensils are located at spots where each is used most frequently. Also, when ample counter space is provided, work can proceed quickly and efficiently.

Merry-go-rounds. The best way to utilize corner spaces, such as shown in Figure 3, is by means of merry-go-rounds. By simply pushing the doors the shelves spin around, bringing shelf contents to the front. In Figure 10, merry-go-rounds are shown in both base and wall positions.

Cutting-board Cabinets. The *A* part of Figure 11 shows a convenient cutting-board cabinet. When the drawer is pulled out, the drawer head drops down and an edge-grained maple board moves up. It can be used for cutting and chopping, and as a base for a grinder.

FIGURE 10. Typical merry-go-rounds in base and wall positions.

Mixer Cabinets. The *B* part of Figure 11 shows a solution to the question of where to store a mixer. The bottom area of such cabinets can be used for the mixer bowls.

Wall Cabinets. Modern wall cabinets are shown in Figures 1, 2, 3, 5, 6, and 7. Such cabinets are primarily for storage space and should be planned for easy access to articles that are used daily. They can be obtained in widths ranging from 15 to 54 inches and in heights of 15, 18, and 30 inches. Double or single doors are available.

FIGURE 11. Cutting board and mixer cabinets.

FIGURE 12. Snack bar and laundry equipment form an island in this kitchen.

Islands. Islands are indicated in the *E* and *F* parts of Figure 4. In Figure 12, laundry equipment and a snack bar constitute an island. Note that shutters can be used partially to divide the work centers.

Suggested Cabinets and Accessories. The following suggestions relate to the work centers previously explained:

I. Sink Center. Suggested items:

Sink cabinet	Pan-storage cabinets	Vegetable bins
Drawer and pan cabinets	Tray-storage cabinets	Cabinets over sink

II. Cooking Center. Suggested items:

Drawer cabinets	Cutlery cabinets	Range-base cabinets
Pan cabinets	Above-range cabinets	

III. Food-preparation Center. Suggested items:

Mixer cabinets	Base cabinets
Cutting-board cabinets	Spice racks
Wall-storage cabinets	Deep-freeze unit
Above-refrigerator cabinets	

IV. Serving Center. Suggested items:

Island snack bar	Base-drawer cabinets
Base-tray cabinets	Tray cabinets

V. Planning Center. Suggested items:

Desk	Wall-storage cabinets

VI. Laundry Center. Suggested items:

Automatic washer	Ironer
Automatic dryer	Wall cabinets

CABINET DIMENSIONS

Typical cabinets and cabinet sizes are shown in Figure 13. Manufacturers of such equipment publish the dimensions for their full line of cabinets. It is wise to secure such data before starting to plan a remodeled kitchen.

FIGURE 13. Typical cabinets and details.

OTHER KITCHEN FACTORS

There are several other kitchen factors which must be kept in mind as we start to consider a remodeling project.

Lighting. Good lighting by both day and night is a most important consideration. If windows give adequate daytime lighting at the main preparation center, the situation is ideal. Sink and work counters are not necessarily placed directly under a window. However, they should be arranged so that the housewife does not work in a shadow.

There are many types of modern lighting fixtures to give well-distributed artificial illumination. Good overhead lighting is needed for general illumination. In addition, separate fixtures in each work area add to the comfort and efficiency of kitchens.

Electrical Convenience Outlets. When planning the lighting for kitchens, the available electrical outlets should be considered. With the ever-increasing use of electrical appliances, adequate wiring facilities are necessary in the modern kitchen.

It is best to plan the necessary electrical connections before the new installation is started. In some existing houses, an additional circuit may be required. This can be installed much more reasonably before other work is done. If future plans include major electrical appliances, such as a freezer, washing machine, or dishwasher, the electrical requirements of these should be considered and provided for in order to save future costs.

Future Plans. Since a modern kitchen is built to last a lifetime, future needs should be visualized. For example, a 27-inch base cabinet can be placed against a sink in order that an automatic dishwasher may be installed in its place at some future time. In the same manner, enough spaces near ranges and refrigerators can be planned so that larger models may be installed some time later without tearing out base or wall cabinets.

CABINET-TOP MATERIALS

Manufacturers of kitchen cabinets generally offer a selection of cabinet-top materials including such materials as Formica, linoleum, and maple wood. Any of these materials can be specified.

WALLS AND FLOORS

Since remodeled kitchens often become additional living rooms, as much thought should be given to the decorating of them as is given to decorating and planning other rooms in houses.

Walls. See Chapter 5 for suggested soilproof types of wall-surface materials.

Many plastic wall coverings, in the form of wallpaper, are also available in a great variety of patterns and colors. Such materials resist all types of staining and can be washed repeatedly.

Floors. See Chapter 6 for suggested floor coverings.

Coverings such as linoleum, asphalt tile, and plastic tile are colorful and easy to keep clean. They also offer a certain amount of resilience which helps to make them comfortable surfaces on which to stand.

SOFFITS

In Figure 6, the dark band between the tops of the wall cabinets and the ceiling is the soffit. In other words, the tops of the wall cabinets do not reach the ceiling and we must provide soffits to fill the intervening space.

Ordinarily, the tops of wall cabinets are about 7' 0" above the floor. Thus, in a kitchen area having an 8' 0" ceiling height, we would need soffits about 1' 0" deep. Ceiling heights vary and soffit depths differ accordingly. However, if a ceiling is more than 8' 6" above the floor, it should be lowered, as explained in Chapter 4. Otherwise, the new cabinets will make the room appear out of good proportion. Such a condition can be visualized by imagining that the soffit had been omitted in Figure 6.

The *A* part of Figure 14 shows a section view of a soffit built in an existing kitchen area. The framing is composed of 2 by 4's and the sheathing is ¼-inch plywood.

The first step in the construction of such a soffit is to determine the distance that point *a* must be above the floor. This will vary according to the brand of steel or wood cabinets to be installed. Next, determine the required length of the soffit—how many cabinets (as indicated in Figure 6) it must cover. The widths of soffits also vary according to the brand of cabinets to be installed but are never much less or much more than 13 inches.

FIGURE 14. Details of soffit.

Nail the 2 by 4 marked *b* over the wall plaster, making sure that the 3½-inch nails are driven at locations where they will enter the studs. Nail the 2 by 4 marked *c* over the ceiling plaster, making sure that the nails are driven at locations where they will enter the joists.

Cut short pieces of 2 by 4 to fit at *d* between *c* and *e* pieces. These short pieces should be spaced 16 inches on centers. The pieces at *j* should be spaced 16 inches on centers, notched to fit over piece *e,* and nailed to piece *b.*

The plywood sheathing can be applied as explained in Chapter 5. Use a piece of molding where the plywood meets the ceiling.

The *B* part of the illustration indicates how 2 by 2's can be used for the framing.

Both the *A* and *B* parts of the illustration show the soffits at right angles to the ceiling joists. But, if soffits must be constructed on two adjacent sides of a kitchen area, the joists will be in a different position on one side.

The *C* part of the illustration indicates a case where the joists are parallel to the soffit and not spaced so that the piece marked *g* can be nailed to one of them. In a case like this several short pieces, such as the one marked *j,* should be nailed to the studding so that braces can be nailed to them. The other ends of the braces should be nailed to the lower framing member of the soffit, as shown at *k.* A few toggle or molly bolts (see Chapter 2), can be placed as shown at *h* to secure the piece *g* in proper position.

FIGURE 15. Hanging cabinets over an island.

HANGING CABINETS

Figure 15 shows an island composed of a range and a planning center. The cabinets above the island must be hung from the ceiling because they are away from the wall.

Figure 16 indicates one method by which off-wall cabinets (Figure 15) may be securely hung. The elevation view shows the wall line and

FIGURE 16. Details of hanging cabinets.

the two pipe hangers necessary. The section view indicates the construction of the soffit and the casing for the cabinets. Note that the tops of the pipe hangers must be so located that the fastening screws will penetrate a ceiling joist.

As shown in Figure 16, the soffit can be used to house indirectlighting equipment, or it can be extended to the ceiling as indicated in Figure 15.

FILLER STRIPS

To make possible the installation of standard-sized wall and base cabinets in any kitchen area, regardless of its dimensions, filler strips of varying widths and heights are available. Such fillers create a finished appearance and do away with dust-catching gaps between cabinets. They are also valuable as a means of overcoming the difficulties caused by out-of-plumb structural details. Typical sizes and types are shown in Figures 13 and 17. A typical application is illustrated in Figure 24.

FIGURE 17. Base- and wall-cabinet filler strips.

KITCHEN-AREA REMODELING

The kitchen areas in most old houses are closely associated with pantries, laundry rooms, or back porches.

The pantries date back to an era prior to the introduction of useful storage cabinets. They are inconvenient to use, cause hundreds of extra steps, and are difficult to keep clean. In connection with modern kitchens, such spaces can be used otherwise and to much better advantage.

The laundry rooms also date back to an early era when hot water came from reservoirs in kitchen cook stoves and when "washing" was a major chore. Such rooms can now be used for other purposes and to much better advantage.

Back porches date back to a time when architects thought a great deal of "gingerbread" decoration added to the beauty of houses. In our modern way of life, we have no need for such porches.

In order to discuss the remodeling of old kitchens as a means of preparing them for modern equipment and to make them convenient and

FIGURE 18. Remodeled kitchen area.

efficient, let us assume the floor plan shown in the X part of Figure 18. Let us further assume that the dimensions of the kitchen are approximately 8′ 0″ wide and 14′ 0″ long, that the pantry is about 6′ 0″ by 7′ 0″, and that the laundry room is close to 8′ 0″ by 7′ 0″.

The kitchen dimensions are ample, so far as the needs of modern equipment are concerned (see Figures 22 and 23). A modern sink can be placed in the same location as the old sink in order to save plumbing expense. Plumbing is an important item, so far as remodeling expense is concerned, and we should always try to use existing water pipes, vents, and sewer connections.

A first-floor lavatory, including a water closet and washbowl, is a handy addition to any old house. Part of the pantry space could be used for such a purpose. Plumbing connections are not far away. Thus, the new piping would not cost too much.

Because of the two doors which lead to other areas of the house, the corner of the kitchen where they are located cannot be used for a dining area. However, the old laundry room will not be needed as such and could therefore be converted into a pleasant dining area. The partition between a and b could be removed and the door enlarged so that the area could be closely associated with a new patio in the yard.

The Y part of the illustration indicates how the floor plan will appear after the remodeling previously discussed is completed.

The old pantry area has been transformed into a convenient lavatory and two spaces for large storage cabinets. The partition between a and b has been removed. Glass doors have been installed so that they afford a view of and open out into the new patio. A new single window has been installed at K. Windows H and J were not changed.

Work centers can be installed in the locations marked A, B, and C. The center at C can be a combination of range and snack bar, somewhat similar to the island center shown in the E part of Figure 4.

Structural Considerations. If the joists in the kitchen ceiling extend continuously from wall EG to wall DF, the removal of partition ab can be accomplished without complications. However, if shorter joists, such as the ones indicated by the dashed lines, have their bearing on partition ab, then a beam must be substituted for the partition.

The A part of Figure 19 shows how the partition ab supports the ends of such joists as indicated in the Y part of Figure 18. When the partition is removed, a beam such as shown in the B or C parts of Figure 19 must be used. Either of these beams will support the joists and will not extend below the ceiling surface. The ends of a beam, such as shown at B, must be supported by two 4 by 4 columns placed in each wall at a and b. The ends of a beam, such as shown at C, must be supported by one 4 by 4 column placed in each wall at a and b.

FIGURE 19. Details of joist support when bearing partitions are removed.

Before the partition can be removed and while the beam is being installed, the joists must be temporarily supported as explained in Chapter 7.

In order to install a new and wider door in the partition between E and M, as shown in the Y part of Figure 18, the old studs must be removed and a new rough frame for the door constructed, as indicated in Figure 20. If the joists run from wall DF to wall EG, their ends, over the door opening, must be temporarily supported while the new framing is being installed.

If balloon framing is encountered, the header shown in Figure 20 must be extended to R and S.

In order to replace the two double-hung windows, shown at K in the

X part of Figure 18, with one large window, the old window frames can simply be removed and a new frame, having the same over-all dimensions, substituted for them.

The partition and door opening for the new lavatory should be constructed as shown in Figure 20, except that two 2 by 4's can be used instead of the 4 by 8 beam.

BOTTOM OF PLATE

R

4"x8" HEADER

S

STUD NEAR M
(SEE Y PART OF
FIGURE 18)

2-2"x4"
STUDS

CORNER

DOOR OPENING TO
SUIT FRAME

M

TOP OF SILL

E

WESTERN FRAMING

FIGURE 20. Details of opening for new door in frame wall.

PRELIMINARY PLANNING

In the foregoing explanations, we discussed the remodeling of a kitchen area. However, the remodeling work did not change the size or shape of the kitchen proper. In such cases, all of the explanations in the balance of this chapter are next in regular order.

In cases where the sizes or shapes of old kitchens are to be changed, the planning order should be as shown in the following four steps, all of which are explained in this chapter under like headings:

1. Preliminary planning   3. How to plan a new kitchen
2. Kitchen-area remodeling   4. Financial considerations

Plan to Save Steps. Most of the kitchen time of the average housewife is spent either working at or walking between the three major pieces of equipment: the sink, the range, and the refrigerator. Therefore, they should be placed as close to each other as possible. However, adequate counter surface and storage room near these pieces of equipment should not be sacrificed.

Where very large, old kitchens are to be remodeled, it is important to consider condensing the areas. The use of an island or peninsula, as indicated in the *E* part of Figure 4 or as suggested in connection with the *Y* part of Figure 18, tends to partition such areas effectively. Another arrangement is shown in Figure 15.

Plan for Convenience. Every housewife has her own way of doing things. Every family has peculiar likes and dislikes. Thus, kitchens should be planned to suit the convenience and habits of everyone concerned.

Plan for Efficiency. Provide such equipment as will help to best advantage in all the work done in kitchens. Any housewife can write a list of the kitchen work she does and then make plans for her new kitchen accordingly.

Check Points. The following points will be of help in preliminary planning work:

1. Provide plenty of electric outlets for toasters, mixers, clocks, coffeemakers, etc.

2. Keep main work centers small but not confining.

3. Plan refrigerator locations so that their doors do not obstruct activities.

4. Do not stint on counter surfaces.

5. As nearly as possible, kitchen arrangements should be planned so that traffic stays out of main work centers.

6. Keep all accessories close to the point of their use.

7. Provide space for long-handled items.

8. Make sure that all necessary utensils and other small equipment can be stored when not in use.

9. Keep any known future requirements in mind and make provisions for them.

HOW TO PLAN A NEW KITCHEN

The following explanations relate to the planning or arrangement of appliances and cabinets within a kitchen area.

Such planning must be done in one of two ways, depending on whether the shape and size of the kitchen is *known* or *unknown*. For example, the shape and size of the kitchen indicated in Figure 18 is *known,* owing to the fact that the remodeling plans did not include changing the original dimensions. The shape of a kitchen would be *unknown* if remodeling plans included reducing the size of a very large old kitchen.

When the shape and size are *known,* we can plan the arrangement of appliances and cabinets without further consideration. When the shape and size are *unknown,* we must carry on such planning for *two* reasons: to determine the required shape and size and to determine arrangement.

Known Shape and Size. When we know the shape and size of a kitchen area, we can use the *template* or *drawing* method of planning the arrangement.

TEMPLATE METHOD. Once we have decided what appliances and cabinets we want in a new kitchen, this process consists of drawing a plan view of the kitchen to the $\frac{1}{2}'' = 1'\ 0''$ scale and also drawing plan views of all equipment and cabinets to the same scale on stiff paper or cardboard. We can then cut out such equipment and cabinet representations and move them around on the plan view of the kitchen. In this manner, we can try out any number of different arrangements until we find one that is satisfactory. Refrigerators and ranges should be separated from cabinets by 1-inch-wide spaces. Both base- and wall-cabinet arrangements can be planned in this manner.

DRAWING METHOD. This process consists of drawing a plan view of the kitchen to the ½″ = 1′ 0″ scale and then drawing the plan views of the appliances and cabinets on the same drawing. Pieces of tissue paper can be placed over the first drawing and other trials made.

Unknown Shape and Size. When we do not know the shape and size a remodeled kitchen will have, the *drawing* method is best suited to the purpose.

Use the ½″ = 1′ 0″ scale to draw a partial plan view of the old kitchen. Select two walls, such as *FL* and *FG* in the *X* part of Figure 18, which are not likely to be changed. Then, by the use of tissue paper, make several trial arrangements of the desired appliances and cabinets. By this procedure, the minimum size of the kitchen and its shape can be determined. This is a most important part of the planning and must be done accurately. Otherwise, any one or more of several costly and disappointing mistakes could happen. This work is not at all difficult and anyone can accomplish it with ease.

PROBLEM 1. It can be assumed that we want the following appliances in a new kitchen: (NOTE: The cabinet numbers shown here are illustrated in Figure 13.)

Appliances:

> Refrigerator, 28 inches wide
> Range, 40 inches wide
> Sink, 30 inches long

Base Cabinets:

> One 24C, 24 inches wide One 45CB-R, 46 inches wide
> One 36C, 36 inches wide One 18D, 18 inches wide
> One M6R, 36 by 36 inches One desk, 38 inches long
> One UT, 9 inches wide

Wall Cabinets:

> One 3618W, 36 inches wide (to be used above refrigerator)
> One 2430W, 24 inches wide (to match 24C base cabinet)
> One 4218W, 42 inches wide (to be used above range)
> One 2730W, 21 inches wide

One 4230W, 42 inches wide
Three 3030W, each 30 inches wide
One 1330CS, 9 inches wide

It can also be assumed that the size and shape of the kitchen area is *known* and as shown in Figure 21. The problem is to plan the arrangement of the appliances and cabinets to suit our needs and convenience.

FIGURE 21. Floor plan for Problem 1.

SOLUTION. Our first inclination would probably be to place the refrigerator near to door X where it would be handy so far as incoming milk and other perishable groceries are concerned. However, there is a window next to the door on one side, and the space on the other side of it is obviously not suited for appliances or cabinets.

In order to take advantage of the existing plumbing, the new sink should be placed in the same position that the old one occupied. The center line of the new sink should coincide with the center line of the window.

The merry-go-round should be placed in a corner to the right of the sink.

The range and its two side cabinets require a total of more than 8 lineal feet and should therefore be placed along wall AB.

FIGURE 22. Final arrangement of appliances and base cabinets in answer to Problem 1.

FIGURE 23. Final arrangement of wall cabinets in answer to Problem 1.

We can assume that after two or three trial drawings we decided upon the arrangement shown in Figure 22, which allows space for a nook or a table and chairs in one corner near the doors. The arrangement is good because all work centers are conveniently placed and because efficiency is possible.

The arrangement of wall cabinets can be planned by means of more trial drawings. The short cabinets, 4218W and 3618W, are to be placed over the range and the refrigerator. Other wall units can be placed where they will be convenient and according to their widths and the widths of base units directly under them.

ELEVATION M

FIGURE 24. Elevation A in answer to Problem 1.

Figure 23 shows the final arrangement.

Figure 24 shows an elevation view of all the equipment as it is to be placed along wall *AB*. This view can be visualized if we imagine that we are standing at *M* in Figures 22 and 23.

Note that a filler strip is required to finish off one side of cabinet 4230W.

Note, too, that a soffit is indicated above all wall cabinets.

HOW TO INSTALL CABINETS

The following explanations and illustrations have to do with typical cabinet installation procedures. There are some variations so far as various brands are concerned, but for the most part, all procedures are similar.

Figure 25 shows placement dimensions for base and wall cabinets. These dimensions will be helpful in laying out cabinet positions. Note that the tops of wall cabinets should not be more than 82 inches above the floor.

FIGURE 25. Cabinet-placement dimensions.

Fastening Cabinets to Walls. There are two methods of fastening cabinets to walls. Either method may be used for all ordinary installation work.

HANGER METHOD. Manufacturers supply steel hanger rods which can be fastened to studs by means of wood screws. The cabinets are then hung on the hangers. When masonry walls are encountered, the hangers must be attached to them by means of such masonry fasteners as explained in Chapter 2.

DIRECTLY TO STUDS. A somewhat less complicated method consists of screwing the cabinet backs directly to the studs. The screws should be long enough to go through the plaster and penetrate well into the studs.

Checking Walls. As old-fashioned cupboards are being removed from walls, the plaster should be checked to locate possible low spots. Wherever such irregularities exist, shims must be used so that the cabinets will be level and plumb. Figure 26 shows how a long straightedge can be used for the checking operation.

FIGURE 26. Checking wall irregularities in old kitchen.

Layout. After all old cupboards, the sink, and baseboards have been removed, the exact locations of the new cabinets and appliances should be outlined on the plaster as shown in Figure 27. The top line must be 82 inches above the floor (see Figure 25) and should be drawn with the help of a carpenter's level. Hold the level against the wall and draw the line along its top edge. The 82-inch dimension should be measured from the highest point on the floor. Note that the exact location of each appliance and cabinet is indicated by a rectangle and by its name or number. The locations should be carefully checked as a means of making absolutely sure that they are correct.

Installing Wall Cabinets. Wall cabinets should be installed first, beginning with corner units such as indicated in Figure 28. Place the hanger bars on top of the 82-inch line and screw them to the studs. If hangers are not being employed, drill holes through the cabinet backs and use 1½-inch No. 12 wood screws. Check the cabinet levelness and plumbness after only one screw has been put in. As each cabinet is installed next to a preceding one, put in the top screws (as indicated in the cabinets) only

FIGURE 27. Marking locations of cabinets on walls.

and bolt the adjacent cabinet sides together. Follow this procedure until the location for the first filler strip, if one is needed, is reached. Fillers generally have four holes that line up with holes in the cabinets. The filler is attached to an adjacent cabinet as shown in Figure 29. After all wall cabinets have been hung, leveled, plumbed, and bolted together, insert bottom screws in the backs of them.

Installing Base Cabinets. As in the case of wall cabinets, corner base cabinets should be installed first in U- and L-shaped kitchens. Follow the same procedure as outlined for wall cabinets. Hold the cabinets in posi-

FIGURE 28. Corner cabinets should be installed first.

FIGURE 29. Installation of filler strip.

FIGURE 30. Installation of sink cabinet.

FIGURE 31. Complete installation.

tion so that their top edges are even with the chalk lines on the wall (note the 34½- and 36-inch dimensions in Figure 25). Drill holes in the cabinets where necessary to contact studding. Make sure that the cabinets are level and plumb. Use shims as may be required. Anchor all cabinets to studs using at least two 2-inch No. 10 wood screws, and bolt them together through their adjoining sides.

Installing Sink Cabinet. See Figure 30. To install the sink cabinets, remove the knockouts from the bottom so that the holes coincide with the locations of existing pipes, or make new holes as may be required. Set the cabinet level and plumb. Use shims where necessary.

Figure 31 shows the completed kitchen.

FINANCIAL CONSIDERATIONS

There are three ways in which remodeling may be carried on and paid for. Any one of them can be employed, depending upon homeowners' budgets and preferences.

Outright Payment. If a homeowner desires to pay the remodeling cost all at one time, the following procedures are recommended:

1. Do the planning as previously explained. Then make up drawings, such as indicated in Figures 22 and 23, which show all appliances and cabinets by name and number.

2. Take the drawings to two or more kitchen-cabinet dealers and ask them to make up an estimate of total cost including just the materials or materials and labor, as may be desired.

Unit-by-Unit Purchase. Some homeowners may prefer to buy and pay for one or more appliances or cabinets at a time and in that manner gradually accomplish the remodeling. In such cases, the following steps are recommended:

1. Do the planning as previously explained. Then make up drawings such as shown in Figures 22 and 23.

2. Ask a kitchen-cabinet dealer for an estimate of cost for each of the appliances and cabinets. Such an estimate will be helpful when planning a unit-by-unit installation.

The following unit-by-unit plan is based on Figures 22 and 23.

1. Buy and install the new sink and sink cabinet first. This appliance constitutes a basis for all other and later installations and it will be greatly enjoyed.

2. Next, install the 36C and MGR units to complete one corner. The range and refrigerator can then be moved to their permanent locations and the base units for the *AB* wall will be mostly complete. Also, work surfaces will have been provided.

3. The UT, 45CB-R and 18D units can be the next step. These units will provide more storage and counter surface.

4. The 24C unit can be added next because it provides a chopping and cutting surface.

5. The wall cabinets are less expensive than the base units and can be purchased in groups. For example, the three 3030W units can be installed next.

In like manner, the balance of the units can be purchased and installed as budgets permit. In the meantime, more and more convenience and efficiency are provided.

Extended Payment. If homeowners desire to install all of the appliances at one time and pay the total cost over an extended period, the following procedures are suggested:

1. Make up drawings as previously suggested.

2. Obtain estimates from kitchen-cabinet dealers.

The following financing plans are available in most regions of the country:

1. F.H.A. No down payment, three years to pay.

2. Open-end mortgage. Remodeling cost added to an existing mortgage. Number of payments increased.

3. Open-end mortgage. This plan increases the size of monthly payments.

4. Refinanced mortgage. Many homeowners have paid off so much of

their original mortgage that the mortgagor will be interested in re-financing to include remodeling costs.

TYPICAL PROJECTS

The following projects can be made in home workshops. All required materials are easily available:

Serving Bar. Figure 32 shows the details for the serving bar indicated in the *F* part of Figure 4. Only 2 by 4's, ¼-inch-hardwood plywood and linoleum are required.

FIGURE **32.** Details of serving bar.

Seat. The *A* part of Figure 33 shows the details for a corner seat which can be used along with a table in a dining area such as shown in Figure 22. The same details can be used to make a seat such as indicated in the

B part of Figure 33. Only 2 by 4's ¼-inch hardwood plywood, 2-inch air foam, and seat-cover material are required.

FIGURE 33. Details of seat.

CHAPTER NINE

Attics

It is surprising how the wasted space in attics can be transformed into efficient and attractive living areas to serve the needs of growing families and to make old houses suitable for our modern way of life.

Millions of old houses around the country were built during an era when popular design features included high roofs. Such houses are usually of sound construction and constitute economic advantages in terms of current building costs. The high roofs are generally irregular in shape, but large attic spaces are available for remodeling purposes.

In order to visualize remodeling possibilities and to see how various roof and attic shapes can be used to advantage, we shall briefly study a few examples.

The upper part of Figure 1 shows part of the attic space in connection with an L-shaped house. The entrance to the space is located on the left-hand side but is not visible in the picture.

The gable roof is partially supported and held in position by means of vertical 2 by 4 studs and by horizontal 1 by 5 collar beams. The space is amply long and wide. Three windows assure enough light and ventilation. The distance between the collar beams and the floor constitutes a satisfactory ceiling height. Therefore, the space is ideal for remodeling purposes.

The lower part of the illustration shows the same attic space after it was transformed into a small apartment. Every foot of available space was used. An efficient but compact kitchen was built into one wall. Space for a bed-type couch was provided in a picture alcove. A com-

FIGURE 1

FIGURE 2

FIGURE 3

bination desk and dressing table was built into another wall. The sloping part of the ceiling was made attractive by means of a dark-colored fascia board and light-colored tile. The remodeled area is completely modern and a worthwhile addition to the house. Such an apartment may be used by a young couple or by elderly members of a family.

The upper part of Figure 2 shows an attic space under an exceptionally high valley-type roof. The lower part of the same illustration shows the results obtained by the erection of a lower ceiling and knee walls. Such an area is ideal for recreation and hobby purposes.

The upper part of Figure 3 shows an attic space under a gable and valley roof. The lower part of the same illustration proves that such a space can be transformed into a pleasant bedroom.

Remodeling an attic is an interesting and rewarding project that can be accomplished at reasonable cost. This chapter proposes to outline the items relating to attics which require careful consideration and to explain typical examples of the planning and structural work required.

REASONS FOR REMODELING

The items listed in the following summary constitute practical reasons for attic remodeling:

1. Separate bedrooms for growing children
2. Recreation area for small children
3. Secluded and quiet apartment for elderly members of a family
4. A second bathroom
5. A music or hobby room
6. A study or office for the man of a family
7. Rentable space
8. Additional and clean storage space
9. A sewing room

REMODELING CONSIDERATIONS

Inexperienced mechanics and homeowners are apt to do a great deal of preliminary planning and thinking without taking into consideration several aspects of cost or allied work. This is a common mistake that always leads to unexpected expense, delays, and probable disappointment. As a means of helping readers to avoid such a mistake, the following summary of preliminary considerations is set forth:

Dormers. In many instances, attic spaces do not have enough windows to provide ample light and proper ventilation, especially when partitions are employed to create more than one room. For example, let us assume that the *V* part of Figure 4 shows the plan view of a typical attic space. Two small windows are indicated, one at either end of the space. The *W* part of the illustration indicates a possible remodeling plan that includes two rooms with a hall between them. Both rooms would be inadequately lighted, but unless all of the doors were kept open, proper ventilation could not be possible. Good ventilation is of great importance in attic rooms, owing to the fact that appreciable summer heat gets through even well-insulated roofs.

In order to provide the necessary light and ventilation in such cases, additional windows must be provided. This is accomplished by means of *dormers.*

TYPES OF DORMERS. The *X* part of Figure 4 illustrates what is called a *continuous dormer.* Two or more windows can be installed, depending upon the length of a house. This type of dormer can also be constructed so that the top of its roof, as shown at *m,* intersects the main ridge of the house, as indicated at *n.* Also, the vertical wall, as shown at *t,* can be extended to the vertical plane of the main house wall indicated at *r.* In like manner, the gables of the dormer, as shown at *x,* can be extended to the same vertical plane as the main gable shown at *y.* Such a dormer tends to detract from the exterior appearance of a house and should therefore be constructed only on the rear elevation.

The *Y* part of Figure 4 illustrates what are called *individual dormers.* Depending upon the length of a house, as from *a* to *b,* two or more such dormers can be constructed to provide as many windows. This type of dormer can be constructed on either the front or the rear elevation of a house.

As indicated by *GHJ* in the *Z* part of the illustration, the shape of an attic space is triangular when a gable roof is involved. Near the walls, as at *G* and *H*, the roof is so close to the floor that part of the space, such as between *G* and *L*, is not usable. As shown at *EF*, knee walls are therefore necessary. Thus, the usable space is bounded by the letters *L K C D E F*. If an extended, continuous dormer is constructed, the usable space will be

FIGURE 4. Types of dormers.

increased to that bounded by the letters *G M C D E F*. Such a dormer could be constructed on the *AB* side of the plan shown on the *W* part of the illustration to provide more space, light, and air for both rooms.

Individual dormers do not provide an appreciable increase in usable space.

Dormers of both types are expensive, unless a homeowner plans to eliminate labor cost by doing the work himself.

Area of Attic Space. Unless an attic space, such as bounded by the letters *L K C D E F* in the *Z* part of Figure 4, has an area equal to that of an average-sized room, remodeling is not recommended.

The probable area of remodeled attic space can be estimated by assuming that knee walls should not be less than 4 feet high. Hold a tape measure at vertical points along a rafter until a length of it 4 feet long just touches the floor. This will locate the knee-wall positions. The distance between such walls multiplied by the length of the attic will give the probable area. This area can be compared with the area of an average-sized room.

The width of a remodeled attic area, such as between *L* and *F,* should be at least 10 feet. If the width is less, the area cannot be used to good advantage so far as furniture is concerned.

After estimating the positions of knee walls, it is wise to make a fairly accurate drawing. Use the $\frac{1}{8}'' = 1'\ 0''$ scale. Then, as explained in Chapter 8, cut out templates representing required furniture. Place the templates on the drawing to determine if the available space is ample.

Ceiling Height. Most gable roofs require collar beams such as shown in the upper part of Figure 1 and by *CD* in the *Z* part of Figure 4. Such structural members should not be moved.

Unless the distance between the bottom edges of the collar beams and the floor is at least 7' 6", the space is not suitable for remodeling.

In cases where the bottom edges of the collar beams are more than 9' 0" above the floor, a new ceiling exactly 8' 0" above the floor is recommended. Figure 5 shows an assumed case where the bottom edges of the collar beams are 10' 0" above the attic floor. As indicated, new ceiling joists can be erected so that the ceiling will be 8' 0" above the floor. This ceiling height creates much better room proportions and allows the use of standard-length wall planks and panels.

If the distance from *A* to *B* is not over 15' 0", 2 by 4's can be used as joists. They should be spaced the same distance apart as the rafters. Nail them at both ends to the rafters. As each joist is erected, measure the distance above the floor and use a level so that all joists will be in the same horizontal plane. Nail two continuous 1 by 4's along the top edges of the joists to stiffen them.

If the distance from *A* to *B* is more than 15′ 0″, 2 by 6's should be used as joists.

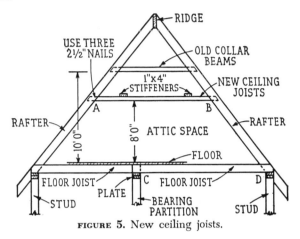

FIGURE 5. New ceiling joists.

SIZE OF FLOOR JOISTS. In most houses, attic floor joists are supported at one end by means of a bearing partition somewhat as indicated in Figure 5. The distance from *C* to *D* is called the *span* of the joists.

It is not uncommon to encounter instances where 2 by 4's are used as attic floor joists. However, when such spaces are to be used as living areas,

FIGURE 6. How to reinforce joists which are too small.

2 by 4 joists are too small and are not permitted by city building codes. Thus, they must be reinforced as indicated in Figure 6.

When spans do not exceed 12 feet, 2 by 6's may be used as reinforcement. For spans ranging from 12 to 16 feet, 2 by 8's are recommended. For longer spans, 2 by 10's should be used.

To install the new joists, scrape away enough of the plaster keys so that the joists contact the lathing. This scraping must be done with care so as to avoid cracking the ceiling plaster. Nail the new joists to the old ones using $3\frac{1}{2}$-inch nails spaced no more than 12 inches apart. Make sure that the ends of the new joists are properly seated on the bearing surfaces, such as shown at C and D in Figure 5.

If joists of any size are spaced more than 16 inches on centers, additional joists must be placed between the old ones so that the floor boards do not have a span of more than 15 inches between joists.

Condition of Roofing. Existing roofing materials, such as shingles, should be inspected to make sure that no roof leaks are possible. Once an attic space is remodeled and decorated, even small roof leaks could raise havoc.

A leak in a shingle roof can be located by examination of the attic side during the time rain is falling. The point where water drips may not be at the leak, for water will often run for long distances along rafters before falling. The path of the water should be traced back to the leak.

A leak from a shingle that is split, or otherwise defective, can be closed with a piece of single-ply tar paper. Raise the end of the defective shingle slightly, using a putty knife, and slip the paper under it. Paste the paper in place by means of roofing cement.

A badly curled shingle should be flattened by splitting, a piece of tar paper placed beneath the split, and the parts of the shingle nailed through its exposed ends, using rustproof shingle nails.

Reroofing. When shingles are in obviously bad condition, reroofing is a logical procedure. This will avoid any possibilities of trouble in the future and give a house a smart, sleek appearance. New asphalt shingles can be applied directly over the old shingles.

Where old wood shingles are involved, the reroofing procedure is as follows.

1. Redrive all protruding nails.

2. Add new nails where necessary to fasten all of the old shingles securely. This is an important part of the work and must be done thoroughly.

3. Slit all curled shingles and nail down the parts.

4. Replace missing shingles with new ones.

5. As indicated in Figure 7, cut back the old shingles at the eaves far enough to permit the application of a 1- by 4-inch wood edging. This board is not shown in the illustration but is under the metal drip edge. Nail the edging firmly to the existing roof boards so that its outside edge projects beyond the edge of the roof boards the same distance that the old wood shingles did.

FIGURE 7. Details of reroofing.

6. Apply pieces of beveled siding, as feathering strips. This procedure assures a smooth and practically level surface on which to apply the new shingles.

7. Nail the metal drip edge in the positions shown in the illustration.

8. Nail the eaves flashing strip over the old shingles as indicated. This strip should be at least 12 inches wide.

9. Apply heavy roofing paper along valleys. For this purpose the paper should be at least 24 inches wide.

10. In cases where a roof intersects a wall, apply a strip of heavy roofing paper, as indicated in the illustration.

11. Apply the new shingles as recommended by the manufacturer. Use rustproof nails which are at least 1¾ inches long.

If an old, badly weathered asphalt-shingle roof is being re-covered, nail down or cut away all loose shingles; remove or redrive all loose and protruding nails, and remove all badly worn edging strips and replace them with new ones.

When asphalt shingles are to be laid on top of old roll roofing, these three steps are recommended:

1. Slit all buckles and nail the segments down smoothly.

2. Remove all loose and protruding nails.

3. If some of the old roofing has been torn away to expose the deck, inspect exposed deck areas carefully for loose or pitchy knots and excessively resinous areas. Cover any defects with sheet-metal patches made from galvanized iron, painted tin, zinc, or copper, approximately 26 gage.

Regardless of the kind of old roofing being prepared for asphalt shingles, the last step is to sweep the roof thoroughly clean of debris. A smooth, sound deck surface is a basic requirement for fully satisfactory asphalt-shingle application.

Climbing Suggestions. No climbing should be done without the type of ladders recommended by the American Ladder Institute and the National Safety Council. Lightweight extension ladders may be used for practically all purposes on one- and two-story houses. They are available in wood and lightweight metal.

When using an extension ladder against a house, the foot of it should be placed away from the house a distance equal to one-fourth the length of the ladder, as shown at Z in Figure 8. For example, if a house is 16 feet high, the foot of the ladder, d, should be placed a distance ad, or 4 feet, from the wall of the house. The ladder height should be adjusted to at least 20 feet, or 4 feet longer than the height it is to reach.

If possible, the top of a ladder, such as shown at C in the Z part of the illustration, should reach about 3 feet above the corner of the roof. Never try to get on a ladder that reaches only to or below a cornice.

As shown at W, a so-called chicken ladder should be made and used to reach various parts of a roof. A ridge piece, such as shown in the X part of the illustration, should hook over the ridge of the roof. The X part of the illustration also shows how the rails of the chicken ladder should be nailed or screwed to the 2 by 6 ridge piece. An extension ladder and a chicken ladder may be moved from place to place where roof work is required.

Make sure that the rails (feet) of a ladder are level. The Y part of the illustration shows how a block of wood can be used to assure safety.

FIGURE 8. Proper use of climbing equipment.

Stairs. The importance of stairs should not be overlooked at the time remodeling is being considered. This one item will have a great deal to do with the enjoyment and use of remodeled attic space.

It is not uncommon to encounter attic stairs which are steep and difficult to walk up or down. Such stairs may have narrow treads and high risers both of which pose a definite hazard.

Figure 9 shows recommended dimensions for attic stairs. To be safe, the treads on such stairs should be at least 10 inches wide. The risers should be about 7½ inches high. Headroom should be no less than 6½ feet so that people of average height will not bump their heads at A. If treads are less than 10 inches wide or if risers are much more than 8 inches high, stairs are difficult to use and somewhat dangerous.

Unless attic stairways are at least 2½ feet wide, the movement of furniture up or down them is likely to be either difficult or impossible.

In most cases, attic stairs cannot be rebuilt without seriously disturbing surrounding partitions, joists, studs, or other structural details. Therefore, rebuilding is not recommended.

Readers are urged to study their attic stairs in the light of the foregoing explanations and to decide for themselves if the stairs are suitable and safe.

FIGURE 9. Stair dimensions.

Disappearing Stairs. In extreme cases where attic steps do not exist, disappearing (folding) stairs may be installed in openings cut into and between attic-floor joists. When not in use, such stairs can be folded into the opening where they are out of the way and out of sight.

Such stairs may be purchased in ready-built assemblies, ready for installation. They can be installed so that they unfold into halls or at other convenient locations.

Heating. The heating of remodeled attic space constitutes another problem that must be given careful attention before final remodeling plans are made. In order to illustrate the problem, we shall assume a one-story house.

The *X* part of Figure 10 indicates how either gravity ducts, starting at *B*, or forced-air ducts, starting at *A*, would have to be installed in partitions to reach the grilles or registers in the attic space. In this case, the first-floor and attic partitions are in the same vertical plane. In order to provide space for the ducts in the sills and plate, portions of partitions and floors would have to be torn out. Such a process is difficult and the patched partitions and floors forever after exhibit the scars.

The *Y* part of the illustration indicates an even more difficult situation that is encountered when attic partitions are not in the same vertical plane as first-floor partitions. A section of attic floor would have to be removed all in addition to the other work previously mentioned.

In either of the foregoing situations, duct installation is difficult and expensive. A better, easier, and less expensive procedure would be to install gas heaters, of the wall type, in the rooms of a remodeled attic. Gas lines could be installed without too much difficulty and the necessary vents could be extended through the roof. In regions where electricity

FIGURE 10. Details of hot-air ducts.

is not expensive, electric heaters could be used to advantage. Or, window-type air conditioners of the type that supply both heated and cooled air could be used.

Insulation. In Chapter 3, there is a full explanation of insulation as applied to remodeled attic spaces.

Chimneys. There are several aspects of chimneys which should be given careful consideration before final remodeling plans are completed.

LOCATION. The location of a chimney may have an important influence on attic remodeling. For example, suppose that a chimney is located at the point indicated by *X* in the *V* part of Figure 4. Such a location would make part of the plan shown in the *W* part of Figure 4 impossible. Therefore, it is wise to measure the size and location of a chimney and to keep such dimensions in mind.

FLASHING. The flashing around a chimney could be rusted or in otherwise bad condition to the extent that some leaking takes place during heavy rainstorms. Such leaking might not be serious enough to have caused concern prior to the time remodeling was contemplated. How-

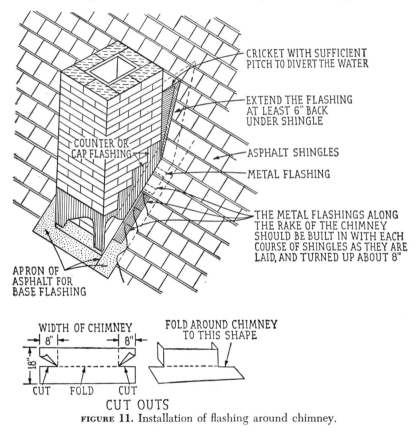

CRICKET WITH SUFFICIENT PITCH TO DIVERT THE WATER

EXTEND THE FLASHING AT LEAST 6" BACK UNDER SHINGLE

COUNTER OR CAP FLASHING

ASPHALT SHINGLES

METAL FLASHING

THE METAL FLASHINGS ALONG THE RAKE OF THE CHIMNEY SHOULD BE BUILT IN WITH EACH COURSE OF SHINGLES AS THEY ARE LAID, AND TURNED UP ABOUT 8"

APRON OF ASPHALT FOR BASE FLASHING

WIDTH OF CHIMNEY

8"   8"

18"

CUT   FOLD   CUT

FOLD AROUND CHIMNEY TO THIS SHAPE

CUT OUTS

FIGURE 11. Installation of flashing around chimney.

ever, even small leaks would ruin the ceiling and wall-surface materials in a remodeled area. Therefore, all flashing should be examined, and if necessary reflashed.

Figure 11 illustrates typical flashing around a chimney. To reflash a chimney, the procedure is as follows:

1. Cut two pieces of metal flashing about 18 inches wide and long enough to bend back to fit the sides of the chimney. The length will

depend on the width of the chimney. These are known as the front-apron and rear-base flashing.

2. Imbed these pieces in roofing cement and nail into place.

3. Step-flash the sides with metal flashing or with metal shingles cut and bent so that they will extend under each course of shingles at the lower end and also into the mortar joints in the chimney.

SWEATING. If a masonry chimney is used as a vent for gas-fired heating equipment, it is quite likely to sweat unless metal flue linings have been installed. Such sweating would ruin wall and ceiling-surface materials in a remodeled area.

MORTAR JOINTS. The National Board of Fire Underwriters recommends that the mortar joints in old brick and concrete-block chimneys should be examined to make sure that they are completely filled with mortar and that the mortar is not cracked or loose.

If joint mortar is loose, it should be scraped out and replaced with new mortar composed of 1 part portland cement and 3 parts clean sand. Moisten the joint surfaces before applying the new mortar and be sure that each joint is completely filled.

Joist Direction. If attic-floor joists are not at right angles to new partitions, 2 by 4 headers must be nailed between the joists as indicated in Figure 12. The headers should be toenailed to the joists using two 3-inch nails on each side and at each end of the headers.

FIGURE 12. Header between joists to support new partition.

Subflooring. All of the floor area involved in remodeling should be covered with a subfloor composed of boards which have a thickness of at least ⅝ inch. Such flooring should be nailed to the joists as suggested in Chapter 2. The nailing is important as a means of preventing floor squeaks.

Dormer Flashing. On some dormers an apron at the bottom and a valley on the roof, as well as side flashing are required (see Figure 13).

The metal apron flashing shown at *A* on the dormer is placed after the shingle course, shown at 1, has been placed. This is followed by placing shingle course 2 and the flashing or shingle tin *B* against the wall. Shingle tins measure about 5 by 7 inches over-all and must be bent at right angles so as to fit tightly against the dormer wall and the roof. Shingle course 3 is then laid and shingle tin *C* placed on top of it. In this manner, each shingle tin is covered by a shingle course. This will cause water to run down on top of the shingle course below.

FIGURE 13. Flashing around dormer window.

After shingle course 8 has been placed, the valley flashing for the roof is fastened into position and the shingling is continued in the same manner as for any roof valley. On the dormer side wall the wood covering will overlap the wall flashing. To ensure drying, the wood covering of the dormer should be cut short enough so that about 1 inch of the metal flashing will be exposed where the dormer meets the roof.

Plumbing. When attic remodeling is being contemplated, an additional bathroom is often one of the desired features. However, the following facts should be understood and kept in mind.

In an average house, the kitchen and bathroom are so situated that all of the plumbing fixtures in both rooms can be served by one soil stack. In other words, there is a mutual partition between the two rooms in which one soil stack is located.

Unless it is possible to plan the position of an additional bathroom so that the plumbing fixtures in it can be conveniently connected to an existing soil stack, a *great deal* of extra labor and material expense will be involved.

In many cities and towns all plumbing installations are subject to strict plumbing codes. Such codes should be studied before any plans for new bathrooms are made.

HOW TO PLAN AND DO ATTIC REMODELING

The following problems and their solutions are typical examples of the visualization, planning, and construction work involved in attic remodeling. We shall make a few assumptions and then discuss the necessary procedures.

PROBLEM 1. It can be assumed that we are going to remodel the attic space of a rectangularly shaped house and that the requirements include two bedrooms, closet space, and individual dormers.

SOLUTION. The various parts of the solution are explained under the following headings all of which are set forth in the order of proper procedure.

FIGURE 14. How to visualize Problem 1.

HOW TO VISUALIZE THE AVAILABLE SPACE. The first step consists of drawing a single-line sketch such as shown in the X part of Figure 14. This sketch should be drawn to scale and indicate the outline of the house (ABCD) and the stair and chimney locations.

The second step consists of drawing a single-line section view such as shown in the Y part of the illustration. This sketch should indicate the shape of the attic space (EFG) and the location of the collar beams.

The third step consists of drawing in the knee walls as shown in the Z part of the illustration. The shape of the available space can now be visualized. It is bounded by the letters *NHJKLM*. The ceiling and knee-wall heights should be indicated at *x* and *y*. At this stage of the planning, we can scale our single-line sketches to determine all of the dimensions in connection with the length and general shape of the available space.

HOW TO VISUALIZE CONSTRUCTION. In order accurately to visualize the structural details involved, it is good practice to draw a section view such as shown in Figure 15. This view should show the floor, the rafters,

FIGURE 15. Principal structural details.

the knee walls, and the collar beams. The drawing provides a better picture of the space and helps in other planning. Actual dimensions should be shown at *A, B, C, D,* and *E*.

PRELIMINARY PLAN VIEW. Using the data obtained from Figures 14 and 15, we can now draw a preliminary floor plan of the space. In Figure 16, the *ABCD* space is the same as shown in the *X* part of Figure 14. The main walls of the house should be indicated as shown at *r, t, x,* and *y*. The stairwell and chimney should also be indicated. Dormers should be spaced so that they constitute good proportion so far as the elevation view of the house is concerned. We shall try them as shown. The floors of the dormer spaces should be flush with the main floor and their walls should be indicated in the same manner as other walls. The depth m depends upon the type of dormer construction to be used. See subsequent illustrations.

Now that the preliminary floor plan is complete, we can study it and discuss the revised plan to be made from it.

Obviously, the bedrooms should be located at E and F. In order to provide privacy for such rooms, some sort of a hall should be planned in

FIGURE 16. Preliminary plan view.

connection with the space at the head of the stairs near H. The hall should be at least 4′ 0″ wide. A closet can be planned near G, in the dark space between the two bedrooms. It should be at least 3′ 0″ wide. After scaling the width of the plan view, we can assume that there is enough space for the hall and the closet. However, if the closet is located along wall KL, its left-hand end wall will not line up with the left-hand wall of the stairwell. Therefore, the dormer locations must be changed.

REVISED PLAN VIEW. Figure 17 shows the revised plan view. The dormer locations have been changed, without destroying good propor-

FIGURE 17. Revised plan view.

FIGURE 18. Typical dormer construction for small windows.

tion, and the hall and closets are indicated. This constitutes a satisfactory plan. Notice that the short partition shown at *X* eliminates the small corner alongside of the chimney. In an actual remodeling project, accurate dimensions should be shown at *A, B, C, D,* etc.

Typical Dormer Construction. Figure 18 shows the structural details for a dormer in which a small window is to be installed. The height of the

FIGURE 19. Typical dormer construction for large windows.

studs at *T* depends upon the exact height required for the window frame. The length of the plate *R* depends upon the horizontal and level distance between the stud corner post and the double rafter *S*.

To construct such a dormer in an existing roof, the roofing and roof boards must be removed around the area of the opening. Then the original rafters, marked *L*, must be taken out. The rafters marked *S* are doubled. The header at *M* can then be nailed into place. Next, the front studs and corner posts, such as at *T*, can be erected. The plate *N* can be installed next. The balance of the work is obvious. All pieces are cut to fit as the assembly is erected. Roof boards can be replaced on the main roof and applied to the roof of the dormer. The sides of the dormer can be sheathed the same as regular exterior walls.

On the inside of the dormer, ceiling joists can be installed. Studs can then be placed under the double rafters to complete the framing.

Figure 19 shows the structural details for a dormer in which a window of ordinary height can be installed. The general construction procedure is the same as previously explained.

FIGURE 20. How to visualize Problem 2.

PROBLEM 2. It can be assumed that we are going to remodel the attic space of a house which has considerably less width than the house specified in Problem 1. The remodeling requirements include: two bedrooms, two closets, and a bathroom.

SOLUTION. We shall assume that an extended, continuous dormer is to be constructed in order to provide more usable space.

HOW TO VISUALIZE THE AVAILABLE SPACE. We shall also assume that the *X*, *Y*, and *Z* parts of Figure 20 were drawn somewhat as explained for similar single-line drawings in the solution to Problem 1. In the *Z* part, the dashed line *FG* indicates the original roof and the letters *FMHG* outline the dormer. The shape of the available space is bounded by the letters *KJLMHC*.

FIGURE 21. Plan for Problem 2.

FIGURE 22. Bathroom layout.

FLOOR PLAN. Figure 21 shows what we can think of as the revised floor plan. As explained in the solution to Problem 1, such a plan should be the result of a preliminary plan and careful study. Note that the dormer contains five new windows, that two closets have been provided, that a hall separates the two bedrooms, and that space for a bathroom

FIGURE 23. Structural details in connection with section *P-P* of Figure 21.

FIGURE 24. Structural details in connection with section *R-R* of Figure 21.

is possible. In an actual plan of this kind, all major dimensions should be shown.

BATHROOM SPACE. In order to make sure that the bathroom space is large enough to accommodate a bathtub of at least 5 feet, a standard water closet, and a lavatory of convenient size, a drawing such as shown in Figure 22 should be prepared. Use the $\frac{3}{4}'' = 1'\ 0''$ scale.

Several such drawings may have to be prepared before a suitable arrangement is found. It should be kept in mind that distances between fixtures, such as indicated at *AB* and *CD,* must be sufficient to allow easy access around them. The door-swing area must also be kept in mind.

If the planned space proves to be too small, the floor plan will have to be studied and changed accordingly.

STRUCTURAL DETAILS. If we imagine that the attic space can be cut through along the *P-P* and *R-R* cutting lines shown in Figure 21, and

DETAIL OF WALL CA

FIGURE 25. Details of wall *CA* shown in Figure 21.

that we can look at the cut surfaces, we can then "see" the section views illustrated in Figures 23 and 24. Such views should be drawn because they help us to visualize the required structural details and because they serve to check the partitions indicated in the plan views. The views also serve as a construction guide.

Figure 25 shows the structural details for part of the wall indicated by *CA* in Figure 21. Drawings of this kind should be prepared because they are helpful when planning the studs, the plate, the sill, and the framing around window openings. (NOTE: The size and types of headers used should conform to local building codes.)

Figure 26 shows the structural details for the partition indicated by *WZ* in Figure 21. Such drawings are helpful in planning the studs, the sill, and the framing around door openings. Note that three-member corner assemblies are necessary at *A*, *B*, *C*, and *D*, where other partitions and walls are intersected.

FIGURE 26. Details of wall *WZ* shown in Figure 21.

The door-opening heights are controlled by the rafters and collar beams. Therefore, stock doors to suit the conditions should be selected and the framing around the openings planned accordingly.

The reader is referred to "Blueprint Reading for Home Builders" by the author and a book on carpentry by J. Douglas Wilson, both companion volumes to this one and published by the McGraw-Hill Book Company, Inc.

CHAPTER TEN

Bathrooms

Bathrooms, like basements and kitchens, have gone through many years of interesting development.

Our grandfathers can remember an era when "plumbing facilities" consisted of backyard installations and when bathing was confined to laundry tubs beside kitchen cookstoves. Few, if any, houses had any provisions for what we now call bathrooms. Plumbing fixtures were unheard of and washbasins were kept in bedrooms and kitchens for the purpose of washing hands and faces.

As cities grew in population, municipal water supplies and sewage disposal were seen to be essential for the prevention of various epidemics. With the advent of the first water mains and sewers, quaint ancestors of our present-day plumbing fixtures made their appearances. Bathtubs were constructed mostly of wood, but had sheet-metal linings. They were unsanitary, inconvenient, and ugly. Other fixtures, including high-tank water closets, were just as crude. However, some progress had been made, and bathrooms became regular parts of many houses.

As time went on, manufacturers took more interest in fixture design, especially from the sanitary standpoint. They produced all-metal and enameled equipment such as shown in the upper part of Figure 1. However, bathrooms were drab and unpleasant areas. Pipes were visible, lighting was crude, and decoration had not been given much thought.

Before long, further improvements in fixture designs came about and more attention was given to the decoration of walls and floors in bath-

FIGURE 1

FIGURE 2

rooms. The upper part of Figure 2 illustrates some of the changes. Yet, bathrooms were still inconvenient, unpleasant, and difficult to keep clean.

During the past 20 years tremendous strides have been made in the design of fixtures and other equipment. In keeping with such progress, bathrooms have also been improved to the point where they are beautiful, functional, adequate, and easy to maintain in sanitary conditions. The lower parts of Figure 1 and 2 indicate some of the improvements we can accomplish by remodeling.

Many old houses are still without bathrooms, and a great number have old-fashioned bathrooms which are inconvenient, inadequate, unpleasant, and unsanitary. This chapter proposes to outline the items relating to modern bathrooms which require careful consideration, to call attention to modern equipment and to show how new or remodeled bathrooms can be planned.

HOW TO VISUALIZE PLAN VIEWS OF BATHROOMS

In order to understand many of the illustrations in this chapter and in order to create such drawings we must learn how to visualize existing, new, or remodeled bathrooms by means of their *plan views*. In other words, we must be able to interpret plan views the same as pictures. An example of this requirement is indicated in Figure 3.

The X part of the illustration shows a plan view of a modern duplex bathroom of the type recommended for large families. Note that all fixtures and equipment are named. The following information is indicated:

1. The over-all size of the bathroom is 14′ 0″ by 10′ 9″.

2. The general space is divided into two areas. One area is 8′ 0″ wide and the other is 6′ 0″ wide.

3. In the 8′ 0″ area there is a bathtub, a water closet and a lavatory. In the 6′ 0″ area there is a water closet and a lavatory.

4. The two areas are separated by a sliding-door partition.

5. Entrance to the general space is by means of one sliding door and one hinged door.

FIGURE 3. How to visualize plan views of bathrooms.

6. There is one window in each area.

7. A tile floor is specified.

8. The two areas afford such privacy that two people may use the general area at the same time.

The *Y* part of the illustration shows a cutaway perspective view (picture) of the general space. Note the *A, B, C,* and *D* corners in the plan and perspective views. The dashed lines *E, F, G, H,* and *J* connect plan and perspective views of the bathtub, water closets, and lavatories.

The two views in Figure 3 should be studied until the perspective view, or picture, can be visualized when looking only at the plan view. Once we have learned such visualization, the planning of new or remodeled bathrooms can be carried on to much better advantage.

BATHROOM SAFETY

Several important safety precautions should be carefully considered and kept in mind when new or remodeled bathrooms are being planned.

Nonslip Flooring. Ceramic tile floors are beautiful and easy to keep clean. Yet, unless special precautions are exercised, they tend to be slippery, especially when wet. Many housewives like to place cloth or other types of small rugs on such floors. Unless the under surfaces of the rugs are treated with rubber or some other nonslip preparation, they are apt to slide on tile and therefore constitute a hazard. The same fact applies to bath mats.

Various forms of asphalt tile and rubber tile or linoleum may be used without as much slipping hazard.

Bathtub Bottoms. Old bathtubs, and even some of the cheaper varieties now available, have curved bottoms which are decidedly dangerous. The one shown in the upper part of Figure 1 is a good example. Such curved surfaces are especially slippery when covered with soap and water. A step too near the side of such a bathtub could result in a serious fall and broken bones.

Flat-bottomed bathtubs, such as the one shown in the lower part of

Figure 1, are recommended by the National Safety Council and by all casualty insurance companies.

Grab Bars. Securely fixed grab bars should be provided on walls for both bathtubs and shower stalls. Metal grab pipes from floors to ceilings should also be installed in front of bathtubs to provide maximum safety for elderly people. Such accessories may add a little to the cost of new or remodeled bathrooms, but the safety they assure is worth whatever they cost.

Thermostatic Valves. Thermostatically controlled valves on shower hot-water outlets may prevent serious scalding.

Towel Bars, Etc. Towel bars, soap dishes, and all fixture handles should be made of metal, since serious cuts may result from broken china.

Light Switches. Locate all light switches near entrance doors and where they cannot be operated from bathtubs or lavatories.

Individual lights should be operated by means of insulated pull cords. Electric switches, cover plates, etc., should be made of insulating materials. Electric heaters should be of the built-in or recessed types.

Medicine Cabinets. Special locked and lighted compartments should be provided for drugs—high enough to be out of children's reach. Ordinary medicine compartments are not safe enough for most drugs. Special wall slots should be provided for the disposal of used safety-razor blades.

Radiators. Steam- and hot-water-heating radiators should be enclosed to prevent any possibility of burns. Casings of various kinds are available for such purposes.

REMODELING CONSIDERATIONS

Inexperienced mechanics and homeowners are apt to do a great deal of preliminary planning and thinking without taking into consideration several aspects of cost or allied work. This is a common mistake that always leads to unexpected expense, delays, and probable disappointment. As a means of helping readers to avoid such a mistake, the following summary of preliminary considerations is set forth.

Piping Economy. Figure 4 illustrates a typical plumbing system such as found in most houses where old bathrooms include water closets,

HOT AND COLD
WATER PIPES
DRAIN   SOIL STACK
LINOLEUM OVER
PINE FINISH
FLOOR
WATER CLOSET
BEND
SECOND FLOOR
BASEBOARD
JOIST
JOISTS NAILED ON
EACH SIDE OF
PARTITION
JOIST
BATH
ROOM   PLASTER
2x8 STUD
CONTINUOUS FROM
FIRST FLOOR TO ATTIC
FIRST FLOOR
JOIST
SUB
FLOOR   SILL
JOIST
KITCHEN   LINOLEUM OVER
MAPLE FINISH
FLOOR

FIGURE 4. Typical soil stack.

bathtubs, and lavatories. All such fixtures are connected to soil stacks which are generally 4-inch cast-iron pipes.

Ordinarily, soil stacks are located in partitions between kitchens and bathrooms or, as shown in Figure 4, in partitions which constitute one wall of kitchens and bathrooms. Note, too, that hot- and cold-water pipes are installed close to soil stacks.

Soil stacks are expensive to install, even at times when houses are under construction and access to the space between studs is easily possible. They are much more expensive if existing partitions have to be opened up so that they can be installed.

In order to economize on piping costs, the locations of new bathrooms should be planned so that existing soil stacks can be used and so that the lengths of water-closet bends do not exceed the length permitted by local building codes. When remodeled bathrooms are being considered, the location of water closets, bathtubs, and lavatories should be planned so that existing drains and closet bends can be employed.

Bathtub Locations. When a modern bathtub is filled with water, the total weight involved constitutes a load that must be carefully considered so far as joists are concerned. Unless due precautions are observed, plaster cracking and other undesirable results are probable.

FIGURE 5. Joists under bathtubs.

The *X* part of Figure 5 shows a situation where joists are at right angles to the length of a bathtub that is located next to a partition. In such cases, most of the load from the bathtub is applied to the joists near the points where they are supported by the plate in the partition. As indicated by the arrow at *P,* some of the bathtub load is applied to the joists at a point approximately 30 inches from the plate. Ordinarily, a situation of this kind may cause the joists to bend only enough to cause small cracks at *R*.

The *Y* part of the illustration shows a situation where joists are parallel to the length of a bathtub that is located next to a wall. In such cases, most of the load from the bathtub is applied to joists S and T. If those joists have a span (distance between points of support) of 12 feet or more, they are apt to bend enough to pull the tub away from the wall and seriously to crack the ceiling plaster attached to their bottom edges. In order to prevent such undesirable reactions, additional joists can be installed, as indicated at M and N. The joists M and N should be nailed to joists S and T using 3½-inch nails spaced about 12 inches apart.

Bathtub Hangers. In cases where new partitions are being installed or where the lath and plaster are to be removed from existing partitions, metal bathtub hangers can be employed to support much of the weight of a bathtub. Such hangers are hung from, or attached to, studs and bathtubs are supported by them.

Codes. Most cities and towns have regulations relating to the installation of all types of plumbing fixtures and to the piping in connection with them. Such codes should be studied before new or remodeled bathrooms are planned.

Windows. Any bathroom should have at least one window. Where duplex bathrooms are involved, each area should have a window.

Condensation. Bathrooms are subject to warm and humid air, and as a result condensation is likely to occur on the walls and ceilings. With this fact in mind, either enamel or waterproof surface materials should be used. The blocks discussed in Chapter 5 are ideal for this purpose.

Roughing-in Drawings. All plumbing manufacturers will supply roughing-in drawings which show where water-supply pipes, waste pipes, and vents must be placed in order to connect with various fixtures when they are set in place. These are very important, especially when we remember that most fixtures are set after all other work is finished.

Cabinets. When new or remodeled bathrooms are being planned, provisions should be made for ample cabinets or other storage spaces, where towels and all other bathroom supplies may be stored.

Heating. See the discussion relating to heating in Chapter 9.

Figure 6 shows several good and poor locations for bathroom hot-air registers.

PART A. The floor register is under a window where the rising warm air mixes with the cold downdraft from the window and outer wall, producing uniform temperature from floor to ceiling.

FIGURE **6.** Register locations.

PART B. The baseboard register is under a window so that hot air is blown upward where it mixes with the cold downdraft from the window and wall to produce uniform floor-to-ceiling temperature.

PART C. The wall register is low on a partition near an outer wall. It blows warm air across the outer wall and the window where it mixes with the normal downdrafts to produce uniform floor-to-ceiling temperatures.

PART D. The floor register is near an inside wall. Heat rises to the ceiling causing cold drafts from the window and outer wall dropping down and crossing the floor. This causes undesirable heating, especially in bathrooms.

PART E. The baseboard register blows air across the floor and creates an unpleasant draft at the floor level.

PART F. The wall register is high in an inside wall. The heat is delivered at the ceiling level and allows cold drafts from the window and outer wall to sweep across the floor.

Sliding Doors. When bathroom space is limited or where a swinging door conflicts with fixtures, sliding doors can be used to advantage. However, and as indicated in Figure 3, there must be enough partition space for such doors to slide into.

Size of Bathrooms. Bathrooms need not be large. Small bathrooms are easier to keep clean and are considerably less costly. The smaller they are, the less floor-, wall-, and ceiling-surface materials required. However, there should be ample room for each of the fixtures and enough room between them for easy access.

Shutoff Valves. It is a good idea to install shutoff valves in the pipelines, near each fixture, so that faucet repairs can be made without shutting off the entire water supply.

ADVANTAGE OF REMODELING

The advantages obtainable, even by fairly economical remodeling, are fascinating. The difference between old and modern bathrooms is so great that such projects are exceptionally worthwhile.

Study the top parts of Figures 1 and 2. Notice in them the items listed in the following summary, keeping in mind that such items are typical of most old bathrooms:

1. Old-fashioned bathtubs are ugly and dangerous.
2. Visible pipes are unsightly.
3. The wood dado (wall covering) is unattractive, unsanitary, and difficult to keep clean.
4. It is difficult to clean the floors under and in back of old-fashioned bathtubs.
5. Inadequate and ugly lavatories.

6. Unsanitary wood baseboards.

7. Insufficient lighting.

8. Inadequate shower facilities.

9. Unsanitary cracks around lavatories.

10. Unsightly and difficult-to-reach medicine cabinets.

11. Old-style water closets.

12. Poor wall and ceiling decorations.

13. Lack of cabinets and storage spaces.

14. Lack of grab bars.

15. Lack of counter space.

16. Unsanitary bathtub drains.

17. Old-fashioned floor coverings.

18. Old-fashioned windows.

19. Unsanitary toilet seats.

20. Wasted space.

Now study the lower parts of Figures 1 and 2. The great advantages of remodeling are immediately apparent. All of the foregoing disadvantages and undesirable items have been removed or corrected. The remodeled bathrooms are more convenient and they are beautiful. For example, note the following improvements shown in the lower part of Figure 2.

1. The bathtub is modern and safe. It has a seat-type rim and is fully enclosed to serve the dual purpose of a shower.

2. Safe grab bars have been provided.

3. The water closet is noiseless and sanitary.

4. The sliding window is glazed with attractive translucent glass.

5. The space can be converted into two areas by means of a folding curtain.

6. The pullman-type lavatory provides storage drawers and counter space.

7. A dressing table adds to the convenience of the remodeled area.

8. Wall storage cabinets have been provided.

9. A modern and sanitary floor has been provided.

10. The tile walls are beautiful and easy to keep clean.

11. Wall decorations add to the beauty of the area.

12. All dust-catching cracks have been avoided.

FIGURE 7

MODERN FIXTURES AND ACCESSORIES

The best way to visualize and study modern fixtures and accessories is by means of the catalogues distributed by manufacturers, or by visiting their display rooms. However, a few suggestions are given in the following paragraphs.

Lavatories. As illustrated in Figures 2 and 7, lavatories are available with and without cabinets. They may be obtained in several colors and sizes, but their price range calls for careful planning. They should not be selected until the size and shape of a new or remodeled bathroom has been determined.

Water Closets. There are a great many types of water closets. They differ in shape, width, height, color, quality, and action. Some have tanks, while others are flushed by means of valves. The noiseless types are becoming more popular, although they are generally more expensive.

Bathtubs. Modern flat-bottomed bathtubs of the types shown in Figure 8 are available in all colors and to suit practically any available space.

FIGURE 8. Typical bathtubs.

The type shown in the *A* part of the illustration is made to have either one, two, or three sides against partitions.

The type shown in the *B* part of the illustration is made for recesses. However, other similar types are available for corner installations.

NOTE: Removable wall panels through which the supply, waste, and vent pipes for bathtubs are accessible should be provided.

Shower Stalls. Shower stalls, entirely separate from bathtubs, can be purchased complete and ready to install in various sizes and qualities. Usually, such stalls require floor space that is 3 feet square. As indicated in the lower part of Figure 2, glass enclosures are also available for use in connection with bathtubs.

Medicine Cabinets. Figure 9 illustrates a modern medicine cabinet with mirror, sliding doors, and tubular lights. Such cabinets are made to be installed between the studs of a partition.

FIGURE 9. Modern medicine cabinet.

Water Heaters. A constant supply of hot water is an essential convenience in modern bathrooms. Automatic gas or electric heaters can be obtained in 30- to 40- or more gallon capacities.

Ventilation. Where possible, electric ventilating fans should be provided in connection with new or remodeled bathrooms. The fans should be located in the ceilings, as near to the center of the rooms as possible, or centered next to an exterior wall, or in a corner. For bathrooms of ordinary size, fans with 8-inch blades are adequate.

LOCATION OF BATHROOM ACCESSORIES

Figure 10 shows the recommended location for several bathroom accessories.

FIGURE 10. Location of bathroom accessories.

MINIMUM-SIZED BATHROOMS

Figure 11 illustrates four of the more or less basic types of bathrooms designed for small areas. With but little modification, one of these types will usually be found to fit remodeling requirements, especially where only limited space is available and when economy is important.

The W part of Figure 11 shows the most economical plan. Plumbing costs can be kept to a minimum because the fixtures are all on one wall,

FIGURE 11. Basic types of minimum-sized bathrooms.

and a maximum of 50 square feet of floor space allows ample access between fixtures. As shown in the illustration, the A dimension is 5' 6" and the E dimension is 9' 0". These dimensions allow a 5' 6" by 2' 6" bathtub, a 20- by 18-inch lavatory, and a standard-sized water closet. The distances shown at B, C, and D are each 12 inches. This plan could be applied to an even smaller floor space by reducing the *A* dimension to 5′ 0″ and by allowing somewhat less than 12 inches at *B, C,* and *D*. However it is wise to allow at least 12 inches between fixtures and between fixtures and partitions.

The *X* part of Figure 11 shows a minimum-space plan for a bathroom between two bedrooms. A corner lavatory could be substituted for the one shown. The one weakness of this plan is that wall space for towel bars is limited. As the illustration is shown, the *A* dimension is 5′ 6″ and the *E* dimension is 9′ 0″. In this plan, the *B* and *D* dimensions should not be less than 12 inches and the *C* dimension not less than 1′ 9″.

The *Y* part of Figure 11 shows a simple, duplex bathroom. The following minimum dimensions are recommended:

A—27 inches	*C*—48 inches	*E*—12 inches
B—30 inches	*D*—12 inches	*F*—48 inches
		G—60 inches

The *Z* part of Figure 11 shows another simple, duplex bathroom in connection with a closet.

The following minimum dimensions are recommended.

A—60 inches	*C*—12 inches
B—12 inches	*D*—36 inches

DUPLEX BATHROOMS

Figure 12 illustrates three basic types of duplex bathrooms designed for large areas and for use by large families. Such bathrooms can be used in odd-shaped areas and serve a double or triple purpose, since up to three people can use them at the same time with full privacy.

The *X* part of the illustration shows a bathroom that has three separate areas all of which may be entered from a hall. All of the areas can be closed to provide complete privacy in each. Minimum dimensions are indicated.

The *Y* part of the illustration shows a three-area bathroom in which two bathtubs and three lavatories add to its convenience. Minimum

FIGURE 12. Duplex bathrooms.

dimensions are indicated. The *A* and *B* dimensions should not be less than 12 inches.

The *Z* part of the illustration shows a two-area bathroom designed for an L-shaped space. The following minimum dimensions are recommended:

A—24 inches $\qquad$ C—42 inches

B—30 inches $\qquad$ D—36 inches

E—57 inches

T Y P I C A L   R E M O D E L I N G   P R O J E C T S

The following problems and their solutions are typical of the remodeling projects which owners of old houses are likely to be interested in:

PROBLEM 1. The X part of Figure 13 shows part of the first-floor plan in connection with a typical old house. We can assume that a kitchen, a dining room, a bedroom, and a living room are located on either side of the central portion indicated in the illustration. We can further assume that kitchen remodeling has eliminated any need for the pantry and that the owner wants to transform the pantry into a bathroom for the first-floor bedroom.

FIGURE 13. Problem 1.

SOLUTION. The first step consists of preliminary planning to determine what the requirements are. We can assume that a bathtub, a lavatory, and a water closet constitute the required fixtures and that entrance to the new bathroom must be possible from both the kitchen and bedroom. We can also assume that the brand and size of fixtures have been selected and determined.

The next step should be accomplished by means of sketches drawn to accurate scale. Draw single-line rectangles to represent the interior of the 8′ 0″ by 5′ 6″ space. Indicate the position of the necessary doors and their widths. Then draw in various arrangements of fixtures, making sure that the symbols are drawn to the same scale as the space outline.

FIGURE 14. Problem 2.

We can assume that the arrangement shown in the Y part of the illustration is satisfactory. In this arrangement, the lavatory and water closet are located so that connections to a soil stack in the kitchen wall can be made without too much trouble or expense. The arrangement allows ample space between fixtures and between fixtures and the partitions. Also, there is ample space for the two doors and a passageway between the water closet and the bathtub.

NOTE: Half bathrooms (sometimes known as powder rooms) can be provided by use of excess hall or other space, as indicated in the Y part of Figure 13.

FIGURE 15. Problem 3.

PROBLEM 2. The X part of Figure 14 shows part of the floor plan for a one-story house. We can assume that the bathroom space is surrounded by a bedroom closet, a hall, and a kitchen. Also, that the letters A, B, and C indicate the positions of the old water closet, bathtub, and lavatory.

We can further assume that the owner wants to remodel the old bathroom and provide an additional half bathroom to serve the needs of a growing family.

SOLUTION. The Y part of Figure 14 indicates one solution to the problem. Note that partitions D, E, and F are planned so that there is room for a water closet and lavatory in the half bathroom and that the three necessary fixtures are well arranged in the main bathroom.

The new half bathroom will require an additional soil stack, but in a one-story house such installation work can be carried on without too much trouble or expense.

PROBLEM 3. The X part of Figure 15 shows part of the floor plan for a one-story house that includes large rooms and halls. This is typical of many old houses. Note that the old bathroom occupies a space that is 9' 6" by 10' 9". The letters R, S, and T indicate the positions of the old water closet, bathtub, and lavatory. The problem is to remodel the old bathroom to suit the needs of an enlarged family.

SOLUTION. The Y part of Figure 15 shows one solution to the problem in the form of a duplex bathroom.

The shaded partitions are new. They divide the space into four areas.

A. This is a small entrance hall to serve the needs of two doors.

B. This area contains a water closet and a lavatory.

C. This area contains the bathtub. Note that a curtain can be hung from the rod indicated to separate areas C and D.

D. This area contains the lavatory and dressing table.

Note that new closets have been provided at E and F and that all areas can be closed off, by means of doors or a curtain, to provide privacy and facilities for more than one person at a time.

CHAPTER ELEVEN

Storage Spaces

The concept of planned storage is an extension of the modern doctrine which states that houses are actually "machines for living," that they must provide much more than mere shelter; they must be focal points for pleasant family life. As such, houses should be planned to provide maximum convenience with a minimum amount of work required to keep the machines functioning smoothly.

A major trend in all types of houses to achieve this end is the use of more and better storage spaces. Several factors are responsible. One is the popular demands for well-organized, uncluttered living. Another is the need for more living space. This is particularly true in houses without attic and basement wherein storage space is at a premium. Even in larger houses, owners have found that such traditional catch-alls as attics and basements are at best inefficient storage spaces and are better suited to use as auxiliary living or sleeping areas. See Chapters 9 and 10.

Given enough well-planned storage spaces, not only can everything be stored neatly and out of sight, but there will be far more actual living area available. For example, note the storage space illustrated in Figure 1. Garments, bedding, and boxes are neatly and conveniently stored and the folding doors do not interfere with furniture or appliance placement in the living area.

Most old houses are so arranged that additional storage spaces may be provided without a great deal of expense. This chapter proposes to outline the items relating to storage spaces which require careful considera-

FIGURE 1. Modern storage closet with folding doors.

tion, to call attention to various types of storage spaces, and to show how they can be planned and installed.

STORAGE-SPACE SAFETY

Several important safety precautions should be carefully considered and kept in mind when new or remodeled storage spaces are being planned.

Lighting. Natural and artificial lighting of storage spaces should be sufficient to make all contents plainly visible. Many serious injuries have occurred because unseen contents fell when disturbed. If the light from adjacent living areas does not make all contents easy to distinguish, electric light fixtures should be installed inside of storage spaces.

Ventilation. Ventilation is especially important in clothes storage spaces to help keep the clothing free from odors and, in humid regions of the country, to prevent the formation of mold or mildew. Air may be kept in circulation by windows or by means of openings in the tops and bottoms of doors.

Dust Prevention. In dusty parts of the country a threshold is needed in connection with "walk-in" storage spaces to help keep contents clean. Shallow "reach-in" storage spaces need doors that are almost as wide as the interior spaces. For doorways more than 2′ 8″ wide, sliding doors are apt to be more dustproof.

Access. Many injurious falls have been the result of difficult access or of crowding in storage spaces. Many more accidents are caused by articles for which no storage space was provided.

Reaching and Climbing. Storage for articles in more or less constant use should be designed so that no reaching or climbing is necessary, to prevent falls and strains. They should be within reach of the average person standing on the floor.

Seldom Used Articles. Storage for articles in seldom or seasonal use should be on the main floor if possible, with ladder or other provision for safe access if they are stored out of reach from the floor.

Outdoor Articles. Outdoor articles such as garden tools and bicycles should be stored on the ground level.

Poisons. Insecticides and other poisons should be stored high, out of children's reach, and kept locked.

Locations. Ordinarily, storage spaces should occupy a floor area that would not be used in other ways. They should be accessible but inconspicuous. However, they should not be located where one side of a chimney forms one of their walls or sides. The reason for this is explained in the following:

During cold weather, when a furnace is in operation, the walls of a chimney will be warm. This is especially true when coal is used as fuel. If a storage space is located next to a warm chimney wall, a circulation of air is created within the storage space which tends to distribute dust over its contents.

If there is no alternative but to locate a storage space next to a chimney wall, an air space at least 6 inches wide should be provided between the chimney and the storage space. This will eliminate undesirable interior circulation.

BASIC TYPES OF STORAGE SPACES

In general, all spaces used for storage of any kind are known as *storage spaces*. This term is in keeping with modern design and construction terminology. However, the older term *closet* is much better known and understood. Therefore, we shall employ the two terms as follows.

All spaces where clothing, linen, towels, etc., are stored will be called closets.

All spaces where general household items such as games, books, sporting equipment, etc., are stored will be called *storage spaces*.

Clothes Closets. All clothes closets are basically the same, regardless of their location. No matter what shape of space is available, one of the six plans shown in Figure 2 can be adapted. Minimum dimensions marked on the plans may be increased and the arrangement then varied by adding hooks, trays, shelves, drawers, racks for shoes, etc. Clothing on hangers is indicated by the lines drawn at right angles to the rods.

For a space limited as to width but fairly deep, the narrow closet with extension rod (*U* part of Figure 2) is a good arrangement. The doorway to this closet should be at least 2 feet wide.

The shallow closet (*V* part of Figure 2) is a typical reach-in arrangement. This is an excellent closet to use when depth is limited. However,

FIGURE 2. Basic clothes-closet types.

the depth should never be less than 2′ 0″. That much space is advisable so that clothes on hangers will not brush against the wall surfaces. This closet requires an opening practically as wide as the closet. For openings more than 2′ 8″ wide, two doors are recommended.

For space that is too shallow to place hangers crosswise, the plan shown in the *W* part of Figure 2 is a good arrangement. Here two extension rods provide the maximum hanging space. The doorway must be practically as wide as the closet.

The corner closet (*X* part of Figure 2) provides considerable hanging space for very little floor area. This closet has no sharp corners that project into living areas.

FIGURE 3. Typical floor plan showing basic and wardrobe-type closets.

A walk-in closet (*Y* part of Figure 2) may be any depth. For more shelf space and less hanger space, one side of such a closet may be fitted with shelves.

The walk-in closet shown in the *Z* part of Figure 2 is similar to the reach-in arrangement shown in the *V* part of the illustration. This closet may be any width that is wider than the door opening. If desired, place the door at *a*, making the shelf L-shaped.

Any of the closets indicated at *B, C, D, E,* or *G* in Figure 3 can be planned and erected following the plans shown at *U, V, W, Y,* or *Z* in Figure 2.

Wardrobe Closets. This type of closet is indicated at *A, E,* and *J* in Figure 3. Either sliding or swinging doors may be used. Generally, rods are installed to extend the full length of such closets, and shelves are erected above the rods. As indicated in Figure 4, storage spaces which have hinged doors are often placed above such closets.

FIGURE 4. Prefabricated closets.

Prefabricated Closets. The *A, B, C, D,* and *E* parts of Figure 4 show typical prefabricated closet units which can be purchased knocked down in cartons, complete with hardware, shelves, rods, and drawers ready for installation. As indicated, the units range from 26 inches to 72 inches wide and have from one to three doors. In all but the 26-inch unit, sliding doors are provided. The units are 8′ 0″ high and 26′ 6″ thick.

They may be used as room dividers or, where no joists must be supported, as partitions between rooms.

The *F* part of Figure 4 illustrates one way in which the units may be used. Two 48-inch units provide ample closet and storage space and create a dressing room at one end of a long bedroom. The units can also be installed at such locations as *A, E,* and *J* in Figure 3. Or, they may be installed along such walls as indicated at *KL* in Figure 3. In fact, these units can be installed wherever closet or storage space is desired.

FIGURE 5. Typical storage space assembled from prefabricated units.

Storage Spaces. The prefabricated units previously mentioned may also be used as storage spaces for all manner of household articles. As indicated in Figure 5, the interiors can be fitted with shelves and drawers. No carpentry work is necessary, owing to the fact that side cleats permit shelves and drawers to be added or subtracted at 6-inch intervals. Cleats, drawers, and shelves are available at building-material dealers where the units are purchased.

CLOSET FITTINGS

It pays to plan carefully the details of closet fittings. Rods, hooks, and trays that are well located make it easier to keep clothing in good condition and to keep the closet in good order.

Rods take care of practically all clothing on hangers. Usually this will include all dresses, except for small children's, all skirts, blouses, trousers, and coats. Table 1 shows the space to allow on the rod for different types

TABLE 1. Rod allowance for garments and location of rod with respect to wall and floor

Garment	Space on rod, inches	Wall to center of rod, inches	Floor to top of rod, inches
Adults'			
Skirts	2	12	45
Jackets	3	12	45
Shirts	1½	12	45
Suits	2	12	45
Trousers	3	12	45
Dresses	1½	12	63
Overcoats	4	12	63
Coats with fur collar	3–6	12	63
Coats without fur collar	2–5	12	63
Evening gowns	2	12	72
Garments in mothproof bags	3	12	72
Children's, 6 to 12 years		10	45
Children's, 3 to 5 years		8	30

of clothing. This table also shows how much space to allow from wall to rod and from floor to rod, depending on the width and length of garments hanging from it. If there is a shelf above the rod, a minimum of 2½ inches should be allowed between the top of the rod and the bottom of the shelf.

In deep, narrow closets there should be an extension pole so that the rod can be pulled out for greater convenience. See *U* part of Figure 2.

There should be enough hooks in a closet to accommodate nightgowns, pajamas, slips, aprons, and other garments that do not belong on hangers. Hooks should be within easy reach of the doorway but not any closer than 5 inches. There should be a minimum allowance of 4 inches between the top of a hook and the bottom of a shelf above it. It is better not to place hooks behind a rod. For the clothing of small children, hooks should not be above a child's eye level. Hooks for garments on hangers cannot safely be put on a door that is less than 30 inches wide.

The distance from hook to hook or from hook to corner will vary with the kind of garments hung on them. For clothing ordinarily kept in a

FIGURE 6. Typical closet fittings.

bedroom closet there should be a minimum of 7 inches between hooks and 3½ inches from hook to corner. For children's clothing, the hooks should be spaced about 9 inches from hook to hook, and 4½ inches from hook to corner.

The *A* part of Figure 6 shows a space-saving method of placing hooks. Hooks in the upper row are on a strip that sets them out from the wall about 3 inches more than the hooks in the row below. If these hooks are placed any closer than 12 inches from a rod, they will reduce the amount of rod space that can be used. The upper hooks will reduce the amount of usable rod space about 8 inches, the lower ones about 4 inches.

The vertical shoerack shown in the *B* part of the illustration is a good one to use when wall space is not so limited as floor space. The lower bar may be covered on the inside with felt to protect the shoes.

The tilted shelf shown in the C part of the illustration fits in the floor space of the closet, below garments on hangers or hooks. For both rack and shelf a width of 18 inches will accommodate at least two pairs of shoes.

Other fittings should supplement the storage space provided in bureaus, chests, and dressers. For folded clothing, shelves are less expensive than trays or drawers; they provide enough protection for most articles.

The width and distance between shelves as well as the depth of trays and drawers varies according to the articles stored. They should be planned to accommodate the largest articles commonly stored in or on them. A minimum for shelves for hats, for instance, would be 12 inches from front to back, a maximum about 15 inches. The distance between shelves used for hats should be 9 inches from the top of the lower shelf to the bottom of the shelf above.

Where walk-in or reach-in closets are involved, dust may create a problem. It is practically impossible to prevent the settlement of dust on the shoulder parts of garments unless bags such as shown in Figure 1 are employed, or unless some sort of cloth or plastic covers are placed over the garments just above hanger levels.

CEDAR CLOSETS

Aromatic-red-cedar closet lining is produced in random lengths up to 8 feet. It is $\frac{3}{8}$ inch thick and comes in a choice of widths from 2 to 4 inches. It is usually put up in bundles or cartons, each containing 40 feet board measure. A 40-foot bundle or carton will cover about 30 square feet of actual space. Table 2 shows the number of 8-foot bundles required for closets of various sizes.

Application. In remodeling work, the cedar can be applied over old plaster or plasterboard in existing closets or directly over the studding in new closets. The cedar strips should be placed horizontally on walls, beginning from the bottom. Courses are placed with the groove edges down. Face nailing is recommended. Use 4d nails and set them just below the surface. Joints need not occur over studs, as the tongue and groove "welds" the pieces together. When cedar is being placed over plaster or

TABLE 2. Number of 8-foot bundles required for various-sized closets

Deep	Wide	High	Bundles
1½	3	7	3
1½	3	8	3
2	3	7	3
2	3	8	4
2	3½	7	4
2	3½	8	4
2	4	7	4
2	4	8	4
2	4½	7	4
2	4½	8	5
2	5	7	4
2	5	8	5
2	6	7	5
2	6	8	6
3	4	7	5
3	4	8	5
3	5	7	5

Closet size in feet is the spanning header over Deep, Wide, High.

plasterboard, short pieces will remain securely in place, even if located between bearing points.

Cedar molding is available for corner treatments. Closet doors should also be lined for best results. To assure greater air tightness of a closet, a condition which increases moth repellency, the door should be weatherstripped.

The cedar lining should be left in its natural state. Application of shellac or other finish would seal in the oil fumes and prevent their functioning as a moth repellent.

CLOSET DOORS

Several types of sliding or hinged closet doors, along with the necessary hardware, are available at lumberyards. However, for simplicity and speed of installation, especially when homeowners are doing the work, prefabricated units such as shown in Figure 4 are recommended. Such units are complete with doors. Wardrobe units such as indicated at *A*, *E*, and *J* in Figure 3 are also available in various sizes with hinged or sliding doors.

Folding Doors. Hinged doors require a considerable amount of swing area. For example, note the *X* part of Figure 7. The 2′ 6″ door requires a swing area that is the equivalent of $5 \times 2\frac{1}{2}$ feet, or $12\frac{1}{2}$ square feet. That much area cannot be used for any other purpose in a room.

As a further example of the floor space required for hinged doors, suppose that the closet indicated in Figure 1 has hinged doors such as shown at *A* and *B* in the *Y* part of Figure 7. Also suppose that the door shown at the left in Figure 1 has a hinged door such as shown at *C* in the *Y* part of Figure 7. The three swing areas required would take up most of the floor space in the *FDE* corner of the room.

Folding doors, such as shown in Figure 1, can be obtained for practically any width of door opening. Following manufacturer's directions, they are easy to install and provide considerably more usable living area in any room.

Sliding Doors. Closet units such as indicated in Figure 4, and at *A*, *E*, and *J* in Figure 3, have sliding doors which slide back of one another and do not require partition space. However, in order to provide a sliding door for the closet opening shown in the *X* part of Figure 7, a length of the partition, such as indicated between *G* and *H*, would have to be torn out and rebuilt. This procedure would require plaster patching and other undesirable work.

If *new* partitions around a closet or storage space are to be erected, sliding-door pockets can be installed without difficulty, owing to the fact that they may be purchased ready for installation and because they constitute part of such partitions.

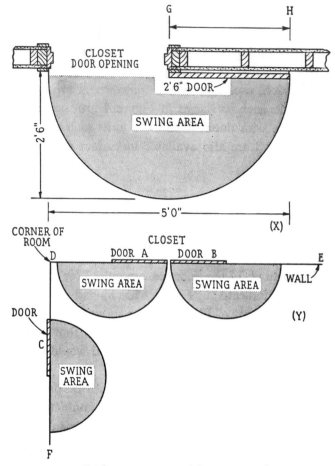

FIGURE 7. Floor area required for swinging doors.

TYPICAL PROJECTS

The following problems and their solutions are typical of the closet re-modeling projects which owners of old houses are likely to be interested in:

PROBLEM 1. The X part of Figure 8 indicates parts of two bedrooms and their positions in connection with a hall. Partition AB is the dividing partition between the two rooms, both of which are large. The problem is to plan and erect a new partition so that three new closets will be created: one for each bedroom and one for the hall.

SOLUTION. The Y part of the illustration indicates the position of the new partition CD. This partition may be located from 3 to 6 feet away from partition AB. Short partitions at J and K divide the space into the required three closets.

FIGURE 8. New partition closets.

Partition CD may be constructed as indicated in the Z part of the illustration. First, place a 2 by 4 sill from C to D. It should be nailed directly to the floor. Then, by means of a plumb bob, locate the position of the 2 by 4 plate directly above the sill. Use 3½-inch nails to fasten the plate to the ceiling. The nails should go through the lath and plaster and penetrate well into joists. Toenail the 2 by 4 pieces L and M to the sill and plate.

In partition CD, two corner assemblies, shown at E and F, are required for the short partitions K and J. It is a good idea to have the frames for the doors on hand so their widths can be measured and the positions of studs *G* and *H* established accordingly. All other studs should be placed 16 inches on centers, or as near to that spacing as possible.

Erect the short partitions, *K* and *J*, using sills, plates, and studs in much the same manner as explained in connection with partition *CD* (see *Y* part of illustration).

Doors *R* and *S* will have to be cut into the old partitions. Remove the lath and plaster in areas somewhat wider than the doors and from floor

FIGURE 9. Details for unit-type closets.

to ceiling. It may be necessary to erect new studs on either side of the door openings. Also, headers will be necessary.

Partitions *CD, J,* and *K* may be covered with any of the surface materials explained in Chapter 5.

The new trim for portions *CD, K,* and *J* should closely match the old trim.

The new closets may be fitted as explained earlier in this chapter.

PROBLEM 2. The *X* part of Figure 9 shows one end of a bedroom, *ABC,* in which closet and storage space is desired. The problem is to plan and install unit-type closets of the type illustrated in Figure 4.

SOLUTION. In a space 10′ 9″ long, one of the 72-inch and one of the 48-inch units can be installed.

The units may be fastened to the floor and walls by means of nails or screws in ample quantity to make them secure. Use a carpenter's level to make sure that the units are level and plumb. Shim as may be necessary.

The two units have a combined length of 120 inches or 9 inches short of the 10′ 9″ (129 inches) space between B and C. Therefore, a filler is required. The Y part of Figure 9 indicates how the filler is applied.

FIGURE 10. Details of under-stairs closet.

Sometimes the ceilings of old houses are more than 8′ 0″ high. In such cases, fillers must be applied between the tops of the units and the ceiling, as indicated in the Z part of Figure 9.

PROBLEM 3. The X part of Figure 10 shows a cutaway view of stairs and of the open space under the stairs. Situations of this kind are common in old houses. The problem is to provide a storage space under the stairs.

SOLUTION. The Y part of Figure 10 indicates how a partition can be framed to enclose the space. The door size will depend upon the available height. The new partition may be covered using any of the surface materials explained in Chapter 5. The new trim should closely match the old trim.

Index

A

Acoustical tile, for basement ceilings, 93, 105–108
  paints for, 102
  for sloping attic ceilings, 108–109
  over sound plaster, 86–89, 98–102
  over unsound plaster, 89–91, 102–105
Added rooms, insulation of, 62–64
Adhesives, for decorative plywoods, 40–41, 124
  for floor tile, 149, 179
  for parquet floors, 166
  for wall blocks, 133
  for wall planks, 129, 131
  (*See also* Glue)
Air conditioners, window-type, 271
American Ladder Institute, 268
American Lumber Standards, 14
Anchor bolts, 43
Anchors, adhesive, 42–43
  iron expansion, 42
  metal strap, 40
Apartments, transforming attics into, 257–258, 261
Ash, 2, 18–19
  ease of working with, 7
  figure in, 10
  nail-holding power of, 29
  shrinkage of, 5
  stiffness of, 9
  warping of, 7
Asphalt tile, 149, 163–166
  for bathrooms, 290
  for kitchens, 233
  laid over concrete, 177–179
Asphaltum, hot, uses of, to dampproof floors, 152
  in insulation, 62, 75
  to waterproof basements, 199, 205

B

Backfills, 192
  causing damp basements, 188
Basements, damp, 187–188, 199–201, 205–206
  insulation of, 204–206
  modern, 180–182
  remodeling of, 41–43, 78, 91, 105–108
    by adding windows, 196–198
    ceilings for, 190
    cost of, 182–186, 209–210
    floors for, 142–143, 187, 191–193, 195–196
    plans for, 184
    precautions in, 183–186
    preliminary considerations in, 186–190
    projects related to, 190–207
    purpose of, 182–183
    typical examples of, 207–213
    wall surfaces for, 123–124, 136–139, 200–203
  temperatures of, 189, 204–206
  wet, 187, 198–199, 201
  (*See also* Recreation rooms)
Basswood, 2–3, 19

Attics, remodeling of, 78, 91, 108–109, 257–261
  and area, 264
  and ceiling height, 264–265
  cost of, 262, 271, 274
  examples of, 258–260
  floors for, 142, 150–152, 168–172
  heating systems for, 270–271
  lighting of, 262
  plans for, 275–284
  reasons for, 261
  wall surfaces for, 123–124
  ventilation of, 55–56, 77, 262

Basswood, ease of working with, 7
  figure in, 10
  nail-holding power of, 29
  shrinkage of, 5
  stiffness of, 9
  warping of, 7
Bathrooms, 285
  attic, 261, 274, 280–283
  condensation in, 294
  duplex, 288–290, 303–304, 308
  half, 307–308
  heating of, 295–296
  modern, 285–288
  plan views of, 288–290, 301–302, 304–
    307
  remodeling of, advantages of, 296
    cost of, 292
    typical, 305–308
  resurfacing walls of, 117, 120–121
  safety precautions for, 290–291
  shutoff valves for, 296
  size of, 296, 302–303
  ventilation of, 77, 294, 300
Bathtubs, 282, 285–288, 290, 296–297,
    299
  hangers for, 294
  location of, 293–294, 301
Batt insulation, 49
  for attics, 58
  for ceilings, 56, 64
  for walls, 64
Battens, 24
Beams, two-piece, nailing of, 35–36
Bedrooms, attic, 257–258, 261, 277–278,
    280–283
  basement, 182
  floors for, 150–152
  resurfacing walls of, 128–136
Beech, 2, 13, 18–19, 150
  ease of working with, 7
  figure in, 10
  flooring grades of, 14
  nail-holding power of, 29
  shrinkage of, 5
  stiffness of, 9
  warping of, 6
Birch, 2–3, 13, 18–19, 150
  ease of working with, 7
  figure in, 10
  flooring grades of, 14

Birch, nail-holding power of, 29
  for plywood, 23
  shrinkage of, 5
  stiffness of, 9
  warping of, 7
Blanket insulation, 49
  for attics, 58, 72–73, 93
  for basements, 93, 106–107
  for ceilings, 56, 64, 70–71, 74
  for crawl spaces, 62, 75
  for floors, 64, 75, 170
  for walls, 64, 69
Bleaches, wood, 26
Blind-nailing, 169–170
Blisters in ceiling plaster, 83
Block-treatment joints, 24
Board-feet content, 16–17
  table of, 17
Brads, for applying plywood, 139
  floor, 33
Breakfast nooks, resurfacing walls of, 120
  (*See also* Dining nooks)
Breaking strength of lumber, 8
Building codes, local, 190, 265, 274, 283,
    294
Butt joints, 24

C

Cabinets, bathroom storage, 294, 297, 300
  cost of, 254
  installation of, 247–253
  kitchen, 218, 227–229
    dimensions for, 230–231
    filler strips for, 237
    hanging, 235–237
    location of, 243–247
    suggestions for, 230
    top materials for, 232
  lumber for, 13, 20
  medicine, 291
  (*See also* Storage spaces)
Carpenter's level, use of, 249
Carpentry work, poor, plaster cracks and,
    82
Carpeting for basement stairs, 202
Cedar, 2, 8, 18, 20
  ease of working with, 7
  figure in, 10
  nail-holding power of, 29

Cedar, red, 13
  shrinkage of, 5
  stiffness of, 9
  warping of, 7
Cedar closets, 319–320
Ceilings, attic, 108–109
    height of, 264–265
  basement, height of, 186, 190–192
    new surfaces for, 91, 93, 105–107
  collar-beam, insulation of, 74
  decoration and apparent height of, 95
  finding center point of, 98–100, 106–107
  insulation of, 51
    in added rooms, 64
  kitchen, height of, 233
    lowering of, 109–112
    resurfacing of, 98–105
  nails for, 33
  new lowered, 94–95, 109–112
  plaster defects in, 78–84
    repair of, 85, 95–98
  plasterboard defects in, 84–85
  resurfacing of, 78, 82–86
    materials for, 86–95, 98–108
  top-floor, insulation of, 56–58, 70–72
Checks in wood, 15
Cherry, 2, 19
  ease of working with, 7
  figure in, 10
  shrinkage of, 5
  stiffness of, 9
  warping of, 7
Chestnut, 2–3, 18–20
  ease of working with, 7
  figure in, 10
  nail-holding power of, 29
  shrinkage of, 5
  stiffness of, 9
  warping of, 7
Chimneys, flashing around, 272–273
  location of, 271–272
  mortar joints for, 273
  storage spaces near, 312
  sweating of, 273
Chip cracks, cause of, 81
Clear finish for plywood, 25
Clips, for fastening ceiling tile, 91
  for fastening wall blocks, 133, 136
  for fastening wall planks, 118, 129, 131

Closets, 308
  attic, 275, 277–281
  cedar, 319–320
  clothes, 312–315
    fittings for, 317–319
    rod allowances for, 317
  doors for, 321–322
  prefabricated, 315–316, 324–325
  typical, 322–326
  wardrobe, 315
  (See also Storage spaces)
Columns or posts, 240
  basement, 187
  screw-type, 206–207
Comfort, insulation and, 51
Compression set, floor cracks and, 145
Concrete, for basement floors, 192
  for basement walls, 192
  fastening furring strips to, 42
  fastening studs to, 210
  forms for, 20
  proper proportions of, 147
  tensile strength of, 147
Concrete blocks, fastening furring strips to, 42
  (See also Foundations, concrete-block)
Condensation, 54–56, 72
  in bathrooms, 294
  common troubles from, 76–77
Conduction, heat flow by, 52–53
Construction, faulty, plaster cracks and, 81–82
Convection, heat flow by, 52–53
Cooling systems, insulation and size of, 51
Cork tile, 149
Corner closets, 314
Corner seats, kitchen, 255–256
Corner treatment for plywood panels, 24–25
Cornice vents, 55–56, 72, 74
Corrugated boards, 119–120
Cottonwood, nail-holding power of, 29
Cracks, in concrete floors, 146–148
    new surfaces for, 152–153
    repair of, 150
  from improper fasteners, 27
  plaster (see Plaster cracks)
  plasterboard, 84
  in wood floors, 143–146
    repair of, 148–149, 153

Crawl spaces, insulation of, 62–63, 75
   ventilation of, 56, 62
Cupboards, old-fashioned kitchen, 224
   toe space under, 225
   (*See also* Cabinets)
Cypress, 2, 6, 8, 18–20
   ease of working with, 7
   figure in, 10
   nail-holding power of, 29
   shrinkage of, 5
   stiffness of, 9
   warping of, 7

D

Dampness, basement, 187–188, 199–201,
   205–206
   ceiling cracks and, 83
   of concrete floors, correction of, 163,
     175
   floor cracks and, 144–145, 148
Darkrooms, basement, 182
Decay in wood, 15, 18
Decoration, bathroom, 285–288, 297
   and ceiling height, 95
   ceiling insulation and, 51
   good taste in, 113
Decorative insulation for basement walls,
   60
Dew point, 54, 76
Dining nooks, 239
   plans for, 222–224
   seats for, 255
   (*See also* Breakfast nooks)
Dining rooms, flooring for, 18
Dishwashers, 225, 227
Door frames, 212, 240–241, 284
Doors, attic, height of, 284
   closet, 321
   fitting wall blocks around, 133–134
   fitting wall planks around, 132
   folding, 321
   plaster cracks around, 113–114
   sliding, for bathrooms, 288–289, 296
     for closets, 321
   for under-stairs closets, 326
Dormers, 58
   flashings for, 273–274
   insulation of, 58
   planning for, 276 281

Dormers, types of, 262–264
Douglas fir, 2–3, 8, 18–20
   ease of working with, 7
   figure in, 9–10
   nail-holding power of, 29–30
   shrinkage of, 5
   stiffness of, 9
   warping of, 7
Downspouts, damp basements from, 188
Drafts in basements, 204–205
Drain tile for wet basements, 199
Drawers, closet, 319
Drawings, roughing-in, for plumbing, 294
   (*See also* Sketching to scale)
Dryouts, plaster cracks from, 83–84
Ducts, cutting structural details for, 204

E

Earthquakes, plaster cracks from, 81–82
Electric heaters for attics, 271
Electrical outlets, in basements, 190
   in kitchens, 232, 242
Elm, 2, 18
   ease of working with, 7
   figure in, 10
   nail-holding power of, 29
   shrinkage of, 5
   stiffness of, 9
   warping of, 6
Enamel, 26, 202
Etching of concrete floors, 195–196
Excavation, basement, to give added ceiling height, 191–192
   to remedy wet basements, 198–199
Exhaust fans, attic, 77
Expansion and contraction, plaster
   cracks and, 80, 82

F

FAS, 13
Fascia board, 261
Fasteners, importance of, 27
   powder-actuated, 43–44
   for wall resurfacing, 118–120, 123–124
   (*See also* Adhesives; Nails)
Fences, lumber for, 20
F.H.A. financing, 254
Figure in wood, 9–10
   for interior trim, 19

Filler strips for kitchen cabinets, 237, 247, 250–251
Fillers, 25, 202
Finish lumber, 12–13
  nails for, 33
Finishes for hardwood plywood, 25–26
Fir, nail-holding power of, 29
  (*See also* Douglas fir)
Fireplaces, basement, 185
Firsts in lumber, 13
Flashing, chimney, 272–273
  dormer, 273–274
Floor drains, existing, plugging of, 204
Floor slabs, 61
Floor tiles, soft, 149–150
  bathroom, 290
  over concrete floors, 163
  over old softwood floors, 152, 160–162
  on plywood, in attics, 152, 170–172
  over worn-out wood floors, 172–173
Floors, of added rooms, insulation of, 64, 73
  basement, insulation of, 61–62
  bathroom, 290
  concrete, bathroom, 296–297
    cracks in, 146–147
    dusting of, 147
    etching of, 195–196
    laying floors over, 150, 163, 168, 173–179
    painting of, 195–196
    peeling of, 147
    repair of, 150, 195
    staining of, 196
  dirty, 146–147
  finding center of, for laying tile, 177–179
  insulation of, 64, 69, 75
  kitchen, 11, 160–162, 233
  remodeling of, 148–153
  sagging, correction of, 152, 189, 206–207
  wood, buckling of, 143
    cracks in, 143–146
    defects in, 142–148
    finish for, 144–145
    hard- (*see* Hardwood floors)
    lumber for, 3, 13–14, 18, 144–145

Floors, wood, nails for, 32–33, 157
  plank, for remodeled attics, 150–152, 168–172
  repair of, 148–149, 153–156
  replacing damaged boards in, 158–160
  soft- (*see* Softwood floors)
  squeaks in, 146, 149, 156–158, 172
  worn-out, tile on plywood over, 172–173
Footings, 190–193, 206
Formica, 232
Foundations, brick, 192, 200
  concrete-block, 187–188, 200
    putting windows in, 196–198
  fastening sills to, 43–44
  footings under, 80
  insulation of, 59–61
  new surfaces over, 136–139, 200–201
  rubblestone, 191
Framing, for basement partitions, 210–213
  for lowered ceilings, 110–111
  rough, lumber for, 18
  for soffits, 233–235
  wall-surface material on, 139–141
  (*See also* Door frames; Window frames)
Freezing, cracks in concrete floors from, 146
Fuel savings, insulation and, 51
Furnaces (*see* Heating plants)
Furring strips, for basement ceilings, 106–108
  for basement walls, 136–138
  fastening to masonry, 41–43
  for lowered ceilings, 112
  lumber for, 20
  nails for, 33
  for resurfacing ceilings, 89–93, 103–104
  for sloping attic ceilings, 108–109
  under squeaking floors, 158
  for wall framing, 139–141

G

Gable vents, 55, 72
Garbage disposal, 225, 227
Gas heaters for attics, 271

Gates, lumber for, 20
Ghost marks in ceiling, 51
Glue, for decorative plywoods, 40–41, 124
  for perforated panels, 123
  for plywood panels, 139
  urea, mixing of, 41
  (*See also* Adhesives)
Grab bars, bathroom, 291, 297
Grooved boards, 119–120
  (*See also* Tongued-and-grooved floor boards)
Grout for basement walls, 200
Gum wood, 2, 18–19
  ease of working with, 7
  figure in, 10
  nail-holding power of, 29
  for plywood, 23
  shrinkage of, 5
  stiffness of, 9
  warping of, 6

H

Hardboard, soft tile floors over, 163–164
Hardwood floors, board-type, over concrete, 152, 173–176
  care of, 176
  laying of, 177
  refinishing of, 153
  replacing of, 149, 153
Hardwood Plywood Institute, 22
Hardwoods, flooring nails for, 33
  for floors (*see* Hardwood floors)
  grades of, 13, 174
  grain of, 3–4
  list of, 2
  nail penetration in, 33
Headers, 283
Heartwood, 18
Heat flow, 51–53
Heat gain, 46–48
Heat loss, 46–48
  through foundations, 60
Heating, bathroom, 295–296
Heating plants, cost of, 185
  insulation and size of, 50
  location of, 189
Hemlock, 2, 8, 19
  ease of working with, 7

Hemlock, figure in, 10
  nail-holding power of, 29
  shrinkage of, 5
  stiffness of, 9
  warping of, 7
Hot-water tanks (*see* Water heaters)
Houses, new, lathing in, 127
  plaster cracks in, 81–82
  old, basements of, 180–182, 184, 189–192, 201
  bathrooms of, 285–288, 305–308
  floor defects in, 145–146, 148
  repair of, 148–149, 152, 172
  kitchens of, 214–217, 224, 237, 249
  lathing in, 127
  lowering ceilings in, 94–95
  plaster cracks in, 78–84, 113
  resurfacing walls in, 128–136
  storage space in, 309, 325–326
  one-story, bathroom remodeling in, 307–308
  heat gain in, 48

I

I-beams in remodeled basements, 194–195, 212
Insulating materials, 48–49
  for attic knee walls and roofs, 58, 72–73
  for basement recreation rooms, 93
  for ceilings, 56–57, 70–72
  for dormers, 58
  for roofs, 59
  for windows, 65
Insulation, of attics, 57–58, 72–73
  of basements, 91
  benefits of, 50–51
  decorative, 60
  definition of, 48–49
  of dormers, 58
  of floors, 142, 163–164, 170–171, 175
  of foundations, 59–61
  importance of, 46–48
  kinds of, 49–50
  mass, 53
  necessary amount of, 54
  principles of, 51–53
  reflective, 53
  of roofs, 58–59

Insulation, of top-floor ceilings, 56–58,
70–72, 91
of walls, 67–68
waterproof, for basement floors, 61–62

J

Jamb blocks, steel-sash, 198
Joining of hardwood-plywood sheets, 24
Joints, fasteners for, 28
plywood, 124
Joist hangers, 44–45
Joists, attic floor, 265–266, 273
under bathtubs, 293–294
ceiling, 110–111, 280
insulation between, 70–72, 106–107,
171–172
dual, insulation between, 69
floor sag and, 152, 206–207
lumber for, 8
nailing of, 36–40
supported by I-beams, 194
temporary support for, 194, 240

K

Kitchen tables, 224
Kitchens, in attic apartments, 257–258
basic types of, 218–221
decoration of, 233
dining nooks in, 222, 239
equipment for, 227–230
floors for, 11, 160–162, 233
islands in, 221, 229–230
modern, 214–218
new, planning of, 243–247, 253–255
remodeling of, 237–241
advantages of, 224–226
cost of, 253–255
for future, 232, 243
preliminary plans for, 241–243
resurfacing ceilings of, 98–105
resurfacing walls of, 116–118, 122
ventilation of, 77
work centers in, 226–227, 239, 242
Knots in wood, 15
painting over, 8
and strength of lumber, 9

L

Lacquer finish for plywood, 26
Ladders, chicken, 268–269
extension, 268
recommended types of, 112
safety hints for use of, 112, 268–269
Larch, 2, 6, 8, 18–20
ease of working with, 7
figure in, 10
nail-holding power of, 29
shrinkage of, 5
stiffness of, 5
warping of, 7
Lateral resistance, fasteners supplying, 28
Lath, nails for, 33
Lathing, 127
Laundries, 237–238
basement, 182, 185–186
kitchen, 221, 229–230
ventilation of, 77
Lavatories, attic, 282
basement, 186
bathroom, 296–297, 299, 301
first-floor, 239, 241
Leaks, plaster cracks from, 83
Level strips under wall blocks, 133, 135
Light switches, bathroom, 291
Lighting, attic, 262
kitchen, 231–232
of storage spaces, 311
valance, in basements, 212–213
Linoleum, for cabinet tops, 232
for floors, 233, 290
Lintels for basement windows, 198
Living rooms, flooring for, 18
Loose fill insulation, 49
for ceilings, 56, 64
for walls, 64
pneumatic application of, 67–68
Louvers, 55, 74
Lumber, availability of, 2
board-feet content of, 16–17
dressed, 11
dry, tests for, 6
finish (see Finish lumber)
floor (see Floors)
grades of, 11–14
grain of, 3–4, 9
green, 4–6, 82, 145

Lumber, hardness of, 3
  kinds of, 2
  standard lengths of, 11, 13–14
  standard widths and thicknesses of, 11,
      13–14
  stiffness of, 8–9
  (*See also* Wood)
Lumber associations, 14
Lumber-core plywood, 22

M

Mahogany for plywood, 23
Maple, 2–3, 13, 18–19, 150–151, 173,
    232
  ease of working with, 7
  figure in, 10
  flooring grades of, 14
  nail-holding power of, 29
  for plywood, 23
  shrinkage of, 5
  stiffness of, 9
  warping of, 7
Masonry, fastening furring strips to, 41–
    43
Mastic, to insulate floors laid over con-
    crete, 175
  for laying asphalt tile, 165
Medicine cabinets, 291
Medusa portland cement, repairing floor
    cracks with, 150
Medusa portland-cement paint, 136, 199–
    200
Medusa rubber-base coatings, 195
Medusa waterproof cement, 191, 199–
    200
Merry-go-rounds, kitchen corner, 227,
    245
Metal lath, nails for, 33
  to reinforce plaster repairs, 125–126
Metal straps, 40
Meters, gas and water, moving of, 185
Miter stiffeners, 44
Mitered joints, 24
Moldings, 132
  base, 167
  wood-faced extruded, 24
Mortgages, 254–255
Music or hobby rooms, attic, 261

N

Nail clinching, 34
Nail holes in plasterboard, 85
Nail points, 34
Nail sets, use of, 170, 202
Nailheads, 35
  sinking of (*see* Nails, countersinking
      of)
Nailing, blind-, 169–170
  of floor boards, 158, 160, 172, 175
  of floor tiles, 162
  general specifications for, 35–40
  perpendicular, 35
  toenailing, 36, 39, 43, 111
Nails, 28
  box, 30
  casing, 30, 33
  for ceiling tiles, 91
  coated, 30
  common, 30, 32
  concrete, 138
  countersinking of, 40, 157–158, 160,
      169–170, 172–173, 202
  cut, 33
  for decorative plywood, 40–41
  finishing, 33, 120, 139, 157, 202
  flathead, 33
  flooring, 32, 149, 152, 160
  framing, 32
  hardened-steel, 42
  powder-actuated, 210
  resistance to, 29
  rule for length of, 31
  shingle, 266–267
  siding, 32
  size of, 30–31
  typical, data on, 32
  for wall blocks, 119
  for wall planks, 118
National Board of Fire Underwriters, 273
National Bureau of Standards, 11
National Safety Council, 268, 291

O

Oak, 2–3, 18–20, 150–151, 173
  ease of working with, 7
  figure in, 10
  nail-holding power of, 29

Oak, for plywood, 23
  quartersawed, 13
  shrinkage of, 5
  stiffness of, 9
  warping of, 7
Offiices, attic, 261
Open recessed joints, 24

P

Paint, ability of wood to hold, 8, 19
  for acoustical tile, 102
  for concrete floors, 195
  curing of, 203
  for hardwood plywood, 25–26
  primer, 202
  for wallboards, 120
  waterproof, for basements, 136, 138,
    188
Paint remover, 200, 203
Panel sheet rock, 124
Panels, plywood, 21, 23–24
Pantries, 237–238
Parquet squares or blocks, 150–151
  over concrete, 166–168
Partitions, basement, framing for, 210–
    212
  bearing, 187, 193–195
  closet, 322–324
  removal of, 239
Party rooms (*see* Recreation rooms)
Patching, of floor cracks, 155–156
  of plaster cracks, 85, 95–98, 125–127
  of plaster holes, 115, 127–128
Peeling of plaster, causes of, 82–83
Perforated panels, uses for, 122–123
Perlite concrete, 153
Pine, 2–3, 8, 18–20
  ease of working with, 7
  figure in, 9–10
  knotty, 13
  nail-holding power of, 29
  northern white, 19–20, 30, 42
  shrinkage of, 5
  stiffness of, 9
  warping of, 7
  yellow, 19
Pipes, 239
  bathroom, 292–293
  cutting structural details for, 203–204

Pipes, kitchen, 253
  relocation of, 185, 189
Pitch discoloration, 16
Planning, by drawing, 244
  by template, 243
  (*See also* areas, as Kitchens)
Plaster, cement, for basement walls, 200–
    201
  cracks in (*see* Plaster cracks)
  frozen, 83
  holes in, repair of, 115, 127–128
  overly retarded, 84
  patching material for, 96–97, 126–127
  poor, cracks resulting from, 81–82
  sound resurfacing of, 85–89, 98–102,
    115–123, 128–136
  unsound, resurfacing of, 89–91, 102–
    105
Plaster cracks, in bathrooms, 293
  ceiling, 78–84
    repair of, 85, 95–98
  lumber and, 8, 10, 79, 82
  wall, 113–114
    repair of, 125–127
Plasterboard, for attic remodeling, 93–94
  defects in, 84–85
  kinds of, 94
  as lathing, 127
  nails for, 33, 94, 105
  panel sheet rock over, 124
  in place of furring strips, 105
Plastic tile, 149, 160
  for kitchens, 233
Plastic wood, 157
Plumb lines for applying wall planks, 129
Plumbing, attic, 274
  bathroom, roughing-in drawings for,
    294
    typical, 292–293
  existing, use of, 245, 293
  expense of, 239
Plywood, decorative, 123–124, 136
    fastenings for, 40–41
  economical use of, 26
  grades of, 22–23
  hardwood, 21–26
  softwood, 18, 21
  for subfloors, 137
    laying tile or planks over, 170–173
Plywood panels, 124

Poisons, storage space for, 311
Pool and billiard tables, 190–191
Popular, 2, 18–20
  ease of working with, 7
  figure in, 10
  nail-holding power of, 29
  shrinkage of, 5
  stiffness of, 9
  warping of, 7
Porch connections, nailing of, 38
Porches, back, 237–238
  flooring for, 18
Portland cement (*see* Medusa portland
  cement)
Powder rooms, 307–308
Power savings, insulation and, 51

                    Q

Quarter round for soft tile floors, 162
Quartersawed lumber, 3, 10, 13

                    R

Radiation, of drafts through foundations,
  60
  heat flow by, 52–53
  of heat by roofs, 59
Radiators, bathroom, 291
Rafter ends, nailing of, 38
Ranges, choice of, 227
  location of, 243–245
Rawlplugs, 42
Recreation rooms, 74
  attic, 259, 261
  basement, ceilings for, 105–108
    example of, 207–213
    floors for, 163–168, 173–179
    size of, 189
    soundproofing of, 68–69, 93, 182–
      183, 189, 193
    walls for, 136–139
Redwood, 2–3, 6, 18–20
  ease of working with, 7
  figure in, 10
  nail-holding power of, 29
  shrinkage of, 5
  stiffness of, 9
  warping of, 7
Reflective insulation, 50
  for attics, 58

Reflective insulation, for ceilings, 57
  for foundations, 61
  for roofs, 59, 68
  for walls, 64
Refrigerators, choice of, 227
  location of, 242–245
Relative humidity, 54
Retaining walls for lowered basement
  floors, 192
Rigid boards for insulation, 50, 62, 64
  of basement walls, 205–206
  over concrete floors, 150
Roof boards, lumber for, 19
Roofing, for flat roofs, 68
  inspection of, before remodeling attics,
    266
  removal of, for dormers, 279
  (*See also* Shingles)
Roofing paper, 266–267
Roofs, condition of, in remodeling attics,
    266
  flat, insulation of, 68
  insulation of, 58–59
  leaky, repair of, 266
  new, application of, 266–268
Room dividers, closets as, 316
Rubber tile, 149, 290

                    S

Sanding, of basement stairs, 202
  of hardwood floors, 176
  of parquet blocks, 168
  of plank floors, 170
Sawdust and shellac to repair floor
    cracks, 148–149, 154–155
Scaffold planks, 112
Screen frames, lumber for, 20
Screws, for fastening furring strips to
    masonry, 42
  for floor planks, 152, 170
  for perforated wall panels, 123
  for plywood, 124
Seconds in lumber, 13
Selects in lumber, 12–13
Serving (or snack) bars, 221, 226, 229,
    255
Settlement of houses, floor cracks and,
    144, 146
  plaster cracks and, 80, 82

Settlement of houses, plasterboard cracks and, 84
Sewage disposal, 285
Sewing rooms, attic, 261
Sheathing, diagonal wall, nailing of, 38–39
  fasteners for, 28
  plywood, nailing of, 39
  wood for, 20
Sheetrock, 94
Shellac, for basement stairs, 202
  sawdust and, to repair floor cracks, 148–149, 154–155
Shelves, cartwheel, 207
  closet, 319
  lumber for, 19
Shingles, asphalt, 266
  around dormers, 274
  nailing of, 39–40, 266–267
  wood, under asphalt, 266–268
  wood for, 20
Shiplap boards, cracks between, 154–156
Shoe racks, 318–319
Shower stalls, 300–301
Shower valves, thermostatically controlled, 291
Shrinkage of lumber, 4–6, 29
  floor cracks and, 143
  plaster cracks and, 79–80
  plasterboard cracks and, 84
  rules for avoiding defects from, 10
Siding, nails for, 32–33
  wood for, 20
Sills, for basement partitions, 210–211
  door, 284
  double, nailing of, 35–36
  fasteners for, 20
  lumber for, 20
  window (see Window sills)
Sinks, 239
  cabinet, 225
  choice of, 227
  location of, 244–245
  old-fashioned, 224
  as work centers, 226
Sisalkraft, 175
Sketching to scale, 129–130, 133–134, 137, 161, 164, 166, 243, 275, 280, 306
  (*See also* Drawings)

Slab insulation, 50
  for flat roofs, 68
Soffits, 233–235, 247
Softwood floors, dished boards in, 145
  putting hardwood over, 153
Softwoods, flooring nails for, 33
  for furring strips, 42
  grades of, 11–13
  grain of, 3–4
  list of, 2
  nail penetration in, 31
Soil, wet, causing damp basements, 188
Soil stacks, 274, 292–293, 306
Sound transmission, 68–69, 170
Soundproofing, 68–69, 78, 91, 93, 142, 170
Spacer strips, 170
Spackle, 202
Splined joints, 24
Spruce, 2
  ease of working with, 7
  figure in, 10
  nail-holding power of, 29
  shrinkage of, 5
  stiffness of, 9
  warping of, 7
Stains, for concrete floors, 196
  for plywood panels, 26
Stairs, attic, 269–270
  basement, 188, 201–202, 209–210
  closets under, 325–326
Staples, 33, 91–92
Starter strips under wall planks, 131–132
Steel wool to clean asphalt tile, 165
Steps, outdoor, lumber for, 20
  (*See also* Stairs)
Storage spaces, access to, 311
  attic, 261, 309
  basement, 182, 207, 209–210, 309
  basic types of, 312–317
  bathroom, 294, 297
  design of, 311
  dust prevention in, 311
  kitchen, 225, 239, 243
  lighting of, 310
  location of, 311–312
  planned, 309–310
  ventilation of, 311
  (*See also* Cabinets; Closets)
Storm sashes, 65–67, 76

Stoves (*see* Ranges)
Straightedge, use of, 249
Structural details, cutting of, for pipes
    and ducts, 203–204
    shrinkage in, 79–80, 84, 143
    typical, 80
Structural insulating board, 49–50
Studies, attic, 261
Studs, attic, 283–284
    for basement partitions, 210–212
    bathroom, 294
    for dormers, 279–280
    wall, fasteners for, 28
        fastening cabinets to, 248, 250, 253
        lumber for, 8
        nailing of, 37–38
Subfloors, attic, 273
    nailing of, 36–37, 158
    plywood, nailing of, 37
    wood, laying plank floors over, 168
    wood for, 20
Surco concrete, 152–153
Sweating, of chimneys, 273
    of foundations, 60–61
    of pipes, 189
    of windows, 55, 76
Swelling of wood, 5–6

T

Temperature, basement, 189, 204–206
Tile, for ceilings, 89, 91, 261
    floor (*see* Floor tiles)
Toe strips, metal, 162
Toenailing, 36, 39, 43, 111
Toilets (*see* Water closets)
Tongue-and-groove joints, 24
Tongued-and-grooved floor boards, cracks
        between, 154–156
    laying of, 168–170
Towel bars, 291
Trim, exterior, woods for, 18
    interior, woods for, 9, 19

U

United States Department of Agriculture,
    12

V

V joints, 24
Valances, 212–213
Varnish for basement stairs, 202
Veneer-core plywood, 21
Ventilation, of attics, 55–56, 77, 262
    bathroom, 77, 294, 297
    condensation control and, 55–56, 74,
        77
    of storage spaces, 311
Vermin, insulation as protection against,
    51
Vertical grain in wood, 3, 10

W

Wall blocks, 118–119, 133–136
    on framing, 139–141
Wall coverings, fabric, 114–115
    plastic, 115, 233
    (*See also* Wallpaper)
Wall panels, 120–122
    perforated, 122–123
    plywood, 123–124
Wall planks, 116–118, 128–133
    fitting around openings, 132
    on framing, 139–141
    plywood, 123–124
Wall plates, nailing of, 39–40
Wallboard (*see* Plasterboard)
Wallpaper, 114
    for kitchens, 233
    removal of, 135
Walls, of added rooms, insulation of, 64,
    69
    attic knee, 275–276
        insulation of, 72–73, 172
    basement, 188, 200–201
        concrete for, 192
        finishing of, 202–203
        insulation of, 60–61
    bathroom, 297
    checking for level, 128–129
    defects in surfaces of, 113–114
        repair of, 114–115
    existing, insulation of, 67–68
    heat flow through, 52–53
    kitchen, 225, 233
        installing cabinets on, 250

Walls, resurfacing of, 115–124
    over sound plaster, 128–136
Walnut, 2–3, 19
    ease of working with, 7
    figure in, 10
    for plywood, 23
    shrinkage of, 5
    stiffness of, 9
    warping of, 7
Wane in wood, 15
Warping, 6–7, 15, 29
Washouts, cracks in concrete floors from, 146
Water, floor cracks resulting from, 144, 148
    plaster cracks resulting from, 83
    plasterboard cracks resulting from, 84–85
    (See also Dampness)
Water closets, attic, 282
    basement, 185
    bathroom, 297, 299, 301
    first-floor, 239
Water heaters, 300
    moving of, 185, 190
Water supply, 285
Waterproof paper, in basements, 205–206
    under crawl spaces, 62–63
    under plank floors, 168
Wax, for concrete floors, 196
    for hardwood floors, 176
    for hardwood plywood, 26
Weatherstripping, 65
Weight shifts, floor cracks and, 143
    plaster cracks and, 80–82
    plasterboard cracks and, 84
Wind force, plaster cracks and, 81–82
Window frames, 241, 283
Window sashes, lumber for, 19
    steel, 196

Window sills, attic, 283
    basement, 198
    kitchen, 225
Windows, attic, 262
    bathroom, 294, 297
    cracks around, insulation of, 65
    dormer (see Dormers)
    double, as insulation, 64–65
    fitting wall blocks around, 133–134
    fitting wall planks around, 132
    kitchen, 231–232, 240–241
    new, in basements, 185, 187, 196–198, 209
    plaster cracks around, 113–114
    storm, 65–67, 76
Woods, defects in, 14–16
    figure in, 9–10
    hard (see Hardwoods)
    nail-holding power of, 28–31
    new, shrinkage of, 4–6
    seasoning of, 5, 79, 144–145
    selection of, 1, 9
    soft (see Softwoods)
    warping of, 6
    (See also Lumber)
"Wood Handbook," U.S. Department of Agriculture, 12
Wood sleepers under hardwood floors, 174–175
Wood slivers for repairing floors, 149, 156
Wooden plugs, in concrete, for nailing furring strips, 138–139
    for plank floors, 170
Woodwork (see Trim)
Work centers, kitchen, 226–227, 242
Work surfaces, kitchen, 224–225, 242
Workbench areas, basement, 182
Workshops, basement, 182

BLUEPRINTS
Plates I to VI

BASEMENT

KITCHEN CABINETS

TOWEL CABINET IN BATHROOM

GLASS PARTITION
(BATH & HALL)

LINEN CLOSET IN HALL

SECTION A-A
F.S.

INTERIOR DETAILS